MW00635772

Concepts in Law and Economics

To Dan Graham,

Concepts in Law
and Economics

A Guide for the Curious

JIM LEITZEL

Whose beneficent influence remains potent. Many thanks, Jim

OXFORD
UNIVERSITY PRESS

OXFORD
UNIVERSITY PRESS

Oxford University Press is a department of the University of Oxford.
It furthers the University's objective of excellence in research, scholarship,
and education by publishing worldwide. Oxford is a registered trade mark
of Oxford University Press in the UK and in certain other countries

Published in the United States of America by Oxford University Press
198 Madison Avenue, New York, NY 10016, United States of America

Library of Congress Cataloging-in-Publication Data
Leitzel, Jim, author.
Concepts in law and economics : a guide for the curious / Jim Leitzel.
p.   cm.
Includes bibliographical references and index.
ISBN 978–0–19–021397–8 (hardback)
1. Law and economics. 2. Law—Economic aspects—United States. I. Title.
K487.E3L45 2015
330—dc23
2015014995

1   3   5   7   9   8   6   4   2

Printed in the United States of America on acid-free paper

To Hilary and Saul, with love

CONTENTS

ACKNOWLEDGMENTS

Almost thirty years ago, I took a class on Law and Economics, taught by Dan Graham at Duke University. Subsequently, I wrote a Law and Economics-style PhD thesis under Dan's guidance. About that time Mike Meurer, who was the first person I knew who held both a law degree and a PhD in economics, joined Duke's faculty; Mike proved inspirational in spurring and directing my early efforts. Dan and Mike have much to answer for.

Part of the underappreciated fallout from the collapse of the Soviet Union was the derailing of my budding career in Law and Economics, as I was drawn to study the Russian economic transition. After the Russian economy was, er, sorted, I came to the University of Chicago. Law and Economics pervades the atmosphere at Chicago, and I proved susceptible to its influence. Chicago gave me the opportunity to teach Law and Economics, which I have been doing for more than a decade. This book is one result of those pedagogical efforts, and it has been much improved by countless interactions with my Law and Econ students and teaching assistants over the years. George Papava, Ravi Gupta, and Petr Barton merit special mention, but without detracting, I hope, from the manifest contributions of many others.

My longtime friend (and occasional co-author) Mike Alexeev of Indiana University teaches Law and Economics, too, and his economic insight and enduring kindness are ideals that I look to emulate. I would feel that way even if he didn't teach Law and Economics—but the fact that he does teach Law and Econ, and that he is very generous, has allowed me to correct some of the grosser errors in the manuscript version of this book. Phil Cook of Duke University, another long-time friend and occasional co-author, helped keep me in the greater Law and Economics arena by recruiting me to work on gun control, and later, by involving me in studying kidney donation. In the interim, Phil stimulated me to work on vice policy, which also provided kindling for the Law and Econ flame. Thanks, Mike and Phil.

Hilary Arnow and Saul Arnow generously formed a family (Artzels?) with me, leading to much happiness, companionship, love, and family-plan cell phone savings on my end. Thanks for all of your support, Hils and Saul. The taking in of the lost became a habit for Hilary and Saul, when Rocky later joined us, despite the lack of phone plan advantages for canine members of the household. If this acknowledgments section seems rushed, it is because I must walk Rocky. If it seems inadequate, it is because I owe more than I can say to Saul and Hilary; this book is dedicated to them.

I am originally from Baltimore, and my Baltimore family, though immeasurably diminished by the loss of both my parents in the past few years, also has been steady in their support: thanks to Janet, John, Susan and Dan, Scott and Travis.

Public Policy Studies in the College at the University of Chicago has been my academic home for a decade and a half, and there's no place like home. Richard Taub, now nominally retired, remains the iconic figure in Public Policy, and I am grateful for his wise counsel and years of encouragement. Lee Price has ably handled the day-to-day running of Public Policy on a year-to-year basis and put up with some of my procrastinations—thank you, Lee. Sabina Shaikh, Chad Broughton, Betty Farrell, Woody Carter, Ray Lodato, Debra Schwartz, Clayton Harris III, and Christa Velasquez are the sorts of colleagues who make academia rewarding. Dean John Boyer continues to improve the College and Public Policy, while Professors Lis Clemens, Adam Green, and Jim Sparrow, temporarily seconded into Mastering the Social Sciences in the College, have been friends to me and to Public Policy, too. Kenyatta Futterman, Kathleen Kish, and Shawn Hawk are other Harper denizens who have eased my path. Thanks to all.

The Economics Education and Research Consortium (EERC) has been a sort of second home for more than fifteen years. EERC sponsors two workshops annually in Russia or Ukraine, and the overlap between frequent workshop participants and my academic and personal friends is staggering. This pleasant intersection includes Mike Alexeev, Rick Ericson, Shlomo Weber, Diana Weinhold, Gary Krueger, Judy Thornton, Olena Nizalova, Tom Coupé, Irina Murtazashvili, Oleksandr Shepotylo, David Brown, Ted Gerber, Russ Pittman, Natalya Volchkova, Victor Ginsburgh, Vladimir Popov, Denys Nizalov, John Earle, Eric Livny, Volodymyr Vakhitov, and David Tarr. Iryna Sobetskaya and Natalia Bystrytska have administered the EERC with care and grace; their tireless efforts and their cheerful presence have made the EERC the welcoming place that it is.

I suffer from law professor envy. Besides Mike Meurer, other law professors whom I can't help admiring, personally and professionally, include Will Baude, Mary Anne Case, and Jeff Stake. Their whereabouts can be traced through CDC data on outbreaks of law professor envy.

ACKNOWLEDGMENTS

Many other old friends, including some whom I have frightfully neglected to my shame and detriment, also have helped me stay more-or-less on track. They include Jed Samuels, Chris Scheidt, Julius Scott, Nina Alexeeva, Geoff Renshaw, Betsy Glennon, Janice Hall, April Harding, Bob Conrad, Cliff Gaddy, Barry Ickes, Stuart Shaw, Chris Young, Steve Smith, Vitaly Yermakov, Vladimir Treml, Vladimir Pantyushin, Will Pyle, and Randy Beard, none of whom have the good sense to live in Chicago. (Randy also has served as a gracious guide through organ donation policy; some of the fruits of his labors appear in chapters 5 and 6.) Phoebe Rice, Brad Henderson, Deidre Ferron, George Tolley, Victor Lima, Joselyn Zivin, Allen Sanderson, Ari Adut, Dimitriy Masterov, Janet Sedlar, Yuval Weber, Judith Miller, Will Baude, Margrethe Krontoft, Andrea Althoff, Rovana Popoff, and Nikkie Eitmann have, at least at times, had the good sense to live in Chicago.

Julia Mahoney, Will Baude, Mark Kleiman, and Mary Anne Case kindly provided some helpful comments at various stages; thanks to all for their generosity and insight.

Oxford University Press was kind enough to recruit some fine anonymous referees, both law professors and economics professors . . . or so I am led to believe. Their discerning comments led to a much better book. Thanks both to the referees and to Scott Parris and Cathryn Vaulman for their help. Scott's stewardship of this book has been inspiring, though I still would like to sneak "fardel" into the text. Any errors that remain in the book are my responsibility, of course, though Law and Economics does indicate many circumstances in which it is desirable not to impose damages upon parties who fail to meet their responsibilities.

J.L.

INTRODUCTION

The Original of Laura

Toward the end of his life, the famed writer Vladimir Nabokov began working on a new novel, which came to be titled *The Original of Laura*.[1] Vladimir had instructed his wife Vera to destroy the unfinished manuscript in the event of his death. Nabokov passed away in 1977, with *The Original of Laura* in a far-from-complete state: the "manuscript" consisted of 138 handwritten index cards. Vera did not get around to destroying the cards before she died in 1991. The manuscript next passed into the control of Dmitri Nabokov, the son of Vera and Vladimir. In 2008, Dmitri, by then in his seventies, acknowledged a pressing duty to decide whether to accede to his father's wishes and do away with the manuscript or to preserve *The Original of Laura* and make it more generally available.

Imagine for a moment that Vladimir Nabokov's direction to his wife about destroying his unfinished novel had been duly recorded in a legal document, his will. Should the law require the executor of the Nabokov estate to heed the unambiguous, written instructions or should the law allow the executor to override the decedent's wishes and release the manuscript? After all, *The Original of Laura* could bring pleasure and enlightenment to millions of people for generations to come. How can anyone justify destroying the draft just because its now deceased creator/owner was a purist about not making incomplete work available to public view? In terms of overall human flourishing—economists might say "efficiency"—it seems as if the decision is between having a world with the additional Nabokovian proto-novel or a world without it. As it safely can be assumed that the manuscript, if released, would do no direct positive harm (scandalized critics of *Lolita* notwithstanding), then the world with the novel should be superior to the world without it. So if the only issue were the isolated case of the Nabokov novel, overall well-being would call for the release of the manuscript.

Even in its incomplete form, *The Original of Laura* exists, so why not make it available?

Laws have effects not just when they are formulated but also into the future. Of course, many of the gains from preserving *The Original of Laura* will arise in the future (in the form of pleasure for future readers)—but so will the incentives fostered by the "law" created or applied in the Nabokov case. How will future authors behave if they know that, should they die, their wishes to have their incomplete manuscripts destroyed will not be honored? Frail novelists might not bother to initiate new projects, understanding that they will not have the final word on dissemination of their writings. Aging authors themselves might destroy unfinished work prematurely, fearing (perhaps wrongly) that they might not survive an acute sickness. On (what turned out to be) his deathbed, Adam Smith (1723-1790), the Scottish father of the economics discipline, asked some friends to destroy most of his unpublished documents. When they dawdled, Smith personally superintended the burning of sixteen volumes of his papers.[2]

A law that permits (or requires) the executor to override Nabokov's wishes ensures the dissemination of *The Original of Laura*. This benefit must be weighed against the possibility that other, perhaps even more worthy literature, will fail to be produced in the future as a consequence. It is hard to know which legal approach—that of honoring an author's wishes for destruction or that of making available already-produced work to a clamoring public—will end up providing the best long-term results.[3] Of course, Vladimir Nabokov's wishes were not part of a legal document or proceeding, so what happened in his case will not have any value as legal precedent. Dmitri Nabokov eventually agreed to release *The Original of Laura*, which was published in November 2009. Perhaps this resolution even suggests a desirable course for the law: for particularly acclaimed writers, declarations of a yearning for posthumous destruction of manuscripts could be converted automatically into a thirty-year waiting period before distribution, with mechanisms in place for exceedingly determined authors to override this default system. Mediocre authors can do as they please.

The Nabokov situation presents one small instance of the chief question motivating the field of Law and Economics: What makes for a good law? Law and Economics compares the likely consequences of laws by evaluating the responses of people to the opportunities presented under different legal regimes. Rules that punish crimes or mandate that compensation be paid to victims of accidents—or require executors to heed the terms of wills—alter the consequences for, and hence the choices of, decision-makers. The more those choices conduce to the common good, the better the law that helped encourage those choices.

A conspicuous omission also characterizes the Law and Economics approach: abstract considerations of justice or fairness are usually not a part of the equation. Faced with the Nabokov dilemma, many people might invoke perceptions of a fair rule or how the rights of authors or readers are implicated. Law and Economics adherents will instead address an economic measure of overall well-being, with fairness or rights only entering via their consequences, their impact on well-being or efficiency—though it might be the case that widely shared notions of fairness and rights achieve their popularity by being broadly consistent with the economist's version of the social good. Finally, the Nabokov puzzle implicitly demonstrates yet another feature that is discernible among Law and Economic analyses: there is not an unambiguous answer as to what rule is best. As John Maynard Keynes noted, economics is "a method rather than a doctrine, an apparatus of the mind, a technique of thinking, which helps its possessor to draw correct conclusions."[4] Experts within the Law and Economics field can disagree about appropriate rules as wholeheartedly as Keynesians and Anti-Keynesians and Post-Keynesians can disagree about appropriate macroeconomic policies.

Choice in the Shadow of the Law

Economics considers people to be goal-directed; they are assumed to make their choices in such a way as to promote their interests, given the alternatives available to them. The interests or preferences of these decision-makers are beyond the scope of economic theory; they are what they are, wacky howsoever they might be, with no objections from the analyst permitted. Economic theory examines how goal-directed people go about choosing the best means to serve their own ends.

While the economics discipline offers a broad theory of human decision-making, the legal system helps to determine the consequences, to the decision-maker and to others, of the various options available. Together, Law and Economics involves the application of the choice theory of economics to the opportunities obtainable within different legal environments. The likelihood that I will choose to return a lost wallet, keep a promise, drive more carefully, or heed the terms in a will is partly a function of the applicable laws and regulations.

Law and Economics engages in comparisons among rules in virtually all imaginable settings—criminal behavior, property disputes, antitrust violations, contracting, and so on. The methodology of choice theory is applied not only to people in general but also to those who specialize in legal work, such as lawyers, police, prosecutors, judges, jury members, and legislators. Is it better to elect or to appoint judges? Should lawyers be allowed to offer their services under a contingent-fee arrangement? These, too, are the sorts of questions that the field of Law and Economics addresses.

The goal of this brief volume is to familiarize readers with the Law and Economics approach. A full survey of the Law and Economics landscape is not presented; rather, the idea is to extract and illustrate the broad themes that permeate the discipline. I try to serve as a Law and Economics guide in the same manner that I try to serve as a Chicago guide when friends come to visit the city in which I have lived for more than fifteen years: I point out the major sights, but I also indulge myself by showcasing some quirky spots that appeal to me. Further, certain landmarks keep coming into view, again and again, whether by accident or through the deliberate planning of the guide: in Chicago, the Hancock building; in the Law and Econ terrain, distributing the costs of accidents, determining the best location to display cultural artifacts, and deciding whether and how to allow people to sell one of their kidneys.

Readers, those putative Law and Economics tourists for whose custom and companionship I am publicly soliciting, are not expected to have backgrounds in law or in economics. My hope is that nonspecialists might be interested because the Law and Economics method offers a lens for understanding why laws are the way they are, and for how public policy can be made more effective. The proffered lens is powerful though perhaps distortionary: I intend to demonstrate that there is value in understanding both the power and the distortions. Further, while many contributions within the domain of Law and Economics are technically demanding, the lens itself, which consists of examining the incentives for decision-making created by different rules, is straightforward and can be grasped and applied by visitors without special equipment or training.

I am an economist and a tour guide, not a lawyer, and certainly nothing in this book should be taken as legal advice. While I try to avoid jargon, some of the terminology might be unfamiliar. I endeavor to explain legal or economic terms of art when they first are presented and also include a glossary. These decisions, I claim, represent rational choices on my part: I want to encourage people to read this book, so I want to make it easy for them to do so. (The brevity of the book, too, is intended to be an inducement to perusal.) I could promise an enjoyable and informative sightseeing experience—but that promise might not be enforceable, and skeptical potential visitors might find it not to be credible. In any event, I hope even skeptical potential travelers will accept my offer to judge the content, and the sights, for themselves.

Outline of the Tour

It is customary for guided tours to provide an itinerary before embarkation. The Contents offers one such itinerary for *Concepts in Law and Economics*, but the Contents is rather bare-bones and excludes the part where you are held captive in a gift shop that is misleadingly referred to as a museum or exhibition. So I will take this opportunity to supplement the Contents with some prosaic description of the remainder of the book:

Chapter 1: E pluribus unum [One Out of Many]

In which laws developed in the style of Jeremy Bentham promote the greatest happiness by making one out of many, by inducing a society of disparate individuals to work almost as seamlessly as a sole human proprietor of an otherwise unpeopled paradise. If those individuals can get together and forge enforceable agreements at no expense, then they can build paradise on earth even when the law is not very adept at deciding who should own what.

Chapter 2: The Sixty-Minute Law School

In which economic efficiency, today's version of Bentham's "greatest happiness," allows one to speak with (unwarranted?) confidence about appropriate rules in all areas of the law, including contracts, torts, crime, and property, without all the rigmarole of attending law school. Making sure that those costs and benefits that your decisions impose on society are themselves reflected in your own rewards—internalizing externalities, in economics jargon—is a standard route to promoting the greatest happiness. Meteorites happen, however.

Chapter 3: What's Done Is Done?

In which law cannot stitch together what man hath rent asunder, though law can limit future rendings. Some current waste serves tomorrow's bounty, in parking spaces as well as inventions. Punish the guilty, but offer some additional goads to avoiding guilt, or to lowering the harms from guilty actions, in the first place. Draconian penalties coupled with low likelihoods of catching and convicting malefactors will not maximize happiness, despite some superficial advantages. Please do not tear down the Taj Mahal: destruction of the Taj will not enhance social well-being, even if you own the Taj and really, really want to tear it down. Please do not mangle my prose in such a way as to bring me into further disrepute—that would be impolite and violate international legal standards. Maximize happiness by stealing the time off of my wristwatch, but not the watch off of my wrist.

Chapter 4: Squeezing a Balloon

In which Professor Sam Peltzman provides the policy version of Newton's third law, where every legislative action is met with an opposite (and equal?)

reaction. Try to subsidize starving artists, or taxicab owners, or home owners, and watch your intention be undermined. Try to subsidize creative behavior, and watch (online!) as technology punishes your hubris—but leaves plenty of scope for creativity in its wake. For democracy's sake, try to subsidize news gathering, fighting both Newton's third law and second law (the one about entropy increasing).

Chapter 5: Deorum injuriae Diis curae [Injuries to the Gods Will Be Remedied By the Gods]

In which offenses against the gods are the concern of the gods alone. Accidental offenses against humans, on the other hand, should mainly be the concern of those humans who can avoid the offenses most cheaply. If your pencil unexpectedly explodes because of a hidden manufacturing defect, well, the consequences should fall at the feet of the manufacturer. If your pencil explodes because you coated it with nitroglycerine, however, you should probably bear the "accident" costs yourself—though if the manufacturer knew that you were likely to coat your pencil with nitroglycerine, then the question of liability becomes more complicated. If you do not appreciate the drug-taking choices of your neighbor, John Stuart Mill suggests that you not try to coerce "improved" neighbor behavior. Speaking of offenses against the gods, return those Parthenon marbles to Athens, and go ahead, sell a kidney.

Chapter 6: Humanity's Crooked Timber

In which less-than-rational folks—that's all of us—look to the law for guidance and protection from those who would like to capitalize on our systematic lapses from considered choice. Maybe our fallibilities suggest that happiness expands when we fail to enforce some mutually agreed upon contracts: Should we rethink the return of the Parthenon marbles, too? Can we regulate, not prohibit, heroin sales and kidney markets to maximize happiness, or are we excessively attached to the status quo? And should we really care about happiness, or economic efficiency, anyway?

Conclusion

In which we risk a thick skull when our excessive attachment to what we own extends to an undue commitment to the lens of Law and Economics.

Concepts in Law and Economics

1

E pluribus unum [One Out of Many]

Robin

Economics has a lot to say about an individual living in isolation, outside of what passes for civilization, a Robinson or Robindaughter Crusoe. Such a person—let's call her Robin—has to think about how to allocate her time: how much to fish, how much to hunt, how much to search for berries, how much to devote to improving her primitive shelter, and how much to relax or sleep. If our goodfellow Robin happens to enjoy berries but not fish, then she will spend a lot of time searching for berries, and perhaps even cultivating berry-bearing bushes, though she will not bother to do much fishing. Economics can characterize how Robin will allocate her time, how she will do the best she can given her straitened (albeit idyllic) circumstances.

Robin's "best" is judged relative to her own preferences, not relative to some ideal developed by a philosopher king or an "eat more berries" advocate. Economics takes Robin's preferences as a given, a starting point, and proceeds to illustrate what conditions will be satisfied by Robin's resulting choices. Economics expects that Robin will do her duty, do the best she can— she cannot be made any better off by having an economist counsel her on optimal decision-making, though perhaps advanced information about berry husbandry or fishing techniques would be helpful to Robin. Robin, rational Robin, can be relied upon not to shortchange herself.

So Robin, going about her solitary business in her state of nature, will implicitly illustrate economic concepts. (Indeed, economics textbooks frequently make explicit Robin's implicit optimizing.) What about law? Robin has no use for law. The island—Robin lives on an island, of course—is hers alone, at least as far as human claimants are concerned: Robin need fear no property disputes. Nor can Robin enter into trade agreements, employment contracts, or venture capital deals. Careless behavior by other people does not threaten Robin with unintended damage, and her solitary Eden is a crime-free zone. Delivering law to Robin's environment provides no boon, no benefit—those optimal economic decisions will not change simply by supplementing Robin's locale with a legal code, an enforcer, and a magistrate.

Add a Friday, a Saturday, perhaps an entire week of companions to Robin's erstwhile lonely isle, and the situation changes considerably. On the economics front, there's the whole new possibility of exchange with the Days. Robin might specialize in berry cultivation and gathering, and trade her surplus crop to Wednesday for some firewood. Robin and Thursday might open up a used bookstore together. Society has expanded the possible types of economic endeavors available to her, but Robin's rational approach to decision-making will encompass these novel options as easily as it handled her life in solitude.

In contrast, the newcomers dramatically alter Robin's legal landscape. She now finds that she can benefit from law, or at least from the right species of law. If Wednesday obtains some of Robin's berries but reneges on his promise to deliver firewood, Robin might appreciate being able to ask a judge to order Wednesday to provide compensation. Robin and Thursday might be able to stave off disputes by detailing how they will share their bookstore profits, in a manner that will be enforceable by a court. The crimes of Monday, a notorious ne'er-do-well, might be kept in check by a police force, and Saturday's convivial but loud parties might be quieted to some extent, too. Robin can be counted on not to shortchange herself, though the Days might not share Robin's regard for her own well-being. Law can compensate, by making sure that the Days do not ride roughshod over Robin's interests, while the newcomers pursue their own ends via rational means. And the law can help ensure that Robin does not lay waste to the Days.

Much of what well-functioning law does is to harmonize the activities of a group of people, so that the group behaves not unlike a single individual pursuing her own ends. As a rational person does not cheat herself, so a society, well-knit by law into something akin to an individual, will not cheat itself. Our solitary Robin will do the best she can, where "best" is judged relative to her own preferences. The standard Law and Economics view is that law should— and often does—make it the case that agglomerations of individuals do the best that they can, where best is judged by the preferences of those individuals. Instead of talking about "best," however, analysts versed in Law and Economics tend to use the term "efficient."

Efficiency

The analogy between a single individual and a society suffers from the fact that different people have different preferences. One person's bookstore is another person's bête noire; one person's berry is another person's burden. If push-pin (an antiquated child's game) is better than poetry for Robin in isolation, then, well, in her solitary society, push-pin is better than poetry. But once there are two (or more) people, Robin might prefer push-pin, and Friday might prefer poetry. If they both have to participate, simultaneously, in either poetry or push-pin, there's a bit of a conflict. What does this multi-person society prefer, push-pin or poetry? How can we define or measure overall human flourishing, when different humans thrive in incompatible ways?

Jeremy Bentham

Jeremy Bentham (1748-1832), a renowned precursor to the modern Law and Economics discipline, was a utilitarian philosopher who believed that the goal for society should be to promote the "greatest happiness"—a close analogue to what economists now call "efficiency." In Bentham's view, people are guided in their decisions by the desires to gain pleasure and to avoid pain; laws influence human behavior by altering the pleasure/pain calculus attached to various actions. The best law is the law that brings the greatest overall surplus of pleasure over pain; "The general object which all laws have, or ought to have, in common, is to augment the total happiness of the community."[1]

Bentham also gave to the world the "push-pin versus poetry" trope in suggesting that social scientists should take human preferences as given and not seek to impose their own standards on what they think other people should value:

> The utility of all these arts and sciences,—I speak both of those of amusement and curiosity,—the value which they possess, is exactly in proportion to the pleasure they yield. Every other species of preeminence which may be attempted to be established among them is altogether fanciful. Prejudice apart, the game of push-pin is of equal value with the arts and sciences of music and poetry. If the game of push-pin furnish more pleasure, it is more valuable than either.[2]

In the Introduction the question was raised as to whether instructions in a will should be carried out faithfully by those left behind. What if those instructions are, following a public autopsy (witnessed by your

(Continued)

friends) of your cadaver, to have your head mummified; your skeleton preserved and dressed in your customary black clothes; the whole assemblage arranged in the sitting position you commonly assumed in life when thinking and writing, along with your walking stick; and this unusual mise en scène placed in a sort of display case? So Bentham requested, and his requests were carried out, though the unsightly mummification of Jeremy's head led to its replacement at the top of the skeleton by a wax model more true to life than the preserved head itself could muster. The case containing Bentham's earthly remains and the wax head still can be visited at University College London. (The original head is nearby but not on public display.) Bentham's will indicates that he was not shy about living companionship for his post-mortem self: "If it should so happen that my personal friends and other Disciples should be disposed to meet together on some day or days of the year for the purpose of commemorating the Founder of the greatest happiness system of morals and legislation my executor will from time to time cause to be conveyed to the room in which they meet the said Box or case with the contents there to be stationed in such part of the room as to the assembled company shall seem meet."[3]

Pareto Improvements

On the nature of social preferences, economics has one standard answer, and Law and Economics a slightly different one. The economics answer is that most of the time you cannot tell what society prefers, what outcome or rule best advances overall well-being. Robin prefers push-pin, and Friday prefers poetry, and that's the end of the story. Only if one alternative is unanimously preferred to another can it be said that society prefers the first alternative to the second. In the case of unanimous preference for one alternative over another, economists would say that the preferred alternative is a *Pareto improvement* over the less preferred alternative (though there are some complications involving the possibility that some folks view the alternatives as completely equivalent). If we weren't already at the unanimously preferred situation, we would have good reason to move there.

An "alternative" need not refer only to a single good like push-pin or poetry—rather, it describes the complete allocation of society's resources among individuals. We might talk about alternatives in terms of poetry and push-pin, but actual alternatives involve the precise distribution of houses and cars and health care and apples and education and pollution and everything else that people value or disvalue. The notion of alternatives and efficiency can be extended beyond the distribution of existing goods, too. Economists can talk about efficient ways to produce goods—more goods with less effort would represent a Pareto improvement—and of efficient decisions about which of millions of possible goods to produce: Robin and Friday could probably do with something beyond poetry and/or push-pin.[4]

We can go up another level as well and talk about efficient laws or policies, those that do the best job of leading to allocations that satisfy preferences. The provision of a patent system, for instance, might (or might not!) represent an efficient way to motivate the discovery and dissemination of new goods. Laws against theft can dissuade behavior that undermines social welfare. In contrast, the rules underlying Soviet-style central planning eventually revealed their inefficiency, their relative failure to promote the well-being of Soviet citizens. Law and Economics-style analyses tend to evaluate laws based on the economic efficiency of the outcomes that those laws help induce.

Trade and Efficiency

Voluntary exchange provides the exemplar of undertaking a move to a Pareto improving allocation. When Robin and Wednesday agree to their berries-for-firewood trade, each, presumably, thinks they will be better off making the trade than by not making the trade. Assuming no one else is adversely affected by their commerce—a big assumption—then the berries/firewood barter agreement represents a social improvement on the original situation: no one would have any reason to vote against the trade, even if only Robin and Wednesday had a strong motive to support the deal.[5]

After people engage in all their mutually beneficial trades, it becomes harder to identify additional moves that are social win-wins. Stumbling across a Pareto improvement is sort of like finding free money for society: we should certainly pick the money up when we find it, but we should not be surprised that it is hard to find. Most of the time we would expect that the status quo does not admit some reform, some alternative allocation of resources or alternative policy (a policy that will help determine the allocation of resources) that would make everyone better off. That is, for many or perhaps most situations, it will not be possible to identify a Pareto improvement.

When we get as far as voluntary trade and other unanimously supported steps will take us, we are said to be at a *Pareto efficient* (or *Pareto optimal*) situation. ("Efficiency" is standard economics shorthand for Pareto efficiency.) Such a situation, from which no further Pareto improvement is detectable, does not leave money (or well-being) lying about. Starting from a Pareto optimal allocation, there's no other alternative that would receive unanimous support when put to a vote against the status quo. Efficiency implies that there is no evident waste, no free lunch available to, but unexploited by, a hungry society.

Efficiency is both central to the economic evaluation of alternatives and rules, and peculiarly unhelpful. While the economics approach intends to judge allocations and rules by their efficiency, generally two outcomes and rules will not be comparable in terms of efficiency: neither would receive unanimous support in comparison with the other. As long as there are more than a handful of people on your island, once those voluntary trades (that do not harm third parties) are exhausted, it is close to impossible, no matter what your starting point, to find Pareto improvements, alternatives that everyone prefers to the status quo; therefore, many, many allocations of society's resources are Pareto efficient. And when two efficient allocations are compared, once again, we cannot say very much; we just shrug, and declare that Robin likes allocation A while Friday likes allocation B, with society's opinion not being determinable.

The shrugging extends from allocations to rules. If law Alpha will result in that allocation A that is preferred by Robin, while law Beta will result in allocation B preferred by Friday, then how can we say if our two-person society prefers rule Alpha or Beta? Indeed, the problem is even deeper, because we are unsure of precisely what allocation ultimately will result when we adopt a law.

The Art of the Deal

Law and Economics tries to go further, however, in gauging society's overall preferences. Voluntary trade and social benefits are so closely associated that we are tempted to invent imaginary trades after we have run out of real ones.

So let's consider again our two-person, Robin-Friday society, sadly agonizing over the push-pin or poetry dilemma. What is better for the desolate dyad, push-pin or poetry, if only one or the other can be made available, and if Robin likes push-pin, whereas Friday is a poetry aficionado? To formulate an answer, we imagine what would happen if Robin and Friday could undertake one of those mutually beneficial exchanges.

Suppose we are starting off with a status quo of push-pin, which (as we have stipulated) Robin likes a lot, though Friday would prefer poetry. Friday considers suggesting to Robin that they switch to poetry. There is no chance that Friday's proposal will receive unanimous support, as Robin is more than content with push-pin. So Friday has an idea—what if he sweetens the deal? What if Friday offers to pay Robin for her agreement to exchange push-pin for poetry? Friday isn't willing to pay an infinite amount for the trade, but he is willing to pay something. Robin probably wouldn't be interested in embracing versification if the amount offered were very small, like a penny, but she would take Friday up on a considerable tender. Robin might well prefer poetry plus $1,000 to push-pin, even if she likes poetry alone less than push-pin. And if Friday is willing to pay $1,000 for the switch to stanzas, in a sense the shift is a Pareto improvement—with the compensation paid to Robin, both parties prefer poetry to the status quo of push-pin. The reform (jettisoning push-pin for poetry) receives unanimous support, once Friday's "bribe" to Robin is included. As with other voluntary trades, then, society can be said to be better off when Robin and Friday agree to replace push-pin with poetry.

More generally, the idea is to imagine a trade of the sort just described, such that a switch from alternative A to alternative B involves compensation from those who prefer the switch, paid to those who don't, in such a way that everyone ends up welcoming the exchange. This hypothetical voluntary trade, which could involve hundreds, thousands, or millions of people, will share the usual property of actual voluntary trades, that of making all parties involved better off. These trades do not leave any money, even hypothetical money, lying about, and hence can be said to maximize the overall wealth or well-being of society.

Why isn't a shift to an allocation that represents higher societal rewards via our hypothetical trade an actual Pareto improvement? Uh, well, because one side of the trade, the payment portion, was imaginary. The compensation does not take place, the hypothetical indemnification for Robin does not actually materialize—the Law and Economics approach asks only if such a quid-pro-quo trade is possible in theory. If the answer is yes, if the winners could in principle compensate the losers, then alternative B represents higher aggregate wealth or well-being than does the alternative A status quo—but the losers won't be too pleased if society implements B, since they don't actually receive the imaginary compensation, and hence they really will be losers in the exchange.[6]

Adopting the imaginary trade test with hypothetical compensation as a method of judging between alternative distributions of resources is another way of saying that you will maximize the size of the economic pie, overall well-being, satisfaction, or wealth. Outcomes or laws which maximize well-being in this sense are what Law and Economics generally means by "efficient"—a less restrictive, and consequently more deployable, standard than that provided by Pareto efficiency.[7] We don't need unanimous consent to say that allocation B (or rule Beta) is socially preferred to allocation A (or rule Alpha); rather, we only need it to be the case that the overall pie is larger with

B (or Beta). Maximizing the size of the pie via the imaginary trade test does not say anything about the shares of the pie, however—indeed, employing the pretend trade method at times will counsel the adoption of rules that leave some people unhappier, even as total social satisfaction goes up.

Willingness-to-Pay

In determining whether society would be better off by switching from push-pin to poetry, we based our answer on the willingness of Friday to pay for poetry, and on the willingness of Robin to accept payment. If Robin would accept a payment for the switch to poetry that is less than the most that Friday is prepared to offer, then poetry is more efficient, represents greater social wealth, than push-pin. (And this is the case, once again, even if no payments are actually made for the switch, if the compensation is imaginary.) A person's willingness-to-pay (for anything) is based on those stable individual preferences that economists take as a starting point for rationality, along with the resources at the person's disposal. Willingness-to-pay calculations allow the intensity of individual preferences— how much do I really like poetry?—to be considered when judging the social desirability of alternative allocations of resources.

As is probably obvious by now, the imaginary trade approach embeds some important limitations. In particular, initial wealth holdings can be determinative in judging the social desirability of a proposed policy change, even if those initial allocations of wealth are morally dubious. Imagine for a second that Friday is quite poor, with only a few dollars to his (odd) name, and Robin is extremely rich. Friday is not willing to pay very much for poetry—even if he really, really likes it a lot more than he likes push-pin—because he does not have much money. A person's willingness-to-pay (in the economic sense, at least) cannot exceed his ability to pay. Let's say Friday is willing to pony up $10 for the switch to poetry, a sizable chunk of his overall wealth. Robin cares just a bit more for push-pin than for poetry, but because she has lots of money, she would need to be paid, say, $100 to accept the alteration. So Friday is willing to pay less for poetry than Robin needs to consent to the change: the status quo of push-pin, by this reckoning, is more efficient, represents higher overall wealth, than poetry. There is no voluntary trade available, even a hypothetical one, that will make everyone better off.

What if the feelings of Robin and Friday toward push-pin and poetry are as above, but now Friday is wealthy and Robin is poor? In these circumstances, Friday might be willing to pay $1,000 for poetry, and desperate Robin might take as little as $1 to agree to the switch. By the standard reasoning, poetry now is more efficient, represents greater social wealth, than push-pin. (This is true even if Friday amassed his fortune by underhanded, robber-baron-or-worse means.) Using the willingness-to-pay standard as our guide to voluntary (and imaginary!) trades privileges the rich in judging the social desirability of alternative allocations. The intensity of preferences that we account for by utilizing willingness-to-pay recognizes only "effectual" preferences, those that are backed up by sufficient resources. This approach at least has illustrious provenance: Adam Smith noted in 1776 that "A very poor man may be said in some sense to have a demand for a coach and six; he might like to have it; but his demand is not an effectual demand, as the commodity can never be brought to market in order to satisfy it."[8]

Another glaring shortcoming of the willingness-to-pay approach is that in most circumstances, it is impossible to know someone's willingness-to-pay for a policy change. Bidding behavior by rational participants at certain types of auctions might reliably reveal individual valuations, but those circumstances are rare. (For that matter, people might not know, even approximately, their own willingness to pay for some good or service, much less the net worth to them of a policy reform.[9]) So analysts have to infer (make up?) the value of outcomes to people, leaving room for considerable disagreement about desirable rules even among those who are committed to the criterion of Law and Economics-style efficiency.

Nonetheless, willingness-to-pay is a serviceable though flawed method of assessing society's overall preferences; its chief deficiencies are understood, so we can be alert to when they are most likely to skew the analysis.[10] In particular, reforms that involve vast changes—especially declines—in the incomes of many people (or even one person) do not readily lend themselves to unambiguous or uncontroversial comparisons via willingness-to-pay. For many ordinary policy adjustments, however, such as altering a sales tax, say, or improving the safety features of public roads, the use of imaginary trades and compensation to gauge the desirability of proposed reforms can provide valuable guidance. Indeed, the willingness-to-pay approach is the basis for cost-benefit studies, which frequently are mandated before public projects are undertaken. A proposed project passes the cost-benefit test if aggregate benefits exceed aggregate costs, so that implementing the project increases net social wealth. The outcome of such a cost-benefit analysis provides an argument, but not the final word, over whether a project should or should not be implemented.

Why Maximize Aggregate Well-Being?

The imaginary trade approach points to what allocations or rules maximize overall well-being, while ignoring issues of how that well-being is distributed.

Why should we think that wealth or well-being maximization and the social good should be closely connected or identical?

If we use willingness-to-pay to assess reforms, we know that sometimes we will adopt changes that increase social wealth, but are not full-on Pareto improvements, unanimously preferred to the status quo. So, some individuals will see their own payoff or satisfaction suffer from the transition. Nevertheless, if society were to employ the imaginary trade and compensation criterion in evaluating proposed changes, in the long run, it would presumably turn out well for everyone, or just about everyone. While you might lose from one individual reform, you would win on others, and there is much to be said for adopting a standard for judging reforms that continually results in a larger overall pie. If some of those changes really do cause some people's well-being to drop precipitously, then perhaps the hypothetical compensation could, in those cases, become actual compensation, to prevent any seriously adverse distributional consequences arising from an overall pie-promoting reform.

The case for this type of wealth maximization is similar to, though weaker than, the case for the unanimity standard that is established by the criterion of Pareto efficiency. Failure to undertake a reform that represents more pie is (sort of) wasteful. If distributional consequences prevent implementing such a reform, then the fact that reform would increase the size of the pie also suggests that an actual deal, not just an imaginary one, could be constructed that, through compensation, would make nearly everyone better off from the change.

Just Compensation

Compensating potential "losers" when pursuing overall wealth-increasing reforms is reflected to some extent in US property law. If the government takes your property for a desirable public purpose— say, your land is seized to make way for a much-needed road—then the government must provide you "just compensation" for the taking. If the compensation is sufficient, then such takings have the look of win-win Pareto improvements.[11]

What if the government undermines the value of your property without actually seizing it? A new regulation, for instance, often will reduce the worth of certain privately owned assets. Perhaps a new environmental ordinance or zoning law might limit the potential for your land to be developed. The regulation might be sensible, and promote the overall public good, but nevertheless impose a significant economic loss on you, the landowner. Does the regulation constitute a "taking" of your property, such that you are entitled to compensation? This question has taxed courts for many decades, but the theme of the legal answer seems to be that if the economic loss to the property owner is quite substantial, then compensation will be required; for small or moderate losses, however, the losses will remain where they first were imposed, upon you, the hapless landowner.[12] That is, when the distributional effects are sufficiently severe, actual compensation replaces the hypothetical compensation that must be available if a new regulation increases the overall pie.

Employing Efficiency

To what employ does Law and Economics put the idea of efficiency or wealth maximization? There are two customary uses. First, as suggested, the amount of wealth generated, the size of the pie, frequently serves as one standard, perhaps the main standard, by which different legal rules are judged. (That is, Law and Economics scholars adopt the imaginary trade and compensation criterion to compare the allocations brought about by alternative legal doctrines.) By this standard, a rule that is more efficient (produces greater wealth) is better than a rule that produces lower wealth. Second, it is argued—most prominently by Judge Richard Posner—that under some circumstances, the law itself will tend to develop in such a way that it will consist of those rules that promote overall wealth or efficiency.[13]

The argument for an efficiency-promoting dynamic is particularly persuasive when applied to the common law concerning contracts.[14] Typically, negotiating parties can override contract law default provisions, by putting into their contracts the alternative terms that they prefer. The parties have no reason not to shape the contract language in such a manner as to maximize their gain from the contractual relationship—that is, with respect to the contracting parties themselves, at least, combined wealth maximization would seem to be their goal. (Any contract that is not wealth maximizing could be replaced by a contract that offers all the signatories a bigger payoff—compensatory payments are indeed possible among parties who already are entering into contracts—so presumably they will accept, unanimously, the Pareto-improving contract terms.) What this logic suggests is that provisions of contract law that do not achieve wealth maximization will be overridden by the contracting parties. Laws are not static, however; in particular, contract law tends to adjust to incorporate those contract provisions that are most commonly employed. The laws themselves, then, are under some pressure to evolve in an efficient, wealth-maximizing direction. (The heretofore concealed assumption, of course, is that the only parties with an interest in the contract are the participating parties. If other people care but are not involved in the negotiations—say the contract is an agreement among thieves concerning how to split any upcoming takings, with the intended victims of the theft not privy to the bargaining—then there is less reason to believe that the rules of contract law will tend toward efficiency.)

Common Law and Civil Law

The term *common law* has a host of different meanings, some tracing back to twelfth-century tribunals in England. For the purposes of Law and Economics, probably the most important element of common law is that it evolves over time through the verdicts and opinions that are rendered when cases are adjudicated. Court decisions in a common law setting—provided that the court is at a sufficiently high level—hold some precedential value. That is, common law courts are expected to follow their own previous decisions, and lower courts are expected to be bound by the prior rulings of their superior courts. The respect for precedent goes by the Latin phrase *stare decisis*, which translates roughly as "standing by the decision." The fact that court verdicts in common law jurisdictions create binding precedents means that the laws in those venues are, to some extent, made by judges—often through their interpretation and application of legislative or regulatory statutes.

If there were perfect respect for precedent there would be limited scope for the law to evolve via court decisions—though which of a wide variety of potentially relevant precedents to apply would still require some discrimination. The job of a lawyer arguing before a court in a common law setting is to explain why the precedents that favor his or her client are applicable to the current controversy, whereas the precedents that favor the other side offer poor analogies to the case before the court. But in practice, respect for precedent is not absolute, and the highest court in a jurisdiction can overrule its own previous decisions if it subsequently feels they are mistaken. These channels for the evolution of the common law give an impetus toward economic efficiency, if inefficient precedents are more likely to be overturned than efficient ones.[15]

Judge-made common law, which is the chief legal approach taken in Great Britain and many former British colonies, is distinguished at times from *civil law*—another term with multiple, and conflicting, meanings. Civil law generally refers to statutory law, where the law is found in written rules—the Napoleonic Code remains the basis for laws in many areas of the world today. A law student in a civil law country studies code books (listings of statutes), whereas a law student in an area dominated by common law primarily studies previous cases and their adjudication. (An alternative context distinguishes civil law from criminal law; in a civil matter, the defendant is threatened with the possible imposition of monetary sanctions, but not with time in prison. A jail sentence is a possible outcome to a serious criminal charge.)

In practice, the differences between common law and civil law jurisdictions are not quite as stark as the earlier descriptions might suggest. Common law is often code-based, too, and judges in civil law countries still engage in legal interpretations that create precedents. Nevertheless, a surprising but fairly robust empirical finding is that a common law tradition tends to be more conducive to long-term economic growth than does civil law. In particular, common law settings seem to be better able to protect private property from governmental incursions, thus encouraging investments that are central to economic development.[16]

The Coase Theorem

The idea that contracting parties such as Robin and Friday, in bargaining among themselves, will seek to maximize their joint payoff lies at the heart of one of the most fundamental insights of Law and Economics: the *Coase Theorem*. The name comes from Nobel Prize-winning economist Ronald Coase, whose influential 1960 article "The Problem of Social Cost" lent currency to the idea.[17] Coase's article does not explicitly identify the Coase Theorem; rather, later interpreters have attributed the theorem to Coase, but their precise specifications of "the" Coase Theorem differ.

The basic notion is that when people get together to figure out how to allocate resources, or to choose the rules that will later allocate resources, they will be sure to come to an agreement that maximizes their joint wealth. The reasoning should by now be familiar—if they are not maximizing joint wealth, then there is a Pareto improvement available, one that they would unanimously prefer: everyone could get a bigger piece of pie. Society won't stop bargaining until overall wealth is as large as possible.

It's the "getting together" part that prevents us from always achieving efficiency. On issues that affect a large constituency—how much should the local steel mill be allowed to pollute?—just finding a room large enough to hold the potentially interested parties would prove to be a burden. Then there's the arduous negotiations, the lengthy, perhaps ambiguous agreement that emerges, and the enforcing of that agreement. All of these elements of getting together, forging, and implementing a settlement are costly—the resources expended in these endeavors are termed *transaction costs*. So one version of the Coase Theorem is: *In the absence of transaction costs, efficient outcomes are achieved.*[18]

The real world, however, is rife with transaction costs. It might seem, therefore, as if the Coase Theorem comes close to stating a tautology: when there are no problems, there are no problems.[19] Nevertheless, the Coase Theorem furnishes a guide, even in a world where transaction costs are significant. The baseline world of zero transaction costs encapsulates the entire universe of imaginary trades and methods of compensation—and we know that voluntary trades tend to increase efficiency. The Coase Theorem, then, yields a framework for talking about the barriers to good outcomes: Why aren't those imaginary trades available in reality? Is the difficulty that there are too many parties to successfully negotiate, or that the resulting agreement is too complex to easily understand and codify, or is it too costly to enforce?[20] Second, transaction costs are not always written in stone—they can be influenced via law and public policy. Indeed, one of the functions served by property and contract law is to make it easier for parties to craft and enforce agreements. Can we think of legal changes that will overcome barriers to realizing our imaginary, overall wealth-promoting deals?

Alternatively, sometimes the creation of transaction costs is the point of policy. Those contracts among thieves about how to split the gains from their nefarious deeds will not be enforceable in the public courts—society wants to raise barriers to the drafting and implementation of such agreements. If *all* transaction costs were low, however, the thieves' intended victims would be part of the negotiation, too, and they would be unlikely to agree to a deal that involves items being taken from them without compensation.

One of the major sources of high transaction costs is "missing markets." Trucks that drive by your apartment building early in the morning routinely wake up hundreds of people. You and your neighbors would gladly pay to delay these trucks, but who can you pay? There is no immediate market for a noise-free environment, so you cannot just go and buy a little bit more quiet. This is not to say that there aren't roundabout ways of purchasing tranquility—you could petition the local government to enact an anti-noise ordinance, sue the trucking companies, wear earplugs, or move to a quieter neighborhood—but some of these roundabout methods themselves are cumbersome: they involve high transaction costs (or in the case of earplugs, the costs might mostly take the form of discomfort or an inability to hear your alarm clock). Nevertheless, the potential solutions involving the local government and the courts, in a sense, have arisen over time as ways to partially fill in for the missing market in "quiet." That boisterous Coasean crowd gathered in a large room seeking to forge an efficient agreement sounds a bit like a legislature in a representative democracy.

The evident waste or inefficiency that accompanies some situations with high transaction costs often will provoke a search among economists to identify a missing market (like the missing market for a noise-free environment), and generate proposals to create a new market to appropriately fill the void. Problems with traffic congestion? Economists are likely to suggest that people be charged for the use of a road, with higher prices prevailing at more congested times. (Privately owned roads might be part of the proposed solution, too.) People can then, in essence, buy themselves free-flowing traffic, through their willingness to pay a high enough price. Constructing the new market can decrease the waste that arises from congestion.

The introduce-a-new-market principle is broadly applied, beyond reducing traffic congestion through opportunities to purchase congestion-free travel. Wasteful air pollution? Set up a market—tradable emissions permits—whereby people have to buy the right to pollute and where people who are particularly unhappy with pollution can buy up the permits and not use them. Airport delays and overcrowding? Set up a market in which airlines exchange take-off and landing rights.[21] It was the fact that these markets did not exist, according to this Coasean-style approach, that created the problem in the first place. The missing markets are a form of transaction cost that makes it hard to craft voluntary agreements to move to better allocations, those with higher social wealth.

Of course, establishing and operating a market are themselves costly, and they might not be worth the cost.[22] Some seeming waste isn't really inefficient; rather, transaction costs are high, and there might be nothing that can be done about it, so there is no point in complaining about not having everything you could imagine. An allocation (or law) is inefficient only if there is another feasible allocation (or law) that produces a bigger pie, even after the costs of transitioning to that alternative are paid. If wishes were horses, everything would be feasible; but sometimes the reality of high transaction costs cannot be sidestepped or overcome through the clever creation of a new market. Sometimes a few loaves and fishes can't feed a large crowd.

Establishing a Market to Erode Rent Controls

Policies that no longer seem desirable can nevertheless be hard to alter if there are some people who would be harmed by the alteration. Constructing a market that would automatically provide compensation to injured parties might be one way of hastening reform, by converting an overall wealth-increasing change into a unanimously supported Pareto improvement. One such possibility has been put forth as a method to speed a return to market-determined rents for housing, after a period of rent controls.[23]

Rent controls mandate that the rents charged for apartments must be less than what otherwise would be the going market rate. Such regulations foster many problems over the long term, if the legislated rent ceiling is significantly below the unrestricted level. The controlled rents lead to an apartment short-age: given the relatively low price, the number of people who would like to rent apartments exceeds the number of apartments that owners offer to let. The shortage means that landlords would have no trouble finding new tenants, so they have less reason to cultivate the goodwill of their existing renters. Owners are less inclined to maintain apartments, both because they do not need renter approbation to avoid frequent turnover and because they cannot receive higher rents for better maintained apartments or public areas. New housing is less likely to be constructed, and vacant apartments become hard to find as current renters stay in place to continue to take advantage of the bargain rates.

The problems arising from tight legal limits on rents are sufficiently severe that many localities look to ameliorate or eliminate their rent control policies. Such deregulatory attempts can founder, however, because current renters are receiving a significant benefit from the low rents. Any quick end to rent controls will harm those renters, and policymakers will not be anxious to earn the ire of a sizable constituency. A policy that decontrols rents only when the current renter vacates the apartment provides a gradual liberalization, but it is likely to be too gradual, given the strong financial incentive that current renters have to stay in their rent-controlled apartments. Current renters might also lobby for rules that will allow them to transfer their subsidy to relatives or heirs who join or replace them in occupancy.

See a problem, establish a market: allow current renters to sell away their rights to continued access to the cheap rents. Specifically, as the economist Michael Wolkoff (1990) suggests, let current renters transfer, for a negotiated payment, their rights to future controlled rents—those low rents currently kept low by law—to the owners of their apartments. The renters do not have to sell, so the proposal will not make them worse off (assuming that landlord mis-behavior to try to force a sale is no worse than previous landlord misbehavior to try to force a relocation). But if they were looking to move anyway, and only staying put because of the cheap rents, now renters can be paid to vacate their apartment.

The reason such a market solution for hastening the end of rent controls can work is that the situation with the controls in place is far from optimal. The existing renters are receiving a benefit, yes, but the apartment buildings are deteriorating, and the benefit to the renters is less than the costs imposed on the landlords. (This is a common issue with policies that primarily redistribute resources—the recipients receive only a fraction of the money that is paid by those who provide the resources.[24]) With the housing stock mired in a sub-optimal state—that is, with overall well-being lower with the rent controls than without them—it will generally be the case that a deal can be struck. Landlords can offer existing tenants a high enough price that the renters will sell back their rights to the controlled rent, probably in the course of moving elsewhere. But for such deals to be consummated, they need (or nearly need) to be legal: an authorized market has to be brought into being whereby renters can sell their claims to controlled rents back to landlords. Once the landlords have acquired the rights, they will be exempt from the rent control ordinance and able to set what rental rate they please for their apartment.

The Coase Corollary

Establishing a market to overcome waste often involves specifying who owns something valuable. (For the renters, it is their right to sell their "ownership" of low rents that needs to be specified.) In the air pollution example, when the market is introduced, residents could be given the ownership of an air pollution-free environment, a right to clean air. A steel mill that wanted to emit some smoke in the course of its operations, then, would have to pay the residents to relinquish their rights. If the market works smoothly (low trans-action costs), then the steel mill will buy the right to emit (limited) pollution at a price that the residents find attractive, and the resulting outcome will be efficient.

Alternatively, when the market is initiated, the steel mill could receive the right to pollute as much as it wants—in this case, the government creates an entitlement for industrialists to make steel and, in the process, to pollute to their hearts' content. Now if the residents want to breathe clean air, they have to pay the steel mill to restrain smoke emissions. But again, if transaction costs are low, the residents will recompense the steel mill for reducing pollution, and the resulting outcome will be efficient.

What I am terming the *Coase Corollary*—and what many writers in Law and Economics call the Coase Theorem itself—is that the efficient outcomes that arise under the two scenarios outlined earlier—one where the residents have the right to a pollution-free existence, and the second where the steel mills have the right to emit all the smoke they care to—involve precisely the same amount of pollution. It does not matter—in terms of the actual amount of pollution that will be generated—whether you assign the "ownership" of the air to the residents or to the steel mill. A typical formulation of the Coase Corollary would be something like: *In the absence of transaction costs, resource allocation is independent of the distribution of property rights.*

This result is profoundly unintuitive—it took Professor Coase himself a long evening to convince the Law and Economics mavens at the University of Chicago of the truth of the corollary back in 1960.[25] The basic idea starts out with the recognition that there exists, presumably, some amount of pollution that maximizes wealth. Think again of Robin on her island alone, with the possibility of making steel. Robin likes steel, but does not like dirty air; she takes into account the pollution when she decides how much steel to produce—her rational decision-making leads her to choose that efficient amount of pollution.

When the island becomes more peopled, creating a market for clean air ensures that steel makers and residents will again take pollution into account, like Robin did when she was the only affected party. If you give the residents the right to no pollution, and zero pollution is not the efficient amount, then everyone can get together—no transactions costs, remember?—and fashion a different outcome, one involving the socially optimal amount of pollution. The deal will be structured in such a way to yield everyone, residents and steel makers alike, at least as much satisfaction as they had initially, when zero pollution was the status quo: the agreement will generate a Pareto improvement. (In a world with no transaction costs, overall wealth increases can be implemented as Pareto improvements, because the hypothetical compensation can be converted costlessly into actual compensation.) Any proposed allocation that does not involve the socially efficient amount of pollution can similarly (and profitably) be overridden.

The exact same argument holds when the steel mill has the legal right to pollute. If by acting on its own, the factory would produce more than the socially efficient amount of pollution, the residents can get together and design some payments to the steel mill in return for its cutting back pollution to the socially efficient level—and everyone will agree to this arrangement. Zero transaction costs signify that folks always can come to deals, so they will continue to bargain until the pie is as large as possible. Frictionless negotiating implies that a group of many can act as seamlessly as one. The maximum pie comes about when the amount of pollution (and all other goods) is at its socially efficient level, no matter what the starting point: In the absence of transaction costs, resource allocation is independent of the distribution of property rights.

The fact that the amount of steel that society produces, or the amount of any other good (or "bad," like pollution) that society produces, is independent of the initial distribution of property rights does not mean that people don't care about the initial distribution of property rights (even if transaction costs, unrealistically, are nonexistent). People care, profoundly, because they personally will end up with more resources if they are assigned ownership than if someone else is. When the steel mill is given the right to produce and pollute, the homeowners have to pay the steel mill to reduce pollution to the optimal amount. When the homeowners possess the property right to a pristine environment, the steel mill proprietor has to pay them to allow production and pollution to increase to the socially optimal levels. The steel mill owner prefers the former distribution of property rights to the latter, even though the amounts of steel produced and pollution emitted work out to be the same in the end.

The "initial" allocation occurs when the ownership of the rights becomes clear—and such clarity might be achieved rather late in a temporal sense. Imagine that your house is situated in such a way as to provide you with a nice view of the lake. Your neighbor adds a room to her house, however, and in doing so, your lake view is somewhat degraded. Does your neighbor have the right to block your view with her domestic extension, or do you have the right to an unimpeded watery vista? If this property issue has not been settled in advance through legal devices like zoning rules and the issuance of building permits, then it can be decided, after the fact, by a court. You sue your expanding neighbor, and the court will either find for you and your view or for her and her McMansion. If transaction costs are zero, whether or not you end up with your view will not be affected by the court's decision—that's the point of the Coase Corollary. If it is efficient—overall wealth-maximizing—for you to have an unimpeded lake view, and if you lose the court case, then you will simply pay your neighbor enough that she will be willing to remove the view-damaging eyesore. If you win the case and it is efficient for you to have the view, your neighbor might try to offer to pay you to let her keep her bloated home, but she will not be willing to offer enough money such that you will agree. So she will have to remove the addition, under the threat that she will go to jail for disobeying a court order if she does not restore your original, delightful (and socially efficient) view.

Of course, there's a little bit of a self-defeating logic here. If transaction costs are zero, then resource allocation is independent of the distribution of property rights. If we are unsure of the property rights, then they will be settled by a judicial proceeding. But if the court did not happen to assign the property rights where they automatically produce the efficient outcome, then there will have to be a further deal among the interested parties—a further deal involving at least one party who just lost an emotionally and financially draining court case. This person might well be uninterested in additional negotiations—that is, the court-ordered assignment of property rights might be sufficiently adversarial that it creates a sort of psychological transaction cost that renders it arduous to trade those property rights.[26] (High transaction costs can hinder contracts even between two parties, not just when there are multitudes of interested people.) Given these sorts of significant transaction costs to post-trial agreements, courts might want to think carefully about assigning property rights in such a way that efficiency can be served without any further negotiations. (Notice here how the notion of justice or of "rightful" ownership again takes a back seat—or is denied admission entirely—when examining a property dispute through the standard Law and Economics efficiency lens.)

More on Property Rights and Efficiency: The Tragedy of the Commons

Until the government or a court makes it clear whether factories own the right to do what they want with the atmosphere, or whether residents have the right to clean air, anyone, presumably, can pollute as much as they choose. The sky will be like an unregulated public park: all and sundry can do what they please with the air. The atmosphere or the park, in these instances, is known as a *commons*, in the sense that people in common have access to them. This open access suggests that the commons will be overused, that too much activity (relative to the overall wealth-maximizing amount) will occur there (and hence that there might be good reason to regulate access and use). When someone uses the commons—cuts down a tree, say, or dumps trash in the park, or pulls fish from the ocean—the benefits of their behavior mostly accrue to them, while some (even most) of the costs are imposed upon other people, in the form of a park with too little shade and too much trash, and an ocean that is depleted of fish. This tendency for commonly owned assets to be overused, perhaps to the point of destroying their value, was named the *Tragedy of the Commons* in an influential 1968 article by Garrett Hardin. Excessive noise pollution in a city is at least one partial example (that we have already noted) of a Tragedy of the Commons, as every citizen is equipped to emit noise and often can do so without interference.

If transaction costs were zero, there would be no inefficient tragedies. The "all and sundry" individuals who are the source of the overuse would come to an agreement limiting the amount of tree cutting or trash disposal or fishing to the socially efficient amount, just as if the park or ocean were owned by a single person (Robin!) who then manages it in a manner to maximize her wealth. Even when transaction costs are significant, people sometimes can hammer out and enforce agreements that mitigate the tragedy—international treaties restricting ocean fishing are one case in point. The agreements typically take the form of limiting access to the commons, of course. It is open access that leads to overuse, so controlling access can avert a tragedy.

The Reverse of the Medal: Property Rights and the Anticommons

Imagine that you have been waiting in a line outside a foreign consulate hoping to be admitted to apply for a visa. In fifteen minutes time, the consulate will close for the day, and the line is long, but after waiting for three hours, you are now at the front of the queue, the next supplicant who will be admitted. Suddenly you are approached by a stranger who has just arrived; the stranger has a moving and credible tale of woe and expresses an urgent need to get into the consulate that day—something that almost surely will not happen if she does not jump the queue. She asks you for permission to get in front of you.

Alas, she has requested that you give her something that you do not legitimately own, since if you agree, she will not only be in front of you, but in front of dozens of other people who have been dutifully waiting, and many of whom, in all likelihood, will not be served that day. (Perhaps you could just give her your spot in line and depart, without violating any vested rights of those behind you. But if you stay in the queue, allowing her entrance harms the interests of others in line and also brings up questions of fairness—the people behind you might have moving and credible tales of woe, too, and they have been waiting.[27]) You suggest that the newcomer start from the back of the line, and secure the agreement of every individual, seriatim, working her way back to you.

Your suggestion will not be welcomed by the stranger. She will recognize that it will be very hard to obtain the agreement of dozens of people expeditiously, and that all it takes is for one person to fail to accede to her request (or even to dither awhile) for the start-at-the-back option to end without her gaining access to the consulate—even if it is efficient for her to be admitted, in the sense that if she had the right to be first in line, no mutually profitable deals could be worked out where she would relinquish that right. The start-at-the-back option fails because of high transaction costs: a large number of people must be approached and must approve and a single recalcitrant individual can scuttle the deal. If any one of these people is Machiavellian (some might say rational), that person might try to withhold his agreement unless he is paid a considerable sum. Indeed, perhaps every individual would name a high price, in total demanding a much greater amount than entrance to the consulate would be worth even to the desperate stranger. It might be particularly tempting for the final person (oh, that would be you—you are at the front of the line, and she is moving back to front) to demand a large payment, after she had secured everyone else's agreement.

The stranger's predicament at the consulate is replicated any time an enterprise requires the unanimous agreement of a large number of people. Simply contacting and negotiating with everyone will be an ordeal, and people will be tempted to hold out for a high price when they see that the overall objective is hostage to their acquiescence. Building or expanding an airport near a major city is one example. The amounts of land required for such an undertaking are significant; further, the adjacent land is likely to have many different owners. Even owners of the non-adjacent tracts that underlie the new flight paths made possible by the airport construction or renovation might have to agree to the increased noise that will descend upon their property.

The Tragedy of the Commons arises when open access to a resource leads to overuse of that resource. The consulate line or airport expansion stories illustrate the flip side, situations where the existence of numerous interested parties with control rights makes it very costly to access an asset—with the result that the asset is underused. Open access leads to overuse, whereas access allowable only after significant hoop-jumping leads to underuse. This flip side, where many individuals have to agree before an economic resource can be employed in a new way, has been termed the *Tragedy of the Anticommons*.[28]

The legal system goes a long way toward determining how frequently anticommons tragedies arise. When airplanes were first invented, it was unclear if the consent of landowners was necessary for airplanes to fly above their real estate. The courts eventually decided that the answer is no: high-flying planes do not need to secure the permission from every landowner whose property they momentarily overfly.[29] Had the courts instead assigned the property rights to the airspace to the landowners below, a Tragedy of the Anticommons would have ensued—airlines could not easily secure permission from the possibly thousands of landowners whose rights would be implicated even in short flights. Building public highways or railroads also requires assembling rights to land from myriad landowners. Eminent domain rules allow the government to seize land for such projects while providing compensation to the landowners, to ensure that the (sometimes) Machiavellian threat to withhold sale unless an extremely high price is paid will not be credible.

The patent system sets up property rights in inventions: people cannot use your patented invention without your permission. (Unlike property rights in real assets like land or furniture, the rights conferred by a patent are temporary; currently in the United States, most patents last for twenty years.) The patent system therefore provides strong incentives to inventors to find valuable new products or processes, as then they can sell those processes (and hold a legal monopoly, be the sole seller) for a high price. Inventors, however, build upon the shoulders of previous inventors. If there are multiple patent holders whose own patented products are necessary components for a new invention, a Tragedy of the Anticommons potentially presents itself. Inventors might shy away from tinkering around in fields that already contain a "patent thicket" because of the high transaction costs, and potential hold-out demands, that would arise from the need to secure permission from numerous patent holders.[30] Strong and protracted patent rights do not necessarily lead to robust incentives for inventions: even if a specific patent is itself more valuable when patents have a long duration, the lengthy patent life generally will render it more costly to secure a patent, as the consent of untold pre-existing patent holders will be required.

Law can help knit a populous society into a wealth-maximizing whole by establishing clear ownership over economically important assets. (What qualifies as "economically important" can change over time: the airspace well above ground level was not economically important prior to the invention of aircraft, but that airspace acquired economic value as technology progressed.) If transaction costs are low (and clarifying property rights is one method of keeping transaction costs low), then the law need not concern itself unduly with how the rights initially are allocated. If transaction costs are high, efficient outcomes will require that the law assign the ownership rights to the high-value users—because the significant costs of transferring rights will prevent those otherwise desirable exchanges from taking place. Open access or too few exclusive property rights can set up a Tragedy of the Commons, where the value of the property is diminished or destroyed by overuse. Alternatively, too many, diversified property rights can set up a Tragedy of the Anticommons, with property underutilized. Both of these tragedies, when transaction costs are high, prevent assets from being employed in their most valuable fashion.

An Aside on View Blocking

Remember the hypothetical case where your neighbor harmed the view from your home when she added a room to her own house? The Coase Theorem (and Coase Corollary) discussion of this example aimed to indicate that, if transaction costs are low, whether the room stays or goes has nothing to do with the existence of a legal right to an unimpeded view from your home. Whatever the distribution of the relevant legal rights, they will be exchanged until the pie-maximizing solution is found.

But more generally, should the law allow neighboring property owners to construct buildings that harm the views from already existing structures? The Law and Economics approach is to ask what incentives are created by various legal rules, and to see which set of incentives results in the greatest overall satisfaction, in a world (like ours) with transaction costs, a world in which it is neither effortless nor free to arrange deals and exchange property rights. How would such an inquiry proceed in the case of views?

If the law gave an existing property owner the right to an unimpeded view, then that owner would hold veto power over all future development visible from the property. The result would be a race to build quickly (and on high ground!) to establish this potentially lucrative view—a sort of contest to plant a flag. Every ensuing parcel owner within eyesight, then, would have to negotiate with the first flag planter as well as any subsequent nearby property owners: for future would-be developers, the rule that existing views are protected property presents a Tragedy of the Anticommons. To avoid the tragedy of numerous in situ flag planters, people would tend to spread out, thereby limiting the number of pre-existing owners who require tribute from a newcomer in exchange for their blessing of view-altering local development.

Creating a race to plant flags and encouraging sprawl do not sound like highly desirable outcomes, so perhaps giving existing landholders rights to their views is not such a good idea. How bad an idea it might be is limited by the ingenuity of people to find ways to work around the bad legal regime, along with the size of the transaction costs that would have to be incurred to secure better outcomes. One possible work-around to undo the need to negotiate with every other owner of a nearby building would be, well, *e pluribus unum*, have a single owner for all the land (Robin again?) and let that person institute efficient rules. For instance, a property developer could win the initial race, or buy the property from the first flag planter, while also acquiring the rights to much or all of the neighboring property. The developer then could establish a sort of gated community governed by private rules (a covenant), where the extent to which later residents can impede established views is spelled out. Perhaps buildings could be no more than fifty feet high, and would have to be at least thirty feet from other buildings, or some such clause. The contracts between the developer and the owners, then, would offer a more efficient set of property rights to views than an unmitigated regime of full veto rights for all current landowners with respect to any future, visible development.[31]

What if the legal regime does not grant property owners rights to their existing views, but rather allows new property owners to build indiscriminately? This allocation of rights eliminates the (wasteful) race to plant a flag and undoes the promotion of sprawl. Simultaneously, some pre-existing views will be lost (non-consensually) to new development, even if the existence of those views is more socially desirable, more efficient, than the situation without the views. No system of property rights, it seems, brings full efficiency, where the best outcomes can be achieved without any further costly workarounds.

We could imagine an intermediate regime, however, in which pre-existing views are not protected, but egregious interference with views or light or air flow would be controlled, perhaps through public zoning rules. Such a regime would largely end the race to develop, and, to the extent that "egregious interference" matches up with "highly inefficient interference," the protection of efficient (and only efficient) views would be accomplished. Something like this regime seems to be the predominant situation in practice, too. In particular, it is generally not the case—nor should it be the case, by standard Law and Economics reasoning—that initial developers receive property rights in views.[32] One rapidly implanted flag should not bring about permanent control over development for miles around.

What Happens When a Property Right Is Infringed?

More importantly, what happens when my property right is infringed? What happens when the local teenagers, scamps that they are, play baseball in my backyard without my permission?

Well, I threaten them, of course! Get off my lawn, irksome children, or I am calling the police! And what will the police do? If the kids are persistent, and the police zealous, the ballplayers will be arrested. Property owners do not have to tolerate trespassers, nor can the teens just leave $20 after they play a game of pick-up baseball on the lawn and call the whole thing even.

But if the government desires my backyard to build a municipal baseball stadium, and I, the grouchy landowner, will not sell, then the government potentially can take the land (via its eminent domain power), evict the owner (moi), and pay me what it considers "just compensation." No one goes to jail for this non-consensual transaction.

So while the homeowner is the homeowner, how his property is protected from incursions depends on whether it is local teenagers or the state who are the potential infringers. The homeowner is protected against the sporty teens via what is termed (confusingly) a "property rule," and he is protected against the state via what is termed a "liability rule."[33] If your yard is protected against incursions via a property rule, then people cannot simply infringe and pay damages. Rather, you can acquire an injunction, and if they continue to *trespass*, they will be arrested.[34] Alternatively, if your yard is protected against undesired interlopers via a liability rule, then outsiders can infringe without your permission, though they must pay you some (judicially determined) recompense. The same property can be protected simultaneously by a property rule (against incursions by teens, say), and by a liability rule (against government takings).

Which type of protection for owners is best for society, property rules or liability rules? For researchers in the Coasean Law and Economics tradition, transaction costs, once again, are the key to answering that question.[35] If it is easy for would-be infringers to negotiate with a property owner—transaction costs are low—then by all means have them negotiate, instead of just letting them impose their will in exchange for some future damage payment. The negotiations will presumably result in consent to any type of "infringement" that is efficient, as the efficiency implies that there is a price the outsiders would be willing to pay, and the property owner would accept, such that those pie-increasing deals (and only pie-increasing deals) would be consummated. Since the baseballing teens could negotiate at low cost, their infringement should be governed by a property rule: secure the owner's permission, or play elsewhere.

If transaction costs are high, however, then permitting infringement without permission, but subject to an after-the-fact payment, is probably the better protection. If someone crashes into your car, they have infringed your property interest in your car; nonetheless, they (or their insurance company) generally can pay you damages to settle the matter. It is too difficult to negotiate in advance with every other driver, so a liability rule typically governs such interactions. If the price imposed after-the-fact fully compensates you, the car owner, and drivers know in advance that they will be subject to such payments if they cause a crash, then those crashes that do take place once again serve the cause of efficiency. (That is, under these rules, drivers choose the pie-maximizing amount of care in operating their vehicles.[36])

But what about the government taking of my house? It is not obvious that transaction costs are any greater when the state is my bargaining partner than when the teens are. Shouldn't the government, too, have to secure my consent to take my property? Why should the government be allowed to wrest property from unwilling owners, subject only to a compensatory payment?

If I am the sole landowner with whom the government needs to come to an agreement to secure land for the municipal baseball stadium, then there is no more reason to allow the government to infringe and pay damages then to allow the local teens to do likewise. (This is especially true if there are many other suitable locations for a stadium.) If a stadium requires the permission of many landowners, however, then the government faces a version of the Tragedy of the Anticommons. Any single landowner is in a position to hold the entire deal hostage to her agreement. The incentive to hold out, which multiplies transaction costs, provides an efficiency rationale—not necessarily a fully compelling one—to protect your home via a liability rule against incursions undertaken in the service of large municipal projects.[37]

Consider another type of property, so-called intellectual property, in this case, patents. The patent system long has been based on protection by property rules: if someone infringes a patent that you own, you can force them to stop. The property rule protection for patents makes sense if it is easy to identify patents that your new inventions might infringe, and to negotiate with the owners of those patents. But the growing patent thicket in some fields is raising the transaction costs involved in identifying and negotiating with patent owners. Not surprisingly, there has been movement (though rather limited movement) away from property rule protection of patents, to liability rule protection—as should be the case, if indeed, transaction costs have increased significantly.[38]

2

The Sixty-Minute Law School

Turning the accomplishment of many years / Into an hour-glass.
—Shakespeare, *King Henry V*, Prologue

The standard Law School curriculum in the United States involves three years of classes—considerably more classroom legal training than Abraham Lincoln or Clarence Darrow ever had. Occasionally there are calls for reform, most particularly, in the direction of shortening the law school curriculum. President Barack Obama, himself a graduate of a three-year law school, has suggested that two years might be a more appropriate length.[1]

But with economic efficiency as your guide, you can pronounce on legal issues with minimal training. (Admittedly, this ability to pronounce might not translate into the ability to pass the bar exam or to help clients in a meaningful or authorized way.) The chapter 1 tour of Robin's isle and willingness-to-pay, Coase and Commons, has set the table, surreptitiously "covering" the basis for the Property component of legal education. Other components of a legal education you will need to know something about are Contracts, Torts, and Crime.[2] We will expand on Property and take on the Contracts, Torts, and Crime components here, using the Law and Economics efficiency approach to reduce three years of study to, oh, about sixty minutes. . . .

Property, Mostly a Reprise

Happiness or well-being expands when goods or services or assets—stuff—that people value is produced and consumed, at least if the costs of producing the stuff are less than the value of the stuff, and if that stuff can be directed (perhaps through low-cost, voluntary trades) to the person who exhibits the highest valuation. Professor Coase taught us that as long as transaction costs are negligible, then the initial legally constituted owner of stuff will be irrelevant in terms of overall well-being, as the low costs indicate that the highest value user can be identified, and the stuff can expeditiously be transferred to that person's control. Transaction costs can be kept low through a variety of legal mechanisms: well-specified property rights, so that people know who owns what and hence who has the legal right to use stuff or trade stuff (hence the "make a market" solution to economic problems like pollution or rent de-control); good contract law, so that stuff can be traded with confidence; and well-bundled rights, so that there are neither too few owners with control over a given piece of stuff (as when open access leads to a Tragedy of the Commons) nor too many owners (as when a multitude of potential naysayers prevents stuff from being redeployed, a Tragedy of the Anticommons).

Transaction costs are fundamental not only for the desirable assignment and trade of property rights but also for deciding what to do when those prop-erty rights are infringed. Low transaction costs mean that people who want to use your property can easily contact you and negotiate for your permission. This ease suggests that they should be required to seek your permission, that is, that trespasses, intentional invasions of your property, should be illegal. If the incursions are efficiency-enhancing, the interlopers should be forced to prove it, by securing, probably through a payment, your acquiescence. Alternatively, if transaction costs are high, as they are among all those road users who might collide with one another, then your property right to have your vehicle free of non-consensual damage should be protected by a liability rule, whereby acci-dental transgressors first invade your property, and then are required to make good that damage. Those (hopefully few) who intentionally plan to invade your property are in a low transaction cost environment, and they need to secure your permission before using your car for their demolition derby.

Even in mature legal settings, where the law helps to minimize transaction costs, those costs still can be high. In this case, the initial ownership of prop-erty rights—rights to stuff such as a lovely view or rights to an additional room to a house, for instance—might have significant, long-term impacts on overall well-being. If the initial owner is not the highest-value owner, prohibitive transaction costs will, well, prohibit trading the stuff to someone who values the stuff more highly.

Technological change often lies at the root of the creation of property rights, because such change holds the potential to lend new value to previously unavailable or previously abundant stuff. The rights to the mineral deposits under your house were not valuable until mankind progressed to the point where those deposits could be gathered and converted into useful or beautiful things. Should you be the owner of the mineral rights just because you own the property above them? What if the "minerals" actually are oil or gas, which can flow from under your home to a well erected on your neighbor's property? Giving the rights to whoever first extracts the oil and gas can lead to a costly race to harvest these non-renewable resources—a race which occurred in many jurisdictions that adopted the rule that the first to harvest the fuels was the legitimate owner. Alternatively, adopting the view that landowners control everything beneath or above their property runs into problems, too, including, as we have seen, what such a doctrine—once a widely adopted one—would imply for airplanes or satellites flying at high altitude over thousands of pieces of property.

Who Owns Meteorites?

Look out, here comes a meteorite! A piece of cosmic rock has come to earth; who owns it? The answer to the ownership query can hold meaningful monetary implications for the parties involved, because even small meteorites can be quite valuable, perhaps worth thousands or tens of thousands of dollars, due to interest from museums, private collectors, and scientific researchers.

Imagine that I am staying in an apartment that I have sublet for a week from a friend. My sister is visiting, and while I am away, a meteorite comes through the open window and lands at my sister's feet. She picks it up (do not try this at home—freshly arrived meteorites are exceedingly hot!) an instant before I arrive. Does my sister own the meteorite? (What if it fell directly into her open suitcase or purse?) Do I own it? Does my apartment-leasing friend own it? Does the owner of the apartment building own it? Will the government try to claim the meteorite as its own? (The term "royalties" that refers to some payments for oil and gas, among other assets, is derived from the long-standing notion that the king, not the landowners, holds the property right to any valuable minerals on or under land.[3])

Well, these are framed as legal questions, and as I am not a lawyer, I am unsure—recall that you should not take anything I say as legal advice. Apparently the usual but not universal rule in the United States is that the landowner receives title to the meteorite; the federal government allows some types of meteorite hunting on public lands, with finders often being allowed to keep their small meteorites.[4] More generally, Law and Economics cannot say what the law *is*—that is for courts and lawyers—but it can try to inform the issue of what the efficiency consequences of different laws would be, and hence, to the extent that efficiency and desirability overlap, what the law *should be*. As we have seen, Law and Economics sets about this task by inquiring into the incentives those alternative laws would generate.

One attractive feature of making the owner of the land the owner of the meteorite is that it generally is easy to tell who owns a parcel of land. A second benefit of assigning ownership to landowners is that when a meteorite is known to have fallen, immediately vesting the landowner with ownership of the meteorite prevents a mad scramble, a race among seekers of extra-terrestrial treasure. Whether this second feature is attractive or not depends on the likelihood that the meteorite would expeditiously be discovered even in the absence of extraordinary search efforts. For meteorites that fall in well-populated areas (or in my sister's suitcase), it is probable that they will quickly be located. In that (suit)case, preventing the race saves a lot of human effort, without appreciably delaying the uncovering of the spacestone.

But if meteorites were to fall in remote areas where serious recovery efforts will be necessary to secure them, then there is much to be said for offering ownership or a sizable reward to those who first locate the rocks: the monetary incentive is likely to spur socially valuable search that otherwise might not be forthcoming.

All of this armchair Law and Econ-style analysis is predicated on the notion that people know (or suspect) that a meteorite has fallen, and they also know its general vicinity. But meteorites have been landing on earth since its inception, and most of them, presumably, have never been found. That is, there are lots of buried meteorite treasures around the globe, and there is a regular inflow, too: annual meteor showers are among the sources of such periodic additions. Monetary rewards or ownership rights for finders of these meteorites would be quite likely to increase the yield.

Incidentally, in terms of scientific value, it generally is helpful to know precisely where a meteorite was situated when found. (A similar point applies to cultural artifacts—knowledge of provenance enhances the information that they provide.) If finders cannot receive an appreciable reward in the formal market (because they have no legal claim to ownership or to a reward), then many of them presumably will offer their finds on the informal, underground market—with the likelihood that knowledge of the precise location and timing of the find will be lost to future researchers.

Contracts

If transaction costs are negligible and property rights are well-specified, then we would expect that Coasean-style bargaining would lead to efficient or nearly efficient outcomes. The bargains that result might manifest themselves in the form of a contract, as when Robin and the man who is Thursday specify how they will divvy up the responsibilities and the profits of their bookstore business. The terms that rational Robin and Thursday will write into the contract will call for actions that maximize their joint gain from their partnership, along with provisions indicating how to split that gain.

The world is complex, however, and contracts, while often bewilderingly complex themselves, are not nearly as intricate as the future situations that might arise. There's always something. You contract with your teenage neighbor Sarah to mow your lawn later in the week; in the meantime a meteorite slams into the neighborhood, destroying your lawn. So now you do not want your (non-extant) lawn mowed, but the contract still calls for a mowing: if Sarah chooses to be a stickler for contractual terms, she might lightly mow over the abyss that used to be your lawn and then demand payment. That is, the action called for by the contract, specified in advance, is no longer the best (most efficient) action to take, thanks to the intervening meteorite. Had transaction costs been zero, there would have been a contingency written into the contract specifying (probably) that in the event of the lawn being destroyed by a meteorite, Sarah should refrain from mowing and you should refrain from paying. But because transaction costs are positive, and because there are zillions of other contingencies that, like the meteorite, are highly unlikely but nonetheless could materialize, there frequently will be situations in which the actions specified by a contract are not the efficient actions to take given the actual, realized circumstances.

Contractual incompleteness is somewhat discouraging, in that those Coasean-style contracts that were supposed to ensure efficient transfer of well-specified property rights themselves might be riddled with inefficiencies. All is not hopeless, however. Various devices, created or facilitated by contract law, can prevent the waste that arises from inefficient actions. The overarching idea, as before, is to try to persuade the contracting parties to act as if they were a single rational adult, to get them to behave as Robin would—even if her behavior involves changing her plans because an unexpected contingency arises.

One possibility available to contracting parties is to renegotiate after the meteorite hits, or after whatever intervening events have occurred. Just before the inefficient mowing is about to begin, you might intercept your young neighbor and suggest that she demur. Sarah might point to the contract, which in some sense has given her the property right to mow your lawn and receive payment. You might have to buy that right from her. You will not be all that happy, relative to how you would feel if Sarah would simply go away, but you prefer paying her a small amount to leave rather than having to pay her a larger amount for a mowing that holds no value to you. In any event, the possibility of later renegotiation can prevent some inefficient actions from taking place, even if those actions were contractually agreed to in advance. Contracting that turns out to be inefficient might be rectified by further contracting.

Contract law takes some positive measures to promote efficiency, beyond simply permitting contracting parties to renegotiate. The doctrine of *frustration of purpose* allows promisors, in some circumstances, to fail to fulfill their contract-sanctioned promises, without having to pay damages. The meteorite's destruction of your lawn is a circumstance ripe for the application of the frustration doctrine. Imagine (as is likely) that it was assumed (at least implicitly) by both parties to the contract that the continued existence of the lawn in something like its original condition was an underlying supposition of the agreement, that the point of the contract was for the lawn to be appealingly maintained. Then the doctrine of frustration of purpose would permit you, bereft of your lawn by *force majeure* (or force astronomique, in this case), to step away from the contract without having to compensate your neighbor. A similar permission might extend to Sarah, if it was her lawnmower, and not your lawn, that felt the force of the meteorite's destructive power.[5]

Through doctrines such as frustration of purpose, contract law delivers a set of implicit contractual terms that apply to all contracts—unless the parties choose to override the implicit terms with explicit ones. These publically provided default rules are likely to call for the sorts of actions that the parties themselves would have agreed to, had they taken the time and trouble to write into the contract their preferred response to every contingency. Transaction costs preclude extremely complex explicit contracts, but contract law provisions donate the complexity gratis. For those specific contractual situations for which the contract law default is itself noticeably inefficient, and the contingency sufficiently likely, the parties will bear the transactions costs and write the contingency—along with the efficient actions to take given the future occurrence of the contingency—into the contract. The defaults provided by contract law generally can be replaced through contract negotiations and explicit agreements.

Expectation Damages and Efficient Breach

Perhaps the main device that contract law offers for knitting two people into a cohesive Robin-like unity is to mandate that, in most circumstances, a person

who chooses not to comply with the terms of a contract is liable for the payment of monetary damages to her contract partner. The breaching party must
pay the breached-against party. (Oliver Wendell Holmes Jr.: "The only universal consequence of a legally binding promise is that the law makes the promi-
sor pay damages if the promised event does not come to pass."[6]) In the United
States, the amount that must be paid is typically determined by the rule that
the breached-against party must be just as well off after she receives the damages payment as she would have been had the contract been fully complied
with (and hence no damages paid) instead. Damage payments constructed in
this fashion are termed *expectation damages*: the situation that the party expected to achieve through contract fulfillment must be reproduced following
a contract breach.

Expectation damages institute all-but-perfect insurance for contracting
parties. Either they receive contractual compliance, or they receive something
that they value just as much as compliance. Under a theoretically pure version
of expectation damages, a contracting party would not even care whether her
partner complied with the contract or chose to breach. This feature of expectation damages implies that when my neighbor is considering breaking her commitment to mow my lawn—let's say that she unexpectedly received an
opportunity to fly into space the very day lawn mowing was contemplated and
contracted for—the decision she makes will be the efficient one, the decision
that maximizes our joint gains. Thanks to expectation damages, I don't care
whether she mows my lawn or flies into space (in this latter case, paying me
those expectation damages). Since I have what I view as identical outcomes in
either instance, whatever choice she makes—to perform according to the contractual terms or to breach and pay damages—will be the best choice for our
two-person team. Expectation damages successfully form one out of many—
or at least form an efficiency-promoting team out of two contracting parties.
This feature of expectation damages is sometimes referred to as *efficient breach*:
in deciding whether to comply with the terms of a contract, a person who operates in a legal regime that perfectly institutes expectation damages will choose
to breach only when it is better (wealth maximizing) for society that she
breach, as opposed to comply, with the contractual terms.

In practice, expectation damages probably do not leave breached-against
parties as well off as they would have been had the contract been fulfilled.
Courts will not require reimbursement for harms that are not demonstrable.
Lost profits stemming from a contract breach, for instance, even if quite realistic, might be too speculative for courts to protect. Nor are all the legal costs
associated with a contract dispute likely to be recompensed.

Nonetheless, expectation damages are a potent arrow in the quiver of those
who argue that the common law—the law that emanates from the precedential

value of previous judicial opinions—tends to evolve toward rules that promote economic efficiency. Long before any economists were analyzing legal doctrines through the criterion of efficiency, contract law had adopted expectation damages. By ensuring (at least in theory) that a contracting party will be paid enough in damages to be fully indemnified against a breach, legal doctrines impart the appropriate incentives for maximizing social well-being when someone is faced with the decision of whether to comply with or to break a promise.

Oliver Wendell Holmes Jr. on Bad Men and the Law

Famed US Supreme Court Justice Oliver Wendell Holmes Jr. is another precursor to the modern field of Law and Economics. In his 1897 essay "The Path of the Law," Holmes suggested that an amoral person—a "bad man"—would look at the law simply as a set of prices that would be exacted for various behaviors. Such a person would not feel any ethical qualms about breaching a contract (nor about behaving negligently and thereby creating an accident, nor about committing a crime), and Holmes further suggested that the law shared the amoral person's point of view:

> The duty to keep a contract at common law means a prediction that you must pay damages if you do not keep it,—and nothing else. If you commit a tort [accidentally harm someone], you are liable to pay a compensatory sum. If you commit a contract, you are liable to pay a compensatory sum unless the promised event comes to pass, and that is all the difference. But such a mode of looking at the matter stinks in the nostrils of those who think it advantageous to get as much ethics into the law as they can.[7]

Accidents

Rational Robin, alone on her island, has to make decisions as to how much care she will take when she engages in her daily activities. These decisions concern her safety: how likely it is that she will suffer an accident, and how damaging an accident will be if she is unfortunate enough to have one. Robin will step more carefully across her isle when she is transporting a fragile object that she values highly, to be extra certain she does not trip and fall. When walking through ground covered with nettles, Robin will tread cautiously to avoid the prickly plants. (Note that the costs of accident avoidance, the hours spent walking slowly and intently watching, for instance, must be paid as the activity is engaged in, but the costs imposed by accidents themselves are probabilistic, only arising in those hopefully rare instances when Robin actually suffers an accident.) Of course, Robin could always take slightly more care, step ever more slowly or watch ever more attentively. As always, we can be confident that Robin will choose the optimal amount of care, the amount that allows her to avoid most accidents, without requiring her to spend six hours to walk six feet. Our confidence arises from our knowledge that Robin is rational, that she tries to do the best she can for herself according to her own lights, combined with the fact that Robin personally bears both the costs of avoiding accidents as well as the damages inflicted by those accidents she fails to avoid.

When Robin's island is invaded by the Days, not only are there new opportunities for production and exchange, there are new possibilities for accidents. In particular, when Robin goes careening across the island on her weekly bacchanalia, she might injure one of the Days, as well as herself. The optimality of Robin's safety-related decisions will now be called into question, since she no longer personally bears all the costs of her accidents.

Strict Liability

As with lawn mowing or pollution, the key to inducing Robin into making decisions that are good for society, and not just good for her, is to make her responsible for the full costs of accidents again, like she was when alone on her isle. The obvious method of doing so is to have Robin fully recompense any losses that she accidentally imposes upon others. Combined with the necessity that she bear the burden of any safety measures that she undertakes, such a compensation will result in full efficiency: Robin will account for losses that she imposes upon others in the same manner as she accounts for harms that befall her directly, since the legal system will force her to make good those losses in the event of an accident. This legal approach to induce *e pluribus unum* in the accident (or tort) setting is known as *strict liability*. The liability is "strict" in that the court does not inquire into how safely Robin was behaving—she may even have been acting in an extra careful fashion. The court only inquires as to whether or not there was an accident, and if Robin caused it. If the answer to both of these questions is "yes," then under a strict liability standard, Robin will have to recompense others for any damages they incur through the accident. Knowing that strict liability is the applicable legal rule, Robin will make socially beneficial choices in terms of how much care she takes to avoid accidents.

The theoretically pure version of strict liability works like a charm, but (as with theoretically pure expectation damages) real-world complications can alter the pleasing picture. Consider the case where Robin, out walking, runs into Friday and injures him. As Professor Coase might suggest, Robin's behavior didn't really "cause" the accident with Friday—if Friday were not there, he would not have been injured, just as if Robin were not there. The situation is symmetric. (Note that with a strict liability standard, we must determine which party will be held strictly liable: we effectively (and asymmetrically) designate one party to be the victim and the other party to be the injurer.) Further, Robin's behavior did not change the probability that Friday would be injured from zero to one, from absolutely no chance that Friday would be injured to the certainty of harm. In the usual accident case, both parties contribute to raising the likelihood of an accident, and even then their behaviors do not surely result in a collision. Perhaps Robin's walking increased the chance that Friday would be injured from 1 percent to 10 percent—but this time, they were unlucky, and the injury took place. Holding Robin responsible for all injuries to Friday leads her to overcompensate him for the actual damage that her behavior caused—which was to increase the probability of an accident from 1 percent to 10 percent—and also will undermine Friday's own efforts to avoid accidents.

Following the Coasean paradigm, imagine for a second that transaction costs are zero, so that Robin and Friday could sign a contract in advance specifying their actions and any damage payments that would be made in the event of an accident.[8] In most accident situations, a wealth-maximizing contract (that Robin and Friday negotiate and voluntarily enter into) would not impose strict liability on Robin to pay for all harms that befall Friday. Only when Robin's actions really did fully cause the accident, raising the probability that Friday would be injured from zero to one, would the optimal contract call for Robin to indemnify Friday against all injuries.[9] In general, then, Robin would not compensate Friday for his total accident damages. But note also that the contract probably would call for some damage payments any time Robin's actions raised the probability of Friday being involved in an accident—whether or not an accident actually took place. The parties typically are interested in ensuring that Robin has strong incentives to behave with appropriate caution, and not that Robin provide perfect insurance for any accident that might befall Friday.

Of course, transaction costs are not zero in the real world, so we cannot negotiate in advance with every other driver and pedestrian to sign contracts specifying our actions and the monetary transfers following future accidents (or following actions that lead to increased risks of accidents). We rely instead on regulations concerning who can drive and in what manner, as well as rules governing the behavior of pedestrians. Those who break the rules are subject to a fine or worse. We complement these regulations with suits for damage payments in the event of an accident. Under strict liability, the party determined to be the injurer must compensate the victim for any injuries, no matter the extent of care taken by the injurer.

Negligence

An alternative to a strict liability approach toward accidents is for a court to employ a *negligence* standard. In this case, the injurer will have to recompense the victim for any damages from an accident only if the court determines that the injurer was negligent, that is, was not acting with sufficient care. What constitutes sufficient care? The obvious (and efficient) standard for sufficiency would be the amount of care that a rational, Robin-like injurer would choose if all of the costs of accidents (including the costs of trying to avoid accidents) fell directly upon her. This is the same amount of care that would be chosen under a well-functioning strict liability system, too.

The requisite level of care within a negligence regime is called the legal *standard of care*, or reasonable care. Potential injurers will have a strong incentive to be seen as meeting that standard of care, because by achieving the standard, they are immune from paying damages. So if the legal standard of care is indeed set at the socially efficient level, then a negligence regime will result in the best possible care choice by potential injurers. That is, either a strict liability regime, or a negligence regime with the legal standard of care equal to the socially efficient level, brings about full efficiency for people in Robin's position, people who might injure someone while traipsing about their world.

Efficient care choices will not eliminate all accidents. The alternative legal regimes differ with respect to which of the parties has to bear the costs of those accidents that do take place. Under strict liability, the injurer pays for accident damages; under negligence, the injurer will choose sufficient care to avoid being found negligent, and hence the victim will be stuck for any damages arising from those accidents that are not successfully averted.

Further, the two regimes vary in terms of the incentives for potential victims such as Friday to try to avoid accidents. When Robin operates under a strict liability standard, Friday is fully insured against any accident damages—he is completely indifferent about whether he is in an accident or not. (The analogy with a contracting party protected by a theoretically pure expectation damages measure is exact.[10]) Alternatively, with a negligence standard, Friday understands that Robin will not be negligent—and hence Friday will have to bear the costs of any accidents himself. The negligence standard, therefore, provides strong incentives for Friday to behave with proper regard for his own safety. Negligence, in a sense, puts both the injurer and the victim in the situation of facing the full costs of accidents, of making one out of many. The injurer bears those costs if she chooses to be negligent, chooses to fall short of the legal standard of care. The victim sustains the costs of accidents when the injurer, responding to the negligence regime, chooses not to be negligent. So the potential victim, rightly expecting that the injurer will take due care, will behave in a socially beneficial way, too.

As with strict liability, a negligence regime in practice might differ from the theoretically pure version. The courts might set the standard of care inappropriately—an issue that does not arise under strict liability, because the amount of care taken by an injurer is legally irrelevant under a strict liability regime. The amount of damages also might be set incorrectly, and some injurers might not have the resources to recompense damages or might manage to evade identification altogether. (These issues arise under either a strict liability or a negligence regime.) Further, it can be difficult to detect some elements of negligence. For instance, after an automobile accident, often it is possible to determine the approximate speed of the "injuring" vehicle, though whether the driver was adjusting the radio or being otherwise inattentive generally cannot be ascertained. When there are substantial unmeasured dimensions of care, a negligence rule results in too little precaution, as potential injurers will be immune from paying damages once they meet the legal standards on the measured dimensions. They can fiddle with the radio without fear of liability, as long as they do not exceed the speed limit.

The torts discussion thus far has focused on the provision of appropriate incentives for taking precaution, of avoiding recklessness. It was noted, however, that strict liability and negligence regimes differ in terms of whether the injurer or the victim will bear the costs of those accidents that do take place. In practice, tort law serves both of these functions, providing incentives for appropriate behavior and (potentially) compensating victims of accidents. The efficiency lens of Law and Economics tends to direct attention to the provision of appropriate incentives, whereas victim compensation is, to use the standard economics-style locution, "just a transfer," that is, an issue that influences how the social pie is sliced, not one that directly affects the overall size of the pie.

Crime

Most crime is socially inefficient. Imagine a potential criminal negotiating with his intended victim in advance, offering to pay the person for the right to rob him or worse. Generally, there would be no price that, simultaneously, the criminal would be willing to pay and the victim would be willing to accept. If there were such a price, there still would be little justification for the crime, as the exchange could take place in a voluntary manner, governed by contract law. Crime typically involves the non-consensual transfer or invasion of a property right, with the invasion fully intended by the criminal.

(One can envisage some socially efficient, overall wealth-maximizing crimes, however: speeding while driving an imminently expecting mother to the hospital is a standard example. Perhaps breaking into an unoccupied house in a remote, deserted area for shelter from a life-threatening storm might be another. Indeed, these both are situations where the law is unlikely to charge the perpetrator with a crime—though in the latter case, compensation for damage might be ordered to be paid after the fact.[11])

Once again, the method to effectively construct an efficient one-out-of-many is to force criminals to bear all of the costs of their activities. If this were to happen, there would be very little crime; efficient crimes still would be undertaken, but most such "crimes" could be conducted in a consensual manner. Only when there are large barriers to the voluntary exchange—as in the case of entering an unoccupied house for shelter in a remote area—will it be necessary to resort to the expedient of invading a property right unilaterally, and paying damages after the fact.

Punishments for crime are, to some extent, intended to internalize (to the perpetrator) the costs of criminal behavior. Once again, practical matters interfere with the theoretical optimality that complete internalization would provide. Many criminals are not identified or not convicted; as a result, penalties for those who are convicted have to be ratcheted up (over what they would be if all criminals were caught and punished), to maintain, on average, the full internalization of costs. Imposing punishments is itself costly, and these costs are hard to pass on to criminals. Courts make errors, sometimes failing to convict factually guilty defendants and sometimes wrongfully convicting the innocent. These types of errors reduce the difference in payoffs between engaging in crime and abstaining from crime, accidentally spurring the incentive to behave as a criminal.[12] (If the judicial system punished people completely at random, then there would be no policy-based rationale to obey the law.)

Purposes of Punishing Crime

Once again, the Law and Economics efficiency-based approach tends to look at penalties for crime primarily in terms of how such penalties influence incentives to engage in criminal behavior. Fines and prison terms raise the price of engaging in crime, so rational would-be criminals will be dissuaded if the threats of fines or prison are high enough. That is, punishments for crime serve the purpose of deterring crime, and perhaps in an ideal world, those punishments could be calibrated in such a way as to induce the welfare-maximizing amount of crime (which, as we have argued, would be very low, at least if the imposition of the penalties were itself not very costly).

Deterrence is not the only efficiency-based rationale for punishing offenders.[13] In the case of prison terms, there is the potential gain associated with the fact that known offenders are isolated from the public at large, and so are unable (during the period of their incarceration) to commit further crimes against the general population. This *incapacitation effect* can combine with the deterrence effect to reduce crime via incarceration. Indeed, if incarceration does decrease crime (and it seems to, at least as currently practiced in the United States), it can be tricky to know whether the decrease is due to deterrence of the currently free population or to the incapacitation of the currently imprisoned population. Clever statistical analysis of appropriate changes in prison terms, however, can differentiate between deterrence and incapacitation effects, and generally finds that both channels are important in crime reduction.[14] Improvements in electronic monitoring might permit incapacitation effects to become more widely available for offenders (or accused, pre-trial defendants) outside of prison, in home detention, for instance.[15]

Punishment for criminals also can be justified (and enhance overall well-being) on the basis of rehabilitation, the possibility that a prison term, for instance, will reform criminals and turn them into law-abiding citizens. Perhaps prison itself or programs offered to prisoners can spur a change in preferences; alternatively, prison education and occupational programs might increase economic opportunities available to released prisoners within lawful industries, thereby steering them away from crime. Perhaps ideally, prison could serve as an effective treatment for the "disease" of choosing to behave in an anti-social manner. In practice in the United States, however, the prison "treatment" does not seem to be very successful, alas. Rather the opposite, in fact: a person released from prison, who previously had found crime to be an alluring opportunity, is likely to return to freedom with even worse options in legitimate employment, and perhaps with new crime skills and notions acquired through his jail acquaintances. One result is that some three-quarters of people released from US state prisons are rearrested within five years, and most of these are arrested within one year of release.[16]

Efficiency When?

Outcomes are efficient when they maximize joint wealth, when there does not exist another arrangement of resources that would do a better job of satisfying people's preferences. But, as noted, we also talk about laws or rules as efficient, even though those rules do not specify the ultimate distribution of goods and services and other things people value or disvalue. A law is efficient if there is no better law available, where a better law is one that, in operation, would generally induce outcomes that result in greater satisfaction, in comparison with those outcomes induced by the original law. Efficient laws maximize the average or expectation of future wealth: we do not know precisely what the outcome—the complete future allocation of goods and services—will be when we adopt a law, but we prefer laws that offer the best hopes for desirable consequences.[17]

There is a tension between choosing efficient rules, however, and achieving outcomes that make the best use of available resources. Consider the case of imprisonment. We adopt rules that involve putting convicted felons into jail. We noted above that there might be various reasons to impose jail sentences, but surely a major one is that we want the threat of jail to deter potential criminals from actually undertaking their crimes. Crimes are socially costly, so rules that offer some deterrence against crime can be efficient, leading to better outcomes than would arise in a world without legal deterrence of criminal acts.

What should happen, however, after someone has chosen to commit a crime and has been apprehended and convicted? The crime has already taken place, so the threatened jail sentence has failed as a deterrent (at least for this specific crime). Keeping someone in jail is costly, both in terms of resources devoted to maintaining the convict and the prison and in terms of the diminished life satisfaction of the prisoner. Assuming that the criminal will not reoffend (of course, a major assumption), and that other potential malefactors will not learn of lenient treatment and ramp up their own criminal behavior, it would seem that the least costly solution—the most efficient—would involve letting the convict go free. Why waste resources on punishment once the crime has occurred, after deterrence has failed, if those resources cannot decrease crime in the future? The situation is analogous to contracting parties who find that a contingency has arisen that renders their contractually specified actions to be undesirable. It is better at that point to re-contract, to choose actions that are efficient given the actual state of affairs, rather than abide by terms that made sense at the time the original contract was signed, but now are wasteful.

If the rule really were that offenders would not be punished after the fact, then, of course, the law would provide no deterrence against crime. (Similarly, if all contracts would be torn up and renegotiated when it comes time to act, then contracts would not be reliable, either.) The best (efficient) rule requires a commitment to punishing offenders, even if once a crime has occurred, it is wasteful to punish the offender. An efficient rule involves restricting your future behavior, obliging yourself (though perhaps not fully) to later actions that, viewed in isolation, look like a waste of resources.

Retribution?

One potential justification for punishing criminals that has not yet been mentioned is retribution—the notion that criminals deserve to be punished, that it is fair and desirable to punish them, even if no (other) beneficial consequences stem from inflicting the punishment.

The "just deserts" nature of retribution implies that the punishment should fit the crime, that is, that criminals more deserving of punishment should receive harsher treatment.[18] But what people think a criminal deserves is not necessarily connected to the consequences that follow from the deserved punishment; hence, the efficiency-based approach of Law and Economics does not mesh too well with punishment based on retribution.[19] Appropriate deterrence of future crimes, for instance, might call for harsher, or for more lenient sentencing, than what an individual criminal's behavior "deserves." Jeremy Bentham recognized that victims or society in general might like to see a criminal get his just reward, and that giving them this satisfaction would increase the total happiness of society if it did not involve any offsetting pain. "But no punishment ought to be allotted merely to this [retributive] purpose, because (setting aside its effects in the way of control [deterrence and incapacitation]), no such pleasure is ever produced by punishment as can be equivalent to the pain."[20] If punishment is necessary for appropriate amounts of deterrence and incapacitation, however, then that punishment can be designed in such a way (holding the extent of the punishment constant) to satisfy the retributive urges of society.

The philosopher and public intellectual Bertrand Russell posed a thought problem to gauge one's attachment to retribution.[21] Imagine that the public could be led permanently to believe that convicted criminals were being imprisoned, when in fact they were being sent to live far away, Robin-like, in idyllic circumstances. Whether in prison or on this court-imposed holiday, the convicts are in no position to commit further crimes. Assume further that the monetary costs are identical for implementing imprisonment or the alternative, the sub rosa vacation. For Russell, rewarding the criminals would be better for society than imprisoning them. The criminal is happier with the vacation, while the rest of society is indifferent: the expenses are the same, and society (including potential future malefactors) falsely assumes that punishment is being inflicted, so deterrence is not undermined, while the isolation of the criminals in both cases means that they themselves are not in need of deterrence to refrain from further crime. Punishment, per se, is inefficient, reduces wealth, and in Russell's thought experiment, punishment offers no advantages not possessed by the secret holiday—unless you place a positive value on retribution. But Russell puts no stock in retribution: punishment itself is a harm from Russell's (as from Bentham's) perspective—and possesses only instrumental value in terms of deterring crime, reforming criminals, or in placing people in a situation where they cannot commit crimes that they otherwise would commit.[22]

Standards of Proof

In a criminal case in the United States, a defendant is not supposed to be convicted unless his or her guilt has been proven "beyond a reasonable doubt." It is not clear, of course, what that standard amounts to in practice, but one common elaboration is that it is better for ten (factually) guilty criminals to go free than for one innocent person to be imprisoned.[23] This characterization nicely encapsulates the trade-off inherent in choosing a standard of proof: an exacting standard such as "beyond a reasonable doubt" makes it less likely that people will be falsely convicted, but more likely that criminals will escape punishment.

For civil cases such as contract disputes or medical malpractice, the standard of proof is not as demanding. A defendant can be found guilty in a civil trial if the "preponderance of the evidence" supports a guilty verdict. Again, interpreting this Delphic standard is not straightforward; nevertheless, the preponderance of the evidence standard is sometimes suggested to mean that as long as it is more likely than not that the defendant is at fault, a guilty verdict should be returned. The different standards of proof indicate that it is easier to obtain a guilty verdict in a civil proceeding than in a criminal trial, at least if the evidence is identical.

Why do civil trials feature a lower standard of proof than criminal trials? The Law and Economics perspective would suggest that efficiency might offer an explanation. The key to efficiency in this setting is that as a result of a criminal trial, a guilty party might be sent to prison. In civil proceedings, however, jail is not an element of the punishment for a guilty defendant. Rather, someone who loses a civil trial generally will have to pay compensation to the winner or a fine to the state. The compensation is a cost to the loser and an equal gain to the winner—overall social wealth is not (directly) affected by the court-ordered payments, though each party's share of that wealth is determined by the court.

Unlike monetary transfers, jail terms do affect, directly, overall welfare. A jail term is socially costly in at least two ways, as we have seen. First, the person who is sent to jail surely is made worse off by being in jail as opposed to remaining free. Second, the building and maintenance of jails require resources, including the labor effort of guards and the fashioning of iron bars. Were the prison not necessary, these resources could have been put into the service of creating other products that people value. If an innocent person is made to pay monetary compensation, the injustice is regrettable, but overall social resources are not directly affected. If an innocent person is sent to prison, overall well-being is directly lowered. As a false conviction carries more social harm when it occurs in a criminal matter rather than a civil matter, it makes sense, all else equal, for criminal trials to employ a higher standard of proof, to make false convictions less likely.[24]

The discussion so far has centered on the direct effects of compensation and jail terms. Much of the rationale for courts, however, stems from their indirect effects. The prospect of prison or of a court-ordered payment deters forward-looking individuals from engaging in activities that society wants to dissuade. Jails are expensive, but they serve a purpose. Note, however, that it might be possible to dissuade potential criminal offenders with fines, as opposed to jail terms. Fines are not, directly, socially costly: they hurt the party who pays them but are a benefit to the state that receives them (or rather a benefit to the taxpayers of that state). If fines can be used instead of jail terms, while keeping deterrence constant, then it is generally better for society that the fines be employed: no need for all those costly prisons and guards.[25] Further, a shift from jail terms to fines generally should be accompanied by a lowering of the requisite standard of proof, because the social costs of convicting an innocent person are less severe once jail terms are not part of the equation.

A high standard of proof like "beyond a reasonable doubt" might make potential criminals bolder, in that they expect that even if identified, they will be hard to convict, at least in the absence of substantial evidence. At the same time, a strict standard largely frees up non-criminals from having to think about generating evidence of their innocent behavior, or avoiding situations that will appear questionable to others even though they are blameless.[26] A lower standard of proof might lead to lots of record keeping and other forms of evidence generation, as well-intentioned people will need to demonstrate in a verifiable way that they are on the right side of the law.

So much for "Turning the accomplishment of many years / Into an hour-glass." For crime, accidents, contracts, and property conflicts, the law takes a similar approach (even though the approach is not implemented perfectly), and that approach can be digested in sixty minutes or less: require people to face the full costs of their behavior, and in doing so, a large society can function almost as smoothly, almost as efficiently, as Robin, a rational individual operating in isolation.

3

What's Done Is Done?

Bart and Lance

Robin and Friday are not the only people who get involved in accidents. Consider two exercise buffs, Bart and Lance. Bart is skateboarding along a lakeshore path, and Lance is bicycling on the path in the same direction. Lance catches up with Bart and proceeds to pass him. Just as Lance is coming by, Bart swerves a bit to avoid a rock in the path. Lance and Bart collide; fortunately neither of the parties involved suffers physical harm. Their vehicles, however, are not so lucky: Bart's skateboard incurs damages valued at $100, and Lance's bicycle, too, endures $100 in damages.

Who should bear these costs? Should the law require Lance to recompense Bart for the damage to the skateboard? Should the law instead force Bart to pay for the damage to Lance's bike? Or should the damages just remain where they were first incurred, with each of the colliders worse off by $100?

Society has an interest in choosing laws that maximize well-being. But notice that in the case of the Bart/Lance imbroglio, the total damage of $200 has already taken place. Whatever the law decides to do in this case only redistributes those damages between Bart and Lance; there is no direct effect on the size of the economic pie. What's done is done.

Nevertheless, not every distribution of the damages in the Bart/Lance case will lead to the same overall well-being. While there is no direct effect on the size of the pie from the legal allocation of damages, there will be an indirect effect—and potentially a very large one. The indirect effect comes from the precedent that will be set: the decision in the Bart/Lance case will help establish the common law rule that will determine how damages are divided in future accident cases. Subsequent skateboarders and bicyclists will (or should) know these rules, and adjust their behavior accordingly. One possible rule could be that "bicyclists always pay." In that case, future Barts will not be very careful about swerving, given that they will be recompensed for any damages they incur in an accident with a cyclist. Future

Lances, on the other hand, will pass by quite hesitatingly and after announcing their presence—or choose to cycle only in areas free of skateboarders. Another possible rule is "skateboarders always pay," which would create essentially the reverse incentives: Barts would be wary, and Lances relatively carefree. Another rule would be "passers always pay," under which future travelers, irrespective of their mode of transport, would be cautious when overtaking another path user. (The "passers pay" rule holds an informational cost advantage, in that it is easier for would-be passers to know they are about to pass than for the would-be passed to know that their being overtaken is imminent.)

The efficiency analysis of a rule is necessarily forward looking—the allocation of the costs from incidents that have already occurred, whether they are accidents or breached contracts or property incursions, is meaningful to the parties themselves but not, directly, to overall wealth. It is the incentives that today's decision creates for future actors that determine the efficiency consequences of a law. When courts in common law jurisdictions make rulings, they are resolving the present case, while simultaneously announcing (sometimes not all that clearly) the rule that will apply in the future. (Of course, if transaction costs are low, then any inefficient rules will be renegotiated, Coase-style—but in accident situations, as well as in many other settings, the costs of negotiating an agreement among all of those who might be influenced in the future by a rule are prohibitive.) Alternatively, in a civil law setting, different rules for distributing the costs of accidents will lead to different levels of future wealth, though no mere rule is capable of repairing accident damage that already has taken place. Today's rules or rulings influence future actors, and not all rules will induce equally desirable future actions.

Chicago Dibs

There is a tradition in Chicago and other northern cities with respect to automobile parking in the winter. After a significant snowfall, people will dig out a parking area along the curb of a public street. If the parking space was originally vacant and snow-covered, they might clear the space to park in it; if their car was parked in the space and then snowed-in, they might shovel snow out of the way to extricate their vehicle. The tradition is not the snow removal; rather, it concerns what happens after they vacate a parking spot they have cleared. When they move their car, before they drive away, Chicagoans will try to establish their property right to the parking spot with, say, some old kitchen chairs or trash cans. These placeholders are intended to make it known that no one else is supposed to park in the otherwise suitable space. The process is called *dibs*, a word that children use to stake their claim when racing for some goodie. ("I call dibs.")

From one perspective, dibs is simply a form of spontaneous privatization of public property, which generally would be frowned upon. (People do not appreciate it when I remove stop signs or manhole covers and sell them to the metal recycling plant.) Further, hoarding parking spaces is particularly costly after a snowstorm, when the snow has increased the scarcity of parking. The dibs system requires that some perfectly serviceable parking spaces be withdrawn from use when they are most needed! Nevertheless, many Chicagoans, including one long-time mayor, support dibs—even as they would decry most other types of private appropriations of public property.

The case for dibs lies in the incentive that the tradition provides for residents to increase the number of parking spaces in the first place, by digging out a spot for their car.[1] Fewer people would be prepared to engage in the necessary snow removal if, as soon as they exited the space, someone else could claim it. The fact that cleared spaces will be unused (and secured with decrepit furniture) is the cost of dibs, while the incentive to clear those spaces initially is the benefit.

Think of "static" efficiency as the optimal use of the existing parking spaces. "Dynamic" efficiency, alternatively, consists of the appropriate generation of additional parking spaces over time. The institution of dibs sacrifices static efficiency to improve dynamic efficiency. Although the existing parking spots are "done," how they are allocated might determine if more spaces become "done" in the future. Whether the trade-off between static and dynamic efficiency created by dibs is sensible, or whether there might be some alternative system that generates more room to park without the waste of underused parking spaces, is not obvious. In any case, the fondness of many Chicago residents for the dibs system cannot be said to be irrational: it is not simply a case of private appropriation of public property with no social benefit.

The institution of dibs also illustrates the importance of custom and social norms in establishing property rules. The effective law needn't always be what is written down by a legislature or decided by a common law judge. People often resolve their own property disputes in ways that can work pretty well for them, even if their solutions are not what a legislature might choose, or indeed, even if these informal agreements run counter to existing laws.[2] Custom and social norms hold the advantages that they are widely understood and tend to attract the consent of the individuals involved. These features of rules limit disputes and the need for extensive, and costly, enforcement and conflict resolution.

Patents

The patent process starts when an inventor records her invention, including how it works and how best to assemble it. The government, upon finding that the invention is novel and useful, protects the inventor with a patent: a right for a limited time, now generally twenty years, to prevent anyone else from making, utilizing, or selling the invention without the inventor's permission. The grant of a patent creates a legal monopoly: only the inventor or someone authorized by the inventor can use the invention. And as we noted in chapter 1, this monopoly typically is protected by a property rule; infringers cannot simply continue to use the patent by making damage payments.

Monopolies generally are considered to be economically undesirable. In a competitive market, goods are sold at prices that just compensate producers for the costs of production. This feature of competitive markets promotes efficiency, as any good that is more valuable to a buyer than it costs to manufacture will be produced and sold: the pie of net benefits will be as large as possible. Monopolists charge prices higher than costs (because it raises their profits to do so—competitive firms would like to charge high prices, too, but the existence of competitors forces their prices down). The high prices dissuade some buyers, even though those disappointed buyers would be happy to pay what it actually costs to produce the good. So a monopolized market does not maximize net benefits, overall wealth; it is less efficient than a competitive market.

Nevertheless, in the case of patents (and for written works, copyrights), the government provides a monopoly to inventors.[3] This monopoly protection ensures that patented inventions will not be used or distributed efficiently, because the price to buy one of the patented products will exceed the costs of making it available. Someone who invents and patents a better mousetrap will be able to have the better mousetrap market to herself for twenty years. She will sell her better mousetrap for a high price, even if it is inexpensive to produce. With her legally protected monopoly, she needn't fear competitors offering the same (or nearly the same) better mousetrap at a lower price.

Why is the government in the business of creating monopoly power, if monopolies are not economically beneficial? The high profits that monopolists can earn provide a spur to invention. The research and development costs of new products and processes can be immense: in the case of pharmaceuticals that require human trials to gauge safety and efficacy, the costs can run in the hundreds of millions of dollars or more. If the moment an invention were completed anyone could learn how to reproduce and sell it, the resulting low prices would make it impossible for inventors to recoup those research and development expenditures. Patents increase the incentive to invent, at the cost of using the existing inventions—for their first twenty years—at less than their full potential.

In other words, the patent system is a legal version of Chicago dibs. Static efficiency—optimal use of existing inventions—is sacrificed for the purpose of enhanced dynamic efficiency, the production of more inventions over time. Although an existing invention is "done," how it is distributed can determine the amount of inventions that are "done" in the future. Once again, whether the trade-off inherent in patents is sensible, or whether there might be some alternative method that provides more inventions without the static waste, is not obvious.[4]

To receive a patent, an inventor has to reveal how the invention can be made. At the expiration of the patent, therefore, anyone who wants to duplicate and sell the invention will have both the information and the legal right to proceed. So not only do patents provide an incentive to inventors, they also ensure that knowledge of how to manufacture the invention enters the public domain and becomes freely available to all. In the absence of patent protection, inventors might try to keep their innovations secret. High monopoly prices could then be maintained, not through the legal protection offered by a patent, but through exclusive access to information. (Alternatively, inventors might rely on their head-start to be a source of profits, even if others can legally copy the invention. Traditionally, as well as now, most innovations are not patented.[5]) Frustration with the static inefficiency inherent in a patent system does not imply that a world without patents would be preferable.

Nevertheless, for most industries, the modern patent system probably does not generate much of a spur to innovation. (The pharmaceutical and chemical industries are notable exceptions.[6]) Inventions depend on pre-existing inventions; in rapidly advancing areas, an innovation might require the approval of dozens of existing patent holders. Litigation to determine if a new invention infringes one or more existing patents is both expensive and common. Further, most of the social gains from inventions are captured by consumers, not by inventors. Forcing would-be inventors to negotiate through a minefield of existing patents—a patent thicket, an instance of a Tragedy of the Anticommons mentioned in chapter 1—can slow the pace of research and development, to society's detriment.[7]

When a patent expires and the invention enters the public domain, anyone can use it without permission. Recall, however, that it is free access to an asset that leads to overuse, a Tragedy of the Commons. Do we want inventions to be owned to prevent free access?

No. Free access has the potential to lead to inefficiency (tragedy!) if your use of the asset degrades my ability to use the asset: when you remove a fish from the ocean that leaves one less fish that I can take. But the ideas behind inventions are not depleted in a similar fashion. If you use an idea from the public domain, I can still use the same idea. So can everyone else. There is no tragedy associated with placing knowledge in the public domain.

Advance Market Commitments

The trade-off of static for dynamic efficiency that characterizes the intended working of the patent system becomes less attractive the larger are those static losses. High monopoly prices for life-saving drugs present one area in which the trade-off becomes all but unacceptable. A drug might only cost a few cents per dose to produce—once it is known precisely what drug to produce and how to manufacture it! The pharmaceutical company's patent protection, however, will result in a much higher price, perhaps hundreds of dollars per dose, until the patent expires. As a result, many people whose lives could be prolonged by the drug—and who could afford to cover the costs of manufacturing their doses—will not be able to pay for the medicine. For them, the monopoly price is fatally prohibitive.

High prices for pharmaceuticals will be an especially acute problem in poor countries.[8] (In rich countries with good health insurance coverage, fewer individuals, presumably, would find the monopoly drug prices to be prohibitively expensive.) The governments of poor countries might have a strong incentive to ignore patents possessed by pharmaceutical firms located in developed countries. With the information on how to produce the drugs publicly available through the patent records, governments (or firms) that ignore patents could manufacture their own drugs and sell them at the relatively low prices that just cover the production costs. They need not compensate the research and development costs because those costs were absorbed earlier by the patent holder. Even if governments did not engage in this behavior, the realization that they might have a strong incentive to do so can undermine the incentive for pharmaceutical firms to develop drugs aimed at diseases that primarily affect people living in the developing world.[9]

While patents are one way of encouraging firms to invest in research and development, they are not the only way. When the disadvantages of patents are high—as when the losses in static efficiency from monopoly prices are significant—then alternative methods of spurring inventive activity become more attractive. In the case of pharmaceuticals, direct government grants to fund basic research have long played a major role in increasing knowledge. In recent years, such grants have been supplemented by a new institution. A prize system known as Advance Market Commitments has been designed to make certain that inventors of vaccines that save lives in poor countries will be recompensed for their costly efforts.[10]

The idea behind Advance Market Commitments is to ensure high prices to developers of successful vaccines while at the same time allowing consumers in poor countries to access the vaccines at low cost. The price guarantee is funded from a pool of prize money assembled by donors including various nations and the Bill and Melinda Gates Foundation. A pilot program concerning a vaccine for pneumococcal disease was initiated in June 2009. Participating pharmaceutical companies enter into a contract with Advance Market Commitments that delineates the payments that will be received for successful vaccines. This approach overcomes the problem that drug makers might fear their patents will not be respected, by offering a different guarantee of remuneration—a guarantee that simultaneously does not involve the loss of static efficiency (and indeed, the loss of life) associated with charging consumers high prices for drugs that, once "done," are cheap to manufacture.

Incentives to become vaccinated are somewhat attenuated even in rich countries. If everyone else is vaccinated, their protection against contracting a contagious disease also protects me—but they won't take my benefit into account when deciding whether or not to become vaccinated. (In the extreme case, if universal vaccination renders everyone else immune from a disease that only is transmitted from human to human, then I am completely protected, even if I am the one exception to the worldwide inoculations.) Further, children might be the main direct and indirect beneficiaries of vaccines, though adults make the vaccination decisions for the children.[11] The insufficiency of individual incentives to become vaccinated typically is countered with government mandates for vaccination in the developed world. Advance Market Commitments help to bolster the incentive for vaccination in the developing world, by ensuring that the vaccines are available to the purchasers at low prices—and are invented and produced despite what otherwise might be the specter of low prices for the producers. The first doses of pneumococcal vaccines developed within the Advance Market Commitments program were delivered at the end of 2010, and by 2013, some 25 million children had received the immunization.[12] The reach of the pneumococcal program continues to expand, and further vaccines now are being distributed through Advance Market Commitments mechanisms.

Preventive and Punitory Measures

In the skateboarder/cyclist accident setting, we noted that after the accident occurs, the judicial determination of which party will bear the losses has no direct efficiency consequences. Nevertheless, rules about who will pay influence incentives, so those rules will go a long way toward determining how many accidents there will be in the future. Assignment of liability for accidents is a useful tool in maximizing the net benefits of travel—but it is not a perfect tool, and there are other methods that can push society toward providing the optimal amount of safety, the amount that a rational person like Robin would take if all the costs of prevention and of accidents fell upon her.

Why is the assignment of liability alone not enough for full social optimality in the accident setting? First, the judicial system is costly, so some accident victims will not even bother to take their claim to court. Why pursue a claim for $100 in damages if to do so requires substantial time and lawyer fees? Second, some injurers are not identified and hence cannot be induced to recompense victims. Other injurers can be identified but possess insufficient assets to cover the damages arising from their behavior. Still other injurers might be adjudged to be inappropriate parties for the assignment of liability; maybe they are children, or mentally incompetent. People who, though identified, cannot be held liable for damages, whether due to lack of means or for some other reason, are said to be *judgment-proof.*

It is unlikely, then, that the imperfect tort system alone provides appropriate incentives for people to behave with the socially optimal amount of care. Similar observations apply to crime: police, courts and prisons are costly, some perpetrators are not identified, some are beyond accountability, and as a result, the amount of deterrence provided against crime is inefficiently small.[13] This tendency toward underdeterrence cannot easily be overcome by any approach that waits until after an accident or a crime has taken place, and then looks to impose liability or punishment.

The insufficiency of after-the-fact (*ex post*) measures leads societies to complement their judicial systems with before-the-fact (*ex ante*) provisions that are intended to preclude some accident or crime problems from ever materializing. (John Stuart Mill refers to *ex ante* measures as *preventive* and to *ex post* measures as *punitory.*[14]) Rather than wait until what's done is done, *ex ante* regulations try to prevent harm directly. In the case of driving, for instance, licenses are compulsory for legal drivers, and knowledge of driving and traffic laws is a condition for receiving a license. The licensing mandate aims to weed out those drivers who are particularly likely to present an accident risk—perhaps because they are children or they have poor eyesight—before they are involved in any crashes. A requirement that car owners purchase accident insurance is an *ex ante* provision that helps the imposition of liability *ex post* to work more smoothly, by reducing the number of judgment-proof injurers. Licensing of cars and drivers also facilitates the effective operation of after-the-fact measures, by making it easier to identify injurers and by offering a non-monetary

sanction—revocation of a driver's license—to wield against unsafe (and perhaps otherwise judgment-proof) drivers.

One of the advantages of an *ex post* liability system is that only the relatively
small number of people who end up in accidents or who commit crimes have to
deal with the regulatory authorities. Preventive controls apply more broadly, to
people who are very likely to prove problematic and to people who are extremely cautious: many 15-year olds would be perfectly safe drivers, and if drivers' licenses were abolished, many adults (and teens) would still operate motor
vehicles with appropriate caution. *Ex post* controls tend to be well-targeted:
those who drive the most, and who drive in the least safe manner, will also be
those who will be most affected by punitive measures or the imposition of liability. *Ex ante* controls are not so well-targeted, applying to the high-risk drivers
and the low-risk drivers alike. But the imposition of regulatory costs even on
low-risk participants might be preferable to doing without the *ex ante* regulations: the costs imposed on nonconsensual, innocent victims who bear some or
all of the damages of automobile crashes or crimes are even less well-targeted in
terms of providing appropriate incentives. As with patents or the "dibs" system,
a bit of seeming waste today—imposing regulatory burdens on low-risk as well
as high-risk individuals—can lead to better outcomes down the road, as it were.

The possibilities for avoiding or evading preventive controls, without altering the prospects for suppressing the undesired activity, often are significant.
Many individuals drive despite the lack of the legally required license or insurance. A similar ability to frustrate the purpose of *ex ante* controls has been
documented in a wide variety of regulatory settings. The use of childproof caps
on medicines can reduce the likelihood that a child will swallow pills and be
poisoned. Mandating that childproof caps be placed on medicines, then, might
seem like a worthy *ex ante* regulation. There is some evidence, however, that
such mandates result in more medicines being stored with their caps off, or less
vigilance paid by adults to medicine availability in general—with increased
poisonings of children as a consequence.[15]

The broad targeting of preventive controls, combined with the notion that
almost any sort of behavior can be viewed as facilitating later recklessness or
criminality, suggests that societies should be wary of haphazardly instituting
costly *ex ante* measures. (As Mill notes, "The preventive function of government . . . is far more liable to be abused, to the prejudice of liberty, than the punitory function; for there is hardly any part of the legitimate freedom of action
of a human being which would not admit of being represented, and fairly too,
as increasing the facilities for some form or other of delinquency."[16]) *Ex ante*
controls can be adopted by authoritarian governments for repressive purposes;
nevertheless, preventive measures can be a helpful, non-abusive supplement to
ex post punishments in many regulatory settings in democratic societies.

Firearm Regulation

People who misuse firearms are subject to punitive measures.[17] Threaten or shoot someone with a gun and you can be arrested and jailed. Some offenders are not caught, however, and some people are crazed or underage or suicidal and unable to respond to the incentives for pro-social behavior that the system of punishment is intended to foster. As in other policy settings, the insufficiency of *ex post* measures that wait until "what's done is done" suggests a rationale for adopting some preventive firearm regulations: gun controls.

Gun controls in the United States typically aim at keeping firearms away from high-risk individuals, such as children, the mentally unstable, and released former felons. (The much tighter controls in Britain appear to have a more general suppression of firearm prevalence as part of the intention.) The controls tend to be most strict for those types of firearms that offer the fewest social benefits relative to their social costs—extremely powerful and easily concealable weapons are two categories of guns that face the most rigorous regulations.

Firearm controls might spur substitution behavior along the same lines of the mandatory-childproof-caps-for-medicines policy noted above. Perhaps handgun controls will lead criminals to employ rifles or to switch to knives. Nevertheless, there is no reason to believe that these sorts of exchanges will render firearm controls completely inefficacious. Such substitutions are costly for would-be gun owners; barriers are burdensome to overcome or avoid. This observation is obvious in the small: parents attempt to keep dangerous articles, including firearms and medicines, away from their children, in part by safe storage techniques. In general, these efforts are effective, though not perfectly so.

Safe storage of firearms makes it less likely that children acquire and misuse guns compared with a household regime featuring uncontrolled gun access. Even if the children make up for any diminution in their gun access by playing with other dangerous goods such as kitchen knives, the misuse of those substitute goods typically involves less damage than firearm misuse. Public gun controls can have a similar effect, reducing the likelihood that some high-risk users will acquire guns, and inducing a portion of the disappointed would-be gun owners to substitute less-deadly types of weapons.[18] The extreme case of a prison illustrates this phenomenon: often populated by highly motivated and dangerous criminals, prisons nevertheless afford little opportunity for inmates to acquire firearms, and their substitute weapons generally do not hold the same potential for carnage.

Society is not a prison, thankfully. Preventive gun laws involve the broad targeting that accompanies all *ex ante* regulations: low-risk adult gun users are required to follow the same (or nearly the same) firearm rules as high-risk users. Care must be taken to ensure that the interests of low-risk gun users are not sacrificed unduly in the name of combating their more dangerous brethren. Controls will appear particularly irksome if the high-risk users are easily able to avoid or evade the regulations that impose significantly upon the unproblematic majority of gun owners. Mandatory background checks and minimum age requirements are varieties of gun controls that can present obstacles to gun acquisition by high-risk users, without burdening adult low-risk users in a substantive way.

Some *ex ante* firearm regulations can be adopted not to raise barriers to firearm acquisition by high-risk users, but for the purpose of improving the efficacy of *ex post*, punitive controls. The requirements that firearms be marked with a serial number and that sales of new guns be recorded, for instance, make it easier to identify the original source of guns used in committing crimes. Gun registration and licensing, too, can render it more difficult to commit a crime with a gun and remain undetected.[19] Although cognizant of the potential for preventive measures to become excessive, John Stuart Mill nevertheless recommends a sort of registration system for the sale of dual-use products, goods that have both beneficial and nefarious applications: "Such regulations would in general be no material impediment to obtaining the article, but a very considerable one to making an improper use of it without detection."[20]

John Stuart Mill

John Stuart Mill (1806–1873) followed in Jeremy Bentham's footsteps as a utilitarian philosopher and as an economics thinker. (Those footsteps were literal, too, as Bentham was a close friend (and landlord!) to the Mill family from the time when John Stuart was growing up.) Unlike Bentham, John Stuart Mill generally is not considered to be a major pioneer of modern Law and Economics; nevertheless, Mill's influential ideas concerning economics, law, and public policy resound throughout twenty-first-century Law and Economics analyses.

John Stuart Mill's magisterial *Principles of Political Economy*, first published in 1848, established itself as the leading economics textbook for more than half a century. The concluding chapter of *Principles of Political Economy*, together with Mill's 1859 essay *On Liberty*, delineates Mill's position on the conditions under which the government, or society more generally, should intervene in individual decision-making. Intervention might be sensible, according to Mill, for what has become a standard economic rationale: the existence of externalities, and in particular negative externalities, harms to others. When the Days join Robin on her island, rules against theft and bodily harm and pollution are legitimate and do not represent unacceptable incursions on individual liberty. (That is, specific rules regarding negative externalities might or might not be desirable, but there cannot be a general principled objection made to them on the basis of illegitimate interference with human freedom.)

Mill accepted the presumption that people typically are better placed to judge their own interests than is society or a governmental bureaucracy. Paternalistic policies, therefore, are suspect, on the grounds of both liberty and efficacy. Nevertheless, the presumption that people know their own interests is only a presumption, and it might not be universally supportable: Mill identified significant realms in which governments might do a better job of making choices for people than the people would do for themselves, even in the absence of externalities. The immediate, everyday items of existence, such as food and shelter, are concerns where Mill believed individual inclinations should be paramount:

> But there are other things, of the worth of which the demand of the market is by no means a test; things of which the utility does not consist in ministering to inclinations, nor in serving the daily uses of life, and the want of which is least felt where the need is greatest. This is peculiarly true of those things which are chiefly useful as tending to raise the character of human beings. The uncultivated cannot be competent judges of cultivation. Those who most need to be made wiser and better, usually desire it least, and if they desired it, would be incapable of finding the way to it by their own lights. It will continually happen, on the voluntary system, that, the end not being desired, the means will not be provided at all, or that, the persons requiring improvement having an imperfect or altogether erroneous conception of what they want, the supply called forth by the demand of the market will be anything but what is really required.[21]

Nor was Mill quite so willing as Bentham to believe that people would be competent to judge whether poetry or push-pin brought the greatest happiness—perhaps people confuse contentment with happiness, or perhaps happiness comes in different qualities, as well as quantities?

(Continued)

> It is better to be a human being dissatisfied than a pig satisfied; better to be Socrates dissatisfied than a fool satisfied. And if the fool, or the pig, are a different opinion, it is because they only know their own side of the question. The other party to the comparison knows both sides.[22]

Low Probability, High Punishment Regimes

Ex post controls attempt to deter socially undesirable acts by punishing people who perpetrate those acts or by forcing people to make recompense for the damages that stem from their actions. If the controls fully internalize all of the costs of behavior, then the decisions that rational people like Robin make will be both individually optimal and socially desirable.

Imagine that your fast driving surely will result in $100 in damages to someone else's car, but no damages to your own custom-made crash-proof vehicle. If the tort system works costlessly, and every time you drive fast you are forced to compensate the other driver for the $100 in damages, you will choose to drive fast only when society as a whole is better off by your doing so: no one else cares (as the other driver is fully compensated), so if you are better off by driving fast and paying the damages (compared to driving slowly), then society (which includes you!) is also better off. (This result depends upon the assumption of no litigation costs and also on the notion that the compensation really is complete: under these (unrealistic) conditions, the victimized driver is perfectly indifferent between (1) not being in an accident and (2) having an accident, followed by the payment of full compensation.)[23] Indeed, if you and your victim had an opportunity to negotiate in advance and sign a contract, as long as the victim's damages would be fully compensated, he or she would be willing to agree, perhaps in exchange for a small bonus, to a contract allowing you to crash into him or her.

Not all speeders are caught, however. What if, when you drive fast and thereby cause an accident and $100 in damages, there were a probability of only one-half that you would be identified and forced to compensate the victim for the harm you imposed? Now, when deciding whether to drive fast or slow, you will recognize that there is a sporting chance that you will not have to pay any damages if you speed. As a result, you will be tempted to drive fast—tempted to drive fast too much, relative to the amount of fast driving that is socially efficient, that maximizes total wealth.

One way that the law can compensate is by demanding that drivers who drive fast and are in an accident and are identified pay not $100 but $200. On average, then, a person who chooses to drive fast will pay $100—half the time she will pay $200 and half the time she will pay nothing. As long as she does not know in advance whether the current occasion for speeding falls in the will-be-caught or won't-be-caught category, she will have approximately the same incentives to drive slowly as someone who always is identified when driving fast and always pays $100—and that person has incentives to behave in society's interests. So the person who is only caught half the time, but pays doubles the damages, also has incentives to choose in ways that are nearly socially efficient.

The same logic applies to someone who is caught only one in ten times, but is charged $1,000, or to someone who is caught only one in one thousand times, but is charged $100,000: the incentives that they have to drive fast should make them choose in a more-or-less socially desirable fashion.

Catching speeders or other injurers, bringing them to court, and having the judge impose a fine all require significant resources. If the same incentives can be created by only litigating the cases of one of every thousand speeders (and charging them 1,000 times the actual damage they cause in the litigated instance) as can be created by bringing all speeders to trial (and charging them $100 each), then there would seem to be a lot to be said for going the one-in-one-thousand route. We need fewer police officers and courts if we have only occasional trials, without sacrificing the provision of incentives for safe driving. Criminal activity is similar—we might be able to offer the same deterrence against crime by catching only a small percentage of offenders and punishing them harshly—than we could achieve by apprehending and punishing (less severely) all offenders.[24]

Low probability/high punishment regimes, however, generally are not employed and seem to lack popularity—for a variety of good reasons. One problem is that they require relatively severe penalties for minor offenses. This might be acceptable in isolation, but sometimes offenses are linked. If you are speeding and will face a huge fine when caught, you might try to outrace or incapacitate any police officers who attempt to stop you. More severe crimes need to be met with more severe sentences if the law hopes to provide a disincentive against ratcheting up the harshness of violations. By swelling the punishment imposed on minor offenders, low probability/high punishment regimes make it harder to maintain the requisite deterrent for crime escalation.[25]

Severe punishments might not even be feasible. As fines increase, more and more people will prove not to have the resources to be able to pay: with respect to monetary sanctions, such individuals will be judgment-proof.[26] Perhaps most important, there is a whiff (or stench) of unfairness about high fines matched with low probabilities of punishment: most offenders are ignored, but every now and then one offender, essentially chosen at random, is punished extremely harshly, much more extensively than the social damage created by the isolated offense.[27] In the United States, such harsh penalties (relative to the costs of the underlying offense) might be precluded by the Eighth Amendment to the Constitution, which prohibits cruel and unusual punishments.

Courts make mistakes. Sometimes they let factually guilty offenders go free, and sometimes they convict the innocent. This latter type of error—that of convicting an innocent person—becomes more costly when the punishment is raised. There would be reasons to fear low probability/high punishment regimes even if courts worked perfectly. The ever-present possibility of court errors renders this enforcement strategy still less attractive.

Destruction of Property: What's Done Cannot Be Undone?

The discussion of *The Original of Laura* in the Introduction provides a glimpse into the more general issue of when an owner can destroy, or direct in a will that survivors destroy, a valuable asset. Consider the Taj Mahal and imagine that it (or some similar architectural wonder) is privately owned. Once again, assume that the owner stipulates in her will that the Taj be destroyed after her death.

First, note that the right to destroy property is extremely valuable.[28] Every household appliance is eventually destroyed; how many toasters would you be willing to purchase if you knew that you (and then your heirs) were required to retain and maintain, forever, any toaster once acquired? (Perhaps you would be allowed to sell or give away the toaster, but the requirements to maintain the toaster would be binding on new owners, too.) How would you feel about the receipt of a birthday or a holiday card or a credit card solicitation if the law required you to save all such missives everlastingly?

So the right to destroy one's property is vital, and in many cases, well, indispensable. Generally we think that owners are in the best position to evaluate the proper disposition of any asset, including its destruction. Nevertheless, in the case of the Taj Mahal—and in other cases where the continued existence of an asset has significant value to many people—the law might want to put some roadblocks in the way of owners' rights to destroy their property, either before or after their own demise. That is, efficiency might be served by legal barriers to the destruction of particularly valuable property, even when that destruction is desired by the owner.

One possibility for determining if property destruction really meets the usual marker for economic efficiency—the maximization of overall wealth—is to mandate a waiting period during which an auction of the asset would be conducted.[29] Following the auction, the current owner would, perhaps, get to decide whether to accept the high bid and sell the asset, or to go ahead and continue plans for destruction. At least in this manner, owners would have a decent idea about what they are sacrificing for indulging their destructive impulse: the value other people associate with the continued existence of their property. Mandated waiting periods also can prevent fleeting passions for destruction from deciding the issue and perhaps protect the property owner from making a rash or uninformed choice, one that she will later, "in her right mind," regret. (The auction obligation, of course, offers no protection against property destruction undertaken by a determined, spiteful misanthrope.) Such an auction would not be compulsory unless the asset in question is worth a substantial sum; for property of minor value, the owner's interest in destruction should carry the day. Opponents to an asset's destruction could be required to post a sizable bond before a pre-destruction auction is mandated, to ensure that only assets with serious outside protective interest are subject to such a forced auction.

Environmental economists sometimes talk about "existence value," the benefit that accrues to non-owners and non-users (of a national park, say), just from knowing that the park (or an endangered species) exists.[30] In aggregate these valuations could be tremendous. In such cases, a required waiting period/auction prior to the destruction (or to the filing of the will) would allow preservationists an opportunity to agglomerate their own forces to potentially purchase the asset.

Will an erosion of an owner's right to destroy a structure make people less willing to invest in erecting a building that might become an architectural monument? This is not an entirely fanciful notion—commercial real estate builders or owners might well think about what they would be facing if they would want to significantly renovate or tear down a prospective building in twenty-five or thirty years; perhaps these owners would choose to erect or maintain buildings in such a way that they could avoid an uproar if the building were slated for destruction.[31] The forced auction requirement does not preclude destruction, so it probably will not become a substantial incentive to avoiding the creation of a magnificent building; indeed, the usual case will be that the higher the public regard, the better off the creator. Nonetheless, stringent constraints on maintenance or destruction must be considered with an eye toward incentives for future creations.

Should rights to destroy be greater for the original progenitors of property (such as Nabokov) than for later owners? My feeling is "yes," in part because the original creators may be less willing to give birth to their masterpiece in the first place if they cannot direct its possible destruction—creators might value control of their products to a greater extent than do subsequent owners.[32] For already existing assets that have passed from the control of their progenitor, the potential disincentive to creation stemming from restrictions on destruction would seem to exist only in a significantly attenuated form. Perhaps a would-be creator would be reluctant to produce a masterful tour de force if she thought that a much later owner of the piece would not be allowed to destroy it, but that seems fairly unlikely; indeed, controls preventing subsequent owners from recklessly damaging or destroying a valuable work of art, for instance, probably increase the incentive to create the work.

Moral Rights: What's Done Cannot Be Redone?

Imagine that a novel such as Nabokov's *The Original of Laura* has been published long ago (so long ago that its copyright protection has expired); it is in the public domain. This means that anyone can republish and sell copies of *The Original of Laura*, without requiring the permission of the author's heirs or of the original publishers. I decide to offer a reprint, but I have never much cared for chapter 2 of *The Original of Laura*—I consider chapter 2 to be excessively verbose while contributing little to the plot. So in the version I release, the original chapter 2 is omitted and is replaced by three words: "yadda yadda yadda." Can I make this alteration to Nabokov's last novel legally?[33]

With the copyright term expired, Nabokov and his heirs do not have full control over derivative works such as translations or my attenuated version. (Copyright holders do control such derivative works while the copyright remains in effect; so much for my Harry Potter sequel.) Nevertheless, my mutilation of Nabokov's novel might not be legal. Authors hold not just a temporary copyright but also a so-called *moral right* (or in France, the country in which the idea first took hold, *droit d'auteur*). The extent and duration of moral rights vary from country to country, but most countries prohibit, for some length of time, alterations to works when those alterations are likely to bring the author into disrepute. My version of *The Original of Laura* could violate Nabokov's moral rights in those countries that have lengthier terms for moral rights than they do for copyrights.

Most nations have acceded to the Berne Convention for the Protection of Literary and Artistic Works, which provides some degree of global standardization for copyright and related rules. With respect to moral rights, the Berne Convention states:

> Independently of the author's economic rights, and even after the transfer of the said rights, the author shall have the right to claim authorship of the work and to object to any distortion, mutilation or other modification of, or other derogatory action in relation to, the said work, which would be prejudicial to his honor or reputation.[34]

In the United States, moral rights in paintings and other types of visual art are protected in part by a statute, the Visual Artists Rights Act of 1990.[35] These rights last as long as the artist remains alive. It would be a violation of the Visual Artists Rights Act, as well as propriety, to purchase a portrait from an artist, and to immediately proceed to draw a mustache on the painted image. Artists are allowed to waive their moral rights, however, so if you tell the artist in advance about your intended mutilation, and gain her written permission, then the mustache is no longer forbidden in the United States.

Ex ante incentives—to create valuable property, to take appropriate precautions, and to desist from crime—depend on what is expected to happen *ex post*, after the property has been created, after the accident occurs, after the crime has been committed. Extensive moral rights, like extensive patent terms or extensive protections of important architecture, do not necessarily ensure the optimal amount of creativity. Today's contributions, whether mechanical, literary, or artistic, draw upon or supersede prior contributions. Almost all of the plots in Shakespeare's plays are based on previously existing stories. Brilliant buildings often are erected on land that once was occupied by structures that were notable in their own day. What's done may be done, but what can be done to property in the future—including altering it or even destroying it—will determine how much will be done in the here and now.

Defacing or Improving?

In October 2012, a visitor to the Tate Modern Museum in London added some sizable graffiti to a very valuable painting by Mark Rothko. In the immediate aftermath, the culprit claimed that his actions increased the worth of the painting.[36] What if he is right and that the Rothko is indeed substantially more valuable than it was before his alteration? Should the graffiti artist be punished or rewarded?

The Rothko graffiti case provides a textbook example of a low-transaction costs environment. As discussed in chapter 1 (in the section "What Happens When a Property Right Is Infringed?"), the low transaction costs imply that the Rothko's unmolested condition should be protected by a property rule, not a liability rule. If the graffiti will raise the value of the painting, let the graffiti artist meet the Rothko owner and convince him or her of the fact. To act without permission and to only pay a fine (or pay a negative fine, receive a reward) after it is learned what effect the graffiti has on the value of the painting (which is what a liability rule might do) would require courts to guess at value changes—not their strong suit—and some graffiti makers might not be identified or may lack the resources to pay the relevant fine. So the better rule is to make it illegal for someone to deface, or improve, art without the owner's permission.

As it turned out, the Tate vandal renounced his act and spent a year and a half in jail;[37] the Rothko painting was laboriously restored over the course of many months and is back on public display.[38] Whether the (now mostly reversed) vandalism actually has resulted in a more valuable painting is unknown, but the foregone pleasure of museum visitors who were deprived of viewing the Rothko during its lengthy repair represents a significant "cost" arising from the vandalism.

Another unusual case of art amendment took place earlier in 2012, this time in Borja, Spain. A well-meaning octogenarian ruined a more than 100-year-old fresco in a church through an ill-advised restoration attempt. The unexpected twist to the story is that her work turned the church and its "ruined" painting into a considerable revenue-generating tourist attraction. Images of the shockingly poor restoration have been reproduced on mugs and tee shirts and a variety of souvenirs.[39] In this case, the restorer's incompetence apparently has increased the value of the original fresco. Should her accidentally valuable deed be rewarded?

As with the Rothko graffiti artist, we do not want a rule that will incentivize future "restorers" to intentionally maim art simply because they think that the ruined version might be more valuable. Those restorers might well be wrong, so it is better to give owners of artwork veto power over attempted improvements or restorations. Of course, much of the reason that the Spanish fresco became seemingly more valuable is tied to the understanding that the restorer was indeed well-meaning, she aimed to make things better. (Also, had this fresco been a world-class masterpiece, like Da Vinci's *The Last Supper*, then it is extremely unlikely that a botched restoration would add value. The original Spanish church fresco was not viewed as being in the same artistic class as *The Last Supper* or the defaced Rothko.) An intentional maimer's efforts would not generate comparable curiosity value, I imagine.

In the case of the Spanish fresco, the church and the would-be restorer reached an agreement on the revenue windfall created by the inadvertent "improvement." The artist receives 49 percent of the image-related profit, which she intends to use for charitable purposes; her renunciation of personal enrichment helps to reduce any incentive that future restorers might have to sabotage their own efforts. The original painter's descendants reportedly would prefer that the fresco be treated like the Rothko, that is, that the "restoration" be reversed.[40]

Property and Theft

The nineteenth-century French anarchist Pierre-Joseph Proudhon famously declared that "Property is theft!" just decades after property was tied to life and liberty as a fundamental right by one of the US founding fathers, George Mason, who himself was following in the footsteps of John Locke. The Fifth and Fourteenth Amendments to the US Constitution protect individuals against the deprivation of "life, liberty, or property, without due process of law." Love it or hate it, property clearly is something to be reckoned with.

I possess property rights to my watch, and those rights allow me to use my watch, to sell it or lend it or trade it, to destroy it (it is not a very valuable watch!), and to keep other people from doing these sorts of thing without my permission (though if someone uses my watch without my express consent by reading the time off of it while I am traveling on the subway, the law will turn a deaf ear to my plea for damage payments).

The economic rationale for providing me with this bundle of property rights in my watch is straightforward and persuasive. Consider first the idea that the law protects the watch against theft, against unauthorized transfer. If this were not the case, then anyone stronger or more cunning than me (more or less anyone) could simply take the watch. I certainly would not be willing to pay very much money to buy a watch that could be taken with impunity, nor would anyone else. Since watches will only be produced if the manufacturers will be able to sell them at a profit, the general unwillingness to pay much for a watch that is not protected against theft means that few watches would be produced. When the law gives an enforceable property right to watch owners, a right that proscribes unauthorized transfer, the wealth of society increases—watches are made and are sold to people who value the watches more than society values the inputs that are required to manufacturer and deliver the watches: the economic pie is bigger. Laws against theft promote economic efficiency.

An Aside on the State of Nature

The full tale of the timepiece is much more complicated, of course. If there were no laws forbidding theft, I might still try to make or buy a watch, and keep its existence a secret, or develop a private security force that would protect my watch. This sort of solution is rather cumbersome, however, and it is likely that the person who ends up with the strongest private security force will essentially establish sovereignty over the territory—weaker forces cannot offer security against the more powerful force.[41] Further, even with property rights established, I will not fully rely upon legal protections: I will take some personal measures to try to safeguard valuable assets, despite knowing that the law will attempt to apprehend and punish thieves.

This point was elegantly stated by Thomas Hobbes in *Leviathan* in 1651, in the cause of defending his claim that, in the absence of a common authority, people will be at war with one another, and the life of man will be "solitary, poore, nasty, brutish, and short." Hobbes continues:

> It may seem strange to some man, that has not well weighed these things; that Nature should thus dissociate, and render men apt to invade, and destroy one another: and he may therefore, not trusting to this Inference, made from the Passions, desire perhaps to have the same confirmed by Experience. Let him therefore consider with himselfe, when taking a journey, he armes himselfe, and seeks to go well accompanied; when going to sleep, he locks his dores; when even in his house he locks his chests; and this when he knows there bee Lawes, and publike Officers, armed, to revenge all injuries shall bee done him; what opinion he has of his fellow subjects, when he rides armed; of his fellow Citizens, when he locks his dores; and of his children, and servants, when he locks his chests. Does he not there as much accuse mankind by his actions, as I do by my words? But neither of us accuse mans nature in it. The Desires, and other Passions of man, are in themselves no Sin. No more are the Actions, that proceed from those Passions, till they know a Law that forbids them; which till Lawes be made they cannot know: nor can any Law be made, till they have agreed upon the Person that shall make it.[42]

Rivalry

With enforced laws against theft, watches can be produced and sold—so now I have a watch. But what if you see my supercool watch and covet it? Fortunately, we are in a low transaction cost environment: you can offer to purchase the watch from me. If it really is worth more to you than to me, you will offer a price that I find acceptable, and I will transfer the watch, and its bundle of property rights, to you. So those property rights not only create an incentive for assets to be produced, they help smooth the transfer of assets to those who value them most highly. Once again, economic efficiency is served.

What about the fact that you can read the time off of my watch on the street or subway without any legal consequences? Why does the law allow you to take the time off my watch without my permission, but does not allow you to take the watch off my wrist? The obvious response is also the economically relevant one: either you can have my watch or I can have my watch, but we cannot both have my watch simultaneously. In contrast, you can read the time from my watch, and I can read the time from my watch, and so perhaps can many other impatient or tardy or just curious individuals, simultaneously. The fact that you read the time does not diminish my ability to read the time; as we saw with knowledge of inventions, there is no tragedy associated with open access to knowledge of the time. But if you possessed the watch, then I would not have it (though maybe I could still read the time off of your wrist).

The economic concept at issue here is called *rivalry*. A watch or an apple or a house is a good marked by rivalry—if I have the watch, you cannot have it too. If you eat an apple, I do not eat that apple. But knowledge of the time is itself non-rival. I can have that knowledge and you can have it and so can virtually everyone else; your knowledge of the time does not make it harder for me to simultaneously possess that knowledge. I would happily give you the time of day!

Public Goods

Economists differentiate private goods such as apples or watches from *public goods* such as national defense. The terms "private" and "public," however, do not in this instance refer to whether the state provides the good. Rather, two features distinguish public goods from private goods. First, public goods are *non-rival* (as described above): the fact that one person in the relevant community consumes the good does not detract from someone else's enjoyment of the same good. As a sea captain, the value that I get from a lighthouse signal is not diminished because other sea captains also are viewing the signal. Second, public goods are *non-excludable*: if the public good is made available to one person, then it will be available to everybody (again, in the relevant community). When you build the lighthouse for me, you are simultaneously supplying it to all the other sea captains, too.

Private goods like watches and houses and apples are rival goods: if I eat the apple, you cannot eat it. Private goods also are excludable: just because you gave me the apple does not mean that the apple is available to everyone else. Public goods, in their purest forms, are non-rival and non-excludable.

Lighthouses and national defense are the paradigmatic examples of public goods. Many goods fall somewhere in between the purely public and purely private extremes, perhaps because these goods can be made excludable with enough effort. For instance, it is possible for urban parks to exclude people, and some privately owned or gated neighborhood parks do that, with keys provided only to local residents. If I plant nice flowers in my yard the lovely view is available to all passersby, but I could erect a wall in front of the flowers to exclude others. (The non-excludability of national defense is hard to work around: imagine trying to offer defense against foreign attack to everybody in the country except for Harry.) Goods also can display degrees of rivalry. Another person or two on the beach does not detract from my enjoying a seaside afternoon: a day at a nearly deserted beach is a non-rival good. As the beach becomes congested, however, the addition of another person "consuming" the beach does lower the value of my beach going: a day at the beach starts out as non-rival, but eventually displays rivalry as the beachfront populates.

Intellectual Property: What's Done Can Be Done Repeatedly

Property rights in my watch—a rival good—promote economic efficiency by spurring incentives to produce watches, and by ensuring that the watches make their way onto the proper wrists, those belonging to the people who value the watches most highly. But what about my knowledge of the time? As that knowledge is non-rival, there is no direct efficiency rationale for creating a property right in existing knowledge. And sure enough, if people read the time off of my wrist, the law is indifferent.

But what is true of knowledge of the time also is true of knowledge more generally: it is non-rival. The knowledge in question may be the knowledge of how to make a watch, or knowledge to the words of a poem or a song or an entire book. The fact that knowledge is non-rival implies, once again, that there is no direct efficiency gain in creating property rights (and hence constraints against "theft") in existing knowledge. The strong economic case for legal recognition of my watch as property does not extend to knowledge or ideas.

As we have seen, however, there is an economic argument for creating atten-uated property rights in knowledge or ideas. Copyrights or patents that grant temporary ownership to the creator of an idea help to generate an incentive to produce the idea in the first place. Property rights in rival goods like watches both help to get watches produced, and to promote the efficient distribution of watches among wrists. Property rights in non-rival goods such as ideas help to get the ideas produced—but they do so at the cost of hindering the efficient distribution of the ideas. Once produced, we could all possess and use the words to my song or the knowledge of my invention. We are sometimes willing to sacrifice this advantage, in the service of improved incentives to create ideas in the first place.

Our intuitions about the value of "property" probably are developed from rival goods, such as land or watches. The term "intellectual property," as ap-plied to non-rival goods such as ideas or knowledge, perhaps grants copyright and patent with a little more luster than they deserve. The economic case for patents and copyrights exists—but it is much less compelling a case than exists for property rights in rival goods such as watches.

Nabokov and Existence Value

The Taj Mahal and the manuscript of *The Original of Laura* possess some of the characteristics of apples and watches, in that if you own them I cannot. That is, the Taj and the Nabokovian manuscript are, to a degree, rival goods. (The words in the manuscript, as opposed to the physical manuscript itself, like the architectural ideas underlying the Taj Mahal, are not rival goods: everyone can possess them simultaneously.) But I am essentially indifferent as to whether or not you eat your apple or sell it or give it to your horse or put it in your compost heap, while I care if you alter or destroy the Taj or the manu-script: these goods have existence value, for me and for many others. In other words, the existence of the Taj Mahal or the Nabokov manuscript is non-rival: I can enjoy their existence, and you can enjoy their existence, simultaneously, even if only one of us can "possess" or "consume" them at a time. They are non-exclusive, too, in that if the Taj or the manuscript exists, then they exist for all of us, irrespective of whether we ever see them.

The idea that society's wealth is maximized when assets (such as watches and homes) are owned by the person who values them most highly makes sense for standard, rival goods that only one person (or family, say) could con-sume. For these goods, we could invoke the willingness-to-pay approach ex-amined in chapter 1: ask every person to reveal the maximum amount they would be willing to pay for the good, perhaps by holding an auction. If we then sell (or give) the good to the person whose (truthful!) response is the largest amount, we would ensure that the good had moved to its highest value user, and that the social wealth associated with that good is maximized.[43]

The willingness-to-pay method works differently with non-rival goods, including the existence of the Taj Mahal. The existence value of the Taj Mahal is not reflected in the highest individual valuation for its existence, because many people can value its existence jointly. The overall existence value is the sum of the valuations of all people who have any interest, no matter how slight, in the continued survival of the Taj Mahal. Auctioning off the Taj as a commodity to its highest value consumer—who might, for instance, want to mandate in his will that the Taj should be destroyed after his own demise—will not ensure that the Taj has moved to its highest valued use or that social wealth is being maximized. Even the option of trying to get everyone who cares about the existence of the Taj to contribute a little bit to its purchase and maintenance might not suffice. Such a contribution scheme is ripe to fall prey to the free rider problem: everyone recognizes that their small contribution will not be decisive, and that if the Taj is saved, they receive their portion of the existence value whether or not they contribute. The incentives such a scheme creates are likely to generate voluntary contributions that are but a small fraction of total existence value. Indeed, the potential to free ride is one of the reasons that public goods such as national defense are funded through compulsory taxes and not by voluntary donations.

Once again, a commitment to social wealth maximization does not imply a commitment to unfettered property rights, where owners have the right to use or abuse or destroy property in any way that they see fit. For goods like the Taj Mahal with a non-negligible existence value, quite the opposite: social wealth maximization requires some limits on how owners can treat their property.

4

Squeezing a Balloon

Well-founded laws and regulations try to push people's behavior in socially beneficial directions. People have a persistent habit of choosing to advance their own private interests, however, and can be creative in finding ways to avoid or evade rules, or in arranging to comply with the letter of laws while undermining the purposes of those laws. People might even resent being pushed.

The fact that rational people like Robin are so obstinate in pursuing their own ends tends to reduce the effectiveness of rules in serving the objectives intended by the rule makers. You cannot generate socially optimal behavior just by passing a rule mandating that everyone make socially optimal, not individually optimal, choices.[1] At the extreme, society might prove to be immune to the influence of regulation—choices (or outcomes) might be equivalent whether or not regulations are instituted, or despite the precise nature of the regulations. A law might squeeze on one part of a balloon, but then other parts will expand—the amount of air inside the balloon might be independent of the rules that indicate precisely where the squeezing occurs, and with precisely what intensity the squeezing will take place.

Analyses in the Law and Economics tradition frequently uncover mechanisms by which the intended effects of laws are counteracted, perhaps even fully counteracted, through induced behavioral changes.[2] The Coase Corollary—in the absence of transaction costs, resource allocation is independent of the distribution of property rights—presents one prominent result where some outcomes are independent of rules. If the goal of a court is to finalize the allocation of resources, and it hopes to do so by assigning property rights, the Coase Corollary tells us that the hope is misplaced (as long as transaction costs, those barriers to negotiating and enforcing agreements, are low). If the goal of a court is to ensure that one of the parties to the litigation benefits relative to the other party, however, then it can accomplish this goal by assigning property rights to the favored party—the allocation of real resources might be independent of the property rights assignment, but the incomes of the various parties are likely to depend quite significantly on the court's decision.

The frequency of arguments about offsetting effects is such that unintentionally, as it were, the first three chapters have already contained many examples beyond the Coase Corollary. In particular, we identified in passing the potential for induced behavioral changes to undermine the intended effects of stronger controls on firearms, stronger patent protections, and stronger safeguards against asset destruction.

The Peltzman Effect

Over the years many governments have instituted regulations to increase the safety of automobiles.[3] For instance, manufacturers have been required to provide safety belts, airbags, and effectual headlamps. Improved automobile safety, better roads, and advances in emergency medicine have helped to decrease per-mile traffic fatalities: in the United States, there were 5.35 fatalities per 100 million vehicle miles traveled in 1967, and 1.10 fatalities per 100 million vehicle miles traveled in 2011.[4]

How much of the improvement over time in automotive safety can be attributed to legal safety mandates? Economist Sam Peltzman of the University of Chicago examined this question in an influential 1975 article, "The Effects of Automobile Safety Regulation." Peltzman suggested that drivers might respond to the presence of enhanced safety equipment by driving more aggressively. As a result, while motorists end up being safer than they were prior to the addition of newly mandated safety devices, pedestrians are put at slightly greater risk. In terms of overall highway deaths, Peltzman could not identify any decline that could be attributed to those higher safety standards he examined. Many related studies subsequently have been undertaken, and while most do not indicate the complete crowding out of safety improvements via altered behavior that Peltzman described, the studies tend to replicate the finding of some countervailing effects following heightened safety regulation. (Nor does the initial safety-promoting change have to result from regulation. Car manufacturers who develop cost-effective and safer designs will still see some of the potential safety improvement dissipated by more aggressive driving.)

The idea that people will respond to a regulatory intervention in a manner that tends to offset, perhaps fully, the policy's intended outcome, has come to be known as the Peltzman effect. Sometimes this effect is presented vividly by considering the opposite phenomenon: Wouldn't you drive more carefully if the business end of a bayonet extended out of the steering wheel, inches from your chest?[5] At any rate, offsetting adjustments to regulatory pressure arise across the spectrum of regulatory and legal settings, including property, contracts, and criminal jurisprudence. Indeed, versions of Peltzman effects are rife even within the restricted domain of the automotive world. Cars with improved fuel efficiency will be driven more miles, perhaps in the end not reducing overall fuel consumption.[6] Higher prices for new cars that meet enhanced fuel efficiency standards will slow the rate at which older vehicles are scrapped, eroding some of the fuel savings that otherwise would accompany the higher standards.[7]

With respect to countervailing tendencies within intellectual property law, recall the patent story related in chapter 3. A government that wants to encourage inventive activity might make it easier to procure a patent, and increase the length of time that a patent is in effect. While at first this reform might lead to more inventions, the long-run effects are not so clear-cut. Tomorrow's inventive activity depends on the current state of knowledge. The greater the extent to which current knowledge is privately owned (via a patent), as opposed to being freely appropriable from the public domain, the higher the barriers to future inventions. More patents today makes inputs for tomorrow's inventions less available, reducing the amount of inventive activity that tomorrow might see. So in the long run, greater patent protection could lead to fewer inventions—or the same amount, or more. Whatever the final outcome, the Peltzman-like (or Peltzman-lite) point is that there will be some offset in the future from expanded patent protection today.[8]

The Peltzman effect with respect to automotive safety, and the increased patent protection example, both show how processes that develop over many stages are susceptible to the partial or full undermining of regulations via offsetting effects. Highway safety depends on a long chain of measures and actions, including automobile design, road maintenance, driver behavior, and traffic enforcement and penalties for infractions. An intervention in one part of the chain can be offset by an induced response in another part of the chain—and there may well be incentives for such a response. In their motoring behavior, drivers indicate that they have a preference for a certain level of safety, at least under the prevailing legal and technological conditions. If more safety is provided via a shift in technology, it is not surprising that drivers will cut back on their own costly efforts to take precautions. (Again, an extreme case brings the point home. If technology progresses so that cars can safely operate themselves, "drivers" would pay no more attention to safety than, for instance, train passengers typically do.[9]) With respect to patents, the dynamic pattern is that future creativity builds on current efforts. Attempting to spur current creativity through heightened patent protection renders that creativity less available to tomorrow's innovators.

Regulations on land ownership present their own opportunities for offsetting behavior. Consider the Endangered Species Act, which limits development on privately owned land that contains habitat hosting an endangered species.[10] This restriction on development can be quite costly to a landowner, though probably not costly enough to constitute a "taking" that would require the payment of just compensation. But the process for adding a species to the endangered list is a time-consuming one, with significant advance notice to the public. As a result, owners of lands that contain habitat for a species which is likely to enter the endangered list have forewarning that their land might become less valuable for development.[11] Owners therefore have financial incentives to hurry to develop their land, or to destroy the habitat, prior to the anticipated restrictions taking effect—actions that hardly lend themselves to conservation of the threatened species. In practice, these incentives seem to have motivated many such avoidance actions, reducing the effectiveness of the Endangered Species Act in aiding threatened species. But as is often the case, the realization that a policy is being countered in an unexpected fashion produces its own counteracting effect. The Endangered Species Act has been amended to permit some reduction of habitat in return for measures to ensure the sustainability of species; the negotiated agreements, "Habitat Conservation Plans," seem to be effective in protecting endangered species in a manner that is less threatening to landowners' financial interests.[12]

The criminal justice system involves many connected links. There are the rules that indicate what behavior is criminal, the efforts that are arrayed to enforce those rules, and the punishments that are meted out to those who are found to have violated the rules.[13] Alterations in one component of the system can induce partially or fully compensating adjustments in other components. Increase the police presence in a neighborhood, for instance, and residents might reduce their own vigilance.[14] Raise the punishment against minor offenses and prosecutors might become less aggressive, while juries might become more reluctant to convict.

Recall from chapter 3 that the costs of enforcement present a reason to prefer high punishment/low probability-of-conviction regulatory regimes. This is, for a fixed level of "expected punishment" (the probability that an offender is punished multiplied by the severity of the punishment), it saves on enforcement costs to lower the probability of punishment as far as possible. But trying to implement a high punishment/low probability-of-conviction regime is complicated by the connections between the extent of punishment and the probability of detection. Not every conceivable combination of size and probability of punishment will be available to policymakers. Consider trying to increase the punishment for a crime, while maintaining the existing probability that an offender is apprehended and punished. The increased sanction will induce violators to take more pains to escape detection; they will spend more on defending themselves when apprehended, too. Further, as noted, other elements of the judicial system, such as prosecutors, police, judges, and juries, might be less willing to press ahead for convictions when punishments are raised. Canada's elimination of capital punishment was followed by higher conviction rates in murder cases: the lower penalties, presumably, made courts more likely to convict defendants.[15]

Taxes and subsidies are another area in which Peltzman-like effects are rampant. A tax imposed on the consumption of a good will reduce consumption of that good, and tax revenues will not be as great as they would be in the absence of a consumption response. In eighteenth-century Britain, for instance, a tax on windows allowed easy determination of tax bills, as tax assessors could count the windows on a dwelling just by walking around it.[16] The result was the bricking in of windows to avoid the tax—and some of the erstwhile windows, now opaque walls, still can be seen in venerable homes in modern Britain.

Endangered Species

The sustainability of the populations of more than 10,000 plant species and more than 10,000 animal species is under threat.[17] Endangered species include many that are well-known to, and beloved by, humanity—Giant pandas, blue whales, Indian elephants, chimpanzees[18]—and many that are known only to specialists. But people generally value, to some extent, preserving even the little known varieties, and not simply because of some remote possibility that those plants or animals will eventually be found to constitute a source of useful medicines or to provide another tangible benefit to the human species.

Given that people seem to want to protect plant and animal species, why do hundreds of species go extinct every year, with thousands more vulnerable to elimination?[19] For some species, the problem is the now-familiar Tragedy of the Commons: an animal is valuable to humans—perhaps its horn is said to possess aphrodisiacal properties—and many people have the opportunity to capture that value by hunting (legally or illegally) the animal. When hunters decide to target the species, they disregard the (minor in itself) contribution that their efforts will make toward pushing the animal towards extinction—

(Continued)

but in the aggregate, this scenario leads to overhunting and potentially to extinction.

The Coase Theorem suggests that if transaction costs are low, an over-hunting Tragedy of the Commons can be avoided. An indeed, parties have come together to try to place bounds on hunting (or fishing) that will not threaten animals with extinction.[20] Most countries, for instance, abide by a ban on commercial whaling which has been in existence since 1982. Other international efforts are aimed not at the hunting per se, but at the market for the animals or the resulting products, such as ivory from elephants. Most countries of the world are members of the Convention on International Trade in Endangered Species of Wild Fauna and Flora (http://www.cites.org/), which bans commercial trade in nearly 1,000 species.

Another approach to fighting commons-type tragedies is to control access to the overused asset by assigning ownership to a single party such as our old friend Robin. If Robin owns all of the whales or elephants (or just some identifiable subset) in an area, then she will have an incentive to maximize their value, and therefore to limit hunting to sustain the population. The problem here (as with the enforcement of treaty-implemented bans) is that Robin's ownership claims over animals that range over long distances or live in remote regions will be all but impossible to enforce; that is, poaching will be hard to prevent. Sometimes, ownership can work; note that cattle are very valuable to humans, but they are not threatened with extinction, because workable (though imperfect) methods for enforcing ownership claims to cattle exist. Animals in the wilderness (as opposed to zoos or other types of captivity) cannot easily be protected from poachers, however, and the greater the market value of the animals, the greater the incentive to poach.

Imagine that an owner is able to effectively control poaching. How can that owner herself be compensated for her husbandry? One possibility is to try to monetize the widespread existence value that large animals possess for humans.[21] People will pay for sightseeing safaris—and as a result, wildlife protection areas have been introduced, with managers who attempt to protect herds from poachers. Another method by which owners can be compensated for protecting endangered species is more controversial: owners can sell (limited) opportunities to hunt the animals. (This is a version of the cattle model.) That is, it is conceivable that human interest in trophy hunting can be converted into a tool for preserving species, at least for those species for which ownership can be effectively established in a cost-effective manner.[22]

The possibility that voluntary arrangements for hunting can protect animals from extinction is hardly the last word on efficiency and hunting, of course. The animals themselves are not voluntary participants—a condition that is replicated in most human-originated interactions with other animals. The interests of non-human animals are reflected in standard Law and Economics cost-benefit analyses only to the extent that humans share those interests and are willing-to-pay to satisfy them. This neglect of the preferences of non-human animals regrettably is evidenced in policy toward animals, too, which tolerates considerable pain and death for animals for perceived (though often miniscule) human advantages.[23]

The Law and Economics approach to "efficiency" with respect to animals has regressed since Jeremy Bentham's day. Bentham recognized that overall well-being should incorporate the interests of humans and of non-human sentient beings: animals are moral subjects; their welfare should be taken into account when determining the "greatest happiness." Perhaps killing animals for human food is justifiable, if it is done in a manner that is no worse than what (non-human) nature has in store for them. (If people derive pleasure from eating meat, and the animals are not made worse off, then, for Bentham, there is no objection to meat eating.) But this cannot justify the all-too-common practice of torturing animals for long periods while they are alive, any more (as Bentham noted) than such a practice can be justified for human slaves. What quality is required before sentient beings "count" in calculating overall well-being? Bentham answers in the form of a series of questions: "The question is not, Can they *reason*? nor, Can they *talk*? but, Can they *suffer*?"[24]

Art Again: Resale Rights, or *Droit de Suite*

Sometimes a struggling, unknown artist sells her imaginative creations for small sums; later, if that artist happens to develop renown, those once inexpensive artworks can sell for many thousands or even millions of dollars. (Indeed, this sequence of events would appear to apply to almost any artist who becomes exceedingly popular.) Those collectors who purchased the early works can reap large gains by reselling their formerly cheap art. The process might sound unfair—a starving artist, forced by penury to accept low prices for now acknowledged masterpieces, watches those who happened upon her early creations grow rich by reselling her handiwork. If she can no longer produce art, or if she has died, she or her heirs might continue to be impoverished while those early patrons are enriched.

This scenario is sufficiently unsettling that legal remedies have been adopted. Following a French precedent from the 1920s, the Berne Convention for the Protection of Literary and Artistic Works (noted in chapter 3 with respect to the moral rights of authors) makes a provision for resale rights, or *droit de suite*; here is paragraph (1) from the relevant Berne article: "The author, or after his death the persons or institutions authorized by national legislation, shall, with respect to original works of art and original manuscripts of writers and composers, enjoy the inalienable right to an interest in any sale of the work subsequent to the first transfer by the author of the work."[25] In various forms, *droit de suite* has been adopted in many European countries and in the state of California. A typical implementation is that art works that originally sell for at least some minimum value—cheap souvenir paintings therefore would be exempt from *droit de suite*—would, upon later resale (and every subsequent resale), entitle the artist or her heirs to a royalty of a small percentage of the resale price.[26] Notice that the Berne Convention does not indicate a time limit to the *droit de suite*—implementing legislation in various countries generally does apply a time limit—though it does indicate that the right is inalienable, so it cannot be contracted away during negotiations between an artist and an original purchaser.

A mandated *droit de suite* is a regulation that directly impinges at one point in the "life-cycle" of a work of art—when the work is resold—and again comes into play with further future transfers. Not surprisingly, such a regulation can induce offsetting changes at other points along the way. How much is an initial purchaser willing to pay for an original work of art? Surely the possibility that the artwork will increase in value helps to determine a buyer's willingness to pay. If *droit de suite* mandates that any realized increase in value must be shared between the artist and the original purchaser, the original purchase price will fall to reflect the purchaser's reduced claim to those uncertain future gains. An extreme case of *droit de suite*, where one-hundred percent of any resale price increase is reserved for the original artist, makes this clear. Such a rule, if enforced, would essentially eliminate the purchase of art for investment purposes—prices for new (and old!) works would fall, perhaps markedly. Starving artists might be worse off, not better off, through an inalienable resale right. Of course, in the standard implementation of *droit de suite*, the resale royalty is not 100 percent, but only a few percent of the resale price. Nevertheless, an offsetting decrease of initial prices will occur with these smaller resale rights, too.[27]

Induced changes in the market for original sales would, on average, counteract the intention of the *droit de suite*. Not all artists will have the average experience, however. Those whose resale rights will turn out to be most valuable during their lifetime generally will be those who will become wealthy through their art sales even without any resale royalties. Artists who remain unknown and starving will be worse off: they will see a decrease in prices for original sales of their art, but little or nothing in the form of royalties from future resales.[28]

Resale rights that are alienable offer a compromise (though one that runs against the expressed intention of the Berne Convention). Artists who are confident that they will shortly become famous would hold onto their resale rights, and receive lower prices today. Other artists, those who expect little in the way of future resale royalties or who are in particularly straitened current circumstances, could offer to waive their claim, and thereby receive higher prices on original sales.

Using the Law to Serve Distributional Goals

Law and Economics deals foremost with the efficiency consequences of the law, the overall wealth generated under different legal rules. What about the distribution of that wealth, however? As the Coase Corollary suggests, the law can affect the distribution of income even in the absence of transaction costs—parties who are granted property rights will have higher wealth than they would if the rights instead were allocated to others. If transaction costs are significant, so that any initial situation is hard to dislodge through private negotiations, an allocation of property rights will have both efficiency and distributive consequences, affecting both the size of the pie and how the portions are doled out.

Given that the law can redistribute income among members of society, should that possibility be taken into account when laws are designed or judicial decisions rendered? Should a court, in assigning property rights in a low transaction cost environment, assign the rights to the poorer party, in the interests of lowering wealth inequality? After all, if transaction costs are low, overall satisfaction can be maximized as people contract away from the original situation to a socially efficient one. Why not give the initial property rights to relatively poor people, so that they can increase their incomes by trading away their ownership in the course of achieving social efficiency?

Monetary or In-Kind Subsidies?

A somewhat parallel question traditionally has been asked within the economics discipline. Suppose that the state has a goal of assisting poor families. It is noticed that poor families spend a large fraction of their income on food—a larger fraction than is spent by richer families. One possible method, then, of helping the poor, might be to subsidize the price of food. Some of these subsidies, alas, will go to rich people when they buy food. Further, such a subsidy undermines overall economic efficiency, by inducing consumers of all income levels to buy "too much" food (and, therefore, too little of everything else). Some of the food that is purchased will cost more to produce than it is worth to consumers, because the subsidy ensures that buyers will not personally have to pay the full costs of food production. It is in this sense that the subsidy encourages excessive food buying.

A second method to help needy people would be to subsidize the price of food only for poor families, through the use of food stamps, for instance. Under this sort of program, low-income families (and only low-income families) would qualify to buy non-transferable food stamps, say, for 50 cents each, with each stamp being exchangeable for one dollar's worth of food.[29] Once again there is an efficiency cost: poor households will continue, as in the general food subsidy plan, to "overconsume" food. The efficiency costs will be reduced relative to the general food subsidy program, though, because non-poor households will still face the full costs of the food they choose to purchase. (Committed aficionados of Peltzman effects might also suggest that the food subsidies provided only to the poor will be rendered (partially?) ineffective in terms of reducing poverty, because such subsidies will increase the incentive to be poor! The empirical evidence, however, suggests that in general, US anti-poverty programs are effective at reducing poverty, despite their potential for inducing some offsetting behaviors.[30])

Yet a third method of helping poor households again involves identifying which households are poor (as in the targeted food stamp program). Now, however, instead of selling poor households food stamps that provide a food subsidy, this method entails distributing cash directly to those poor households. The cash allocation subsidizes anything that the poor wish to consume, not only food. Economists tend to look kindly upon this solution, as it does not distort the prices facing consumers of food or other goods—those efficiency costs that accompany price subsidies disappear, while the poor are still aided. If you want to help the poor, this reasoning goes, then alleviate their poverty directly, by furnishing them with cash—indirect aid via subsidized goods or services is more costly overall. This point of view also reflects the standard economics approach that preferences are taken as a given. The fact that income transfers subsidize whatever goods poor people wish to purchase, instead of promoting consumption of those goods (such as food) that the authorities want to subsidize, is generally considered a benefit by economists. Nevertheless, transfer programs in practice often involve devices such as food stamps, in part because broad political support for a food initiative is more robust than for a cash subvention plan that can directly subsidize purchases of alcohol or lottery tickets, for instance.

Allowing food stamp recipients to sell their stamps in a free market essentially replicates a cash handout, as the stamps will sell for the value of the subsidy.[31] Whoever ends up using the stamps will have faced the full cost of the food they purchase—some of it at the supermarket register and some of it in buying the stamps—while poor people who are not interested in subsidized food can turn their stamps into cash. More generally, subsidies targeted at certain types of preferred consumption such as food or warm clothing are subject to squeezing-the-balloon-type pressures. Recipients can trade or sell the preferred goods to buy items that better satisfy their own preferences, rather than the preferences of the subsidy providers.

Laws and Distributing Pie

Let's return to the issue of using the law to allocate property rights in a manner intended to discriminate among income groups. Court decisions, then, are like food stamps or energy subsidies, they offer an indirect method of redistributing resources—and this method suffers from the same sort of detrimental efficiency consequences that accompany indirect redistribution plans such as food subsidies. The alternative of simply giving money to the poor tends to dominate the use of the legal system to effect a redistribution of wealth. That is, if you want to help the poor, choose those legal rules that promote efficiency, rules that maximize the size of the pie. Then, identify the poor people and give them cash. Altering the legal rules for the purpose of indirectly helping the poor might serve the distributional goal but at the sacrifice of economic efficiency; better to keep the efficient rules and tackle poverty directly.[32]

Furthermore, those distributional goals themselves might not be well served, either, even when aiding the "little guy" is the intent of the laws. What sort of rules will favor "little guys" like modest apartment renters or applicants for small loans? Contracting partners such as borrowers and lenders, or apartment owners and tenants, have a mutual interest in fashioning contractual terms that lead to the largest surplus in their relationship. While each party, presumably, would be happy to take as much pie as possible, even out of the hand (or mouth?) of their contract partner, they nevertheless have a common interest in baking a substantial pie together: the more pie, the bigger the slices available to each of the parties.[33]

Consider a borrower and a lender who enter into a loan agreement, and down the road, they find themselves in a dispute. Imagine that the contract calls for a balloon payment—a single payment at the end of the loan term that is much more sizable than the previous monthly payments. When the time comes to make the balloon payment, the borrower balks at the (perhaps unexpectedly) large amount of money due. The matter goes to court. What happens if the judge reasons that borrowers tend to be disadvantaged relative to lenders, and on those (unstated, perhaps) grounds, holds that the balloon payment term is not enforceable? The litigating borrower will be ecstatic to win, and the lender conspicuously less pleased with the course of justice.

For future borrowers, however, the precedent set by the court ruling is not such a clear victory. New loan agreements will not employ the now unenforceable balloon payment term, but that is not the end of the story. Appropriately enough, there will be some squeezing-the-balloon-type effects. Other contractual terms will adjust: perhaps the interest rate will be higher, or more collateral will be required. These sorts of adjustments are likely to counteract, for future borrowers, the gains that accrued to the original borrower when she won her court case. Indeed, the induced changes in loan contracts will probably make borrowers as a class worse off than they were when balloon payment terms were enforceable. Prior to the dispute, at the time of contract formation in the original case, presumably[34] the borrower and lender fashioned the contractual terms in such a way as to maximize the total surplus available to the pair—while the interest rate and other terms helped to determine the shares of the surplus accruing to each of the parties. The contract terms they found best included a balloon payment clause—and such a clause is no longer available to future borrowers and lenders. So the constraint on enforceable terms that stems from the court ruling not only will fail to make borrowers as a class better off in the future, it is likely to make borrowers—and lenders—worse off.

Squeezing Copyright

Copyright law grants authors a temporary property interest in any written production that is fixed in a medium, whether that medium is a piece of paper, a webpage, or what have you. The protection afforded by copyright makes it illegal, in many circumstances, for the writing to be reproduced without authorization. The writing can be of almost any sort, as mundane as a grocery list or as profound as an epic poem. Writers are granted this copyright protection automatically: they do not have to register or apply. The length of a copyright term in the United States has been raised substantially in recent years, now reaching the lifetime of the author of the writing, plus seventy years.

The ban on reproduction of copyrighted works admits substantial exceptions; that is, the law recognizes circumstances—so called *fair uses*—where writing can be copied without express authorization or the payment of royalties: short quotations reproduced in book reviews are one example of fair use. Furthermore, copyright protection extends only to the specific expression of an idea—the more general idea itself is not protected. I cannot reproduce and sell without permission a copyrighted romance novel, but I can write my own story following the plot of Boy Meets Girl, Boy Loses Girl, Boy Gets Girl, without authorization.

The economic rationale for copyright protection, as described in chapter 3, is to improve incentives for the creation of written expression—at the cost of granting monopoly control of that expression to the copyright holder for about a century. The fair use exceptions seem to make sense from an efficiency viewpoint, as they permit borrowings of prose that probably would be agreed upon were the copyright holder and the secondary user to negotiate, without requiring that the costly negotiation take place. Fair use also applies to some borrowings that hold substantial social benefit—and hence are likely to promote overall well-being—even if the copyright holder would not have agreed. One might forgive a novelist for not authorizing copying for the purpose of a negative review or a parody, but copyright law does not require permission for those purposes: if the author's approval were required before commentary on a printed work would be allowed, much informative commentary, including negative book reviews, would be squelched. (A further implication is that positive reviews would become less persuasive.[35]) Some non-commercial educational and research purposes also present economically justified and legally recognized fair uses for unauthorized copying.

The legal regime concerning copyright has come under extensive pressure in recent decades. This pressure has arisen primarily from technological innovations concerning the manipulation of digital content: CDs and DVDs and Blu-ray Discs, mp3 files, cheap and widespread computing power, and the Internet. Copyrighted material, including the majority of recently created music, films, and text, has become very inexpensive to copy and redistribute in digital form. Anyone with a digital version of a book, film, or song, and an Internet connection, has the potential to supply all the world with exact reproductions of the digital content. When you sell or even lend your digital creation, you create a potential competitor for future sales—at least if you take no measures to overcome the technological ease of copying and distributing digital content. The competitor will be able to offer an essentially identical product, without having to incur any of the costs of creating the content (beyond the resources expended for acquiring that first access).

Of course, illicit copying always was feasible. Nevertheless, the previous copyright system for books, music, and film had achieved a sort of workable equilibrium where very few people could actually do much in the way of reproduction. Perhaps a professor could provide photocopies (at least after photocopiers became widespread) of a copyrighted book chapter to all the students in her class, but by and large, it was very costly for someone to take copyrighted material and to reproduce it with high fidelity and on a large scale—and without being identified and forced to pay damages for copyright infringement. (Incidentally, the professor's unauthorized behavior might have constituted fair use.) The copyright system worked in part because most people were not in a position to engage in unauthorized copying that would be commercially harmful to the owner of the copyrighted material. (Indeed, copyright protections were largely superfluous—and hence nonexistent— until the spread of the printing press made large-scale reproduction cost-effective.) This is no longer the case.

The greatly eased access to reproducing and distributing copyrighted works threatens returns to content creators and could result in greatly diminished investments in expensive media, such as full-length Hollywood-style feature films. If people can watch movies for free through illegal but widespread Internet downloads, box office and video rental receipts will fall, and studios will be wary about producing costly movies. But there is a significant countervailing incentive, too. The same technologies that have simplified the copying and distribution of copyrighted material have made it easier to create such material in the first place. Books are written on computers and researched on the Internet, basement bloggers can reach extensive audiences, animations and music can be composed and generated at a keyboard, and even lengthy films can be produced and globally distributed at low cost by millions of amateurs and auteurs. The digital revolution has unleashed vast creative forces.

The traditional copyright regime not only precludes many forms of unauthorized copying, it also protects against unauthorized derivative works. (Derivative works come in many varieties: similar content in a different form, such as a translation of a book into a different language, or a film adaptation of a book, or tie-ins such as toys that are based upon comic book or movie characters.) As lamented in chapter 3, I cannot write and distribute a Harry Potter book without the approval of J. K. Rowling, the inventor and copyright owner of the Potter franchise. I cannot take two Beatles songs and concatenate them to make a "new" song, without the permission of the copyright owner. (I can perform and sell recordings of my own version of a Beatles song without permission, however, provided I pay a legally stipulated royalty—songs, once they are commercially released by the copyright holder, are governed under a mandatory licensing/royalty scheme. My unauthorized cover version cannot represent a substantial alteration of the original, however.) Another impact of the digital revolution, though, is that borrowing and reconfiguring material from multiple sources—think of sampling within hip hop music—has become technologically simple. One creative artist, Kutiman, makes intriguing music videos by mixing together samples of amateur and professional musical offerings posted by others on YouTube—the same website on which Kutiman's complex mixes can be found. DJ Earworm produces annual "United State of Pop" videos that mash-up the most popular music videos from a calendar year.[36]

While copyright law gives the original creator the right to control derivative works, it is worth asking why.[37] The core tension within copyright and patent law centers on providing incentives for the creation of valuable ideas and expressions, at the cost of establishing (time-limited) hegemony over existing expressive material. Monopoly control of derivative works by copyright owners might add to the incentive to create the source work, especially if there is a realistic prospect of substantial financial return from derivative productions. The possibility that a movie might spawn a sequel (controlled by the copyright holders of the original movie), for instance, might be determinative in whether the original movie is made in the first place. (I cannot claim that this book was written solely because of the anticipation of the blockbuster movie version, alas.) So allowing people other than the original creator the possibility to market, without permission, a derivative work, might undermine overall creative incentives.

Many derivative works, however, do not threaten the market for the original product or a derivative made by the original copyright holder, and can even improve the market for those products. Much of "fan fiction" falls into this category—fan fiction consists of (usually unauthorized) stories written by devotees of copyrighted works (such as Harry Potter novels or Star Wars movies, say), often distributed over the Internet. Fan fiction generally stokes interest in the original works, boosting sales of the originals and of authorized derivatives. Copyright law grants original authors monopoly control over derivative works, but in some cases, as with fan fiction and music mixes, the monopoly power does little or nothing in terms of improving the incentives for creating the original works—while diminishing the incentives to create the unauthorized derivatives. (And these unauthorized derivatives themselves can hold significant value for consumers, as the millions who have watched Kutiman's and DJ Earworm's videos can attest.) Of course, in cases where derivative works do not harm original creators, the copyright holders are unlikely to proceed with infringement suits against the unauthorized authorial disciples—but the risk remains, along with the consequent chilling of re-creative effort.

To recapitulate, digital technology has brought at least three developments in its wake:

(1) copyright holders are less able to prevent widespread copying and unauthorized distribution of their material;

(2) costs of production and distribution of new creative materials have been markedly decreased; and,

(3) derivative works, sometimes based on multiple copyrighted sources, are much easier to develop and distribute.

The first of these developments could impair incentives to produce books, music, and other content, while the second and third developments, in overall terms, can improve those incentives. The policy dilemma is that responding to the first development with stronger enforcement against copyright infringement can simultaneously suppress the boost to creativity associated with developments (2) and (3).

Creative Commons and Open Access

In situations where unauthorized derivative works do not impose economic harm on copyright holders, the copyright holders (as noted) are unlikely to press infringement suits. This implicit permission can be formalized, removing doubt among potential copiers. A new regime for accomplishing this formalization has been developed, one in which copyright holders agree to make their content available to others, in specified circumstances, without individual authorization. The umbrella term for this approach is Creative Commons (http://creativecommons.org/).

Founded in 2001, Creative Commons has designed a series of licenses that authors and other content producers can attach to their creations. The licenses spell out the conditions under which other people can make use of those creations, without individual authorization—and typically the licenses sanction much more use than copyright law alone allows. For instance, a license might permit others to make derivative works from your copyrighted material, perhaps only if they do so in a non-commercial fashion, with attribution for your contribution, and if they agree to make their own work available to others on similar terms. (This would constitute an "Attribution Non-Commercial Share Alike" license in Creative Commons terminology.[38]) Downstream content creators who desire more access—for instance, to incorporate your work into a commercial product—can always seek your permission, of course, as under a standard copyright regime.

Creative Commons licenses therefore enable many value-creating trades that would have involved higher (and perhaps prohibitive) transaction costs in the absence of the licenses. Upstream and downstream content creators, via the use of a Creative Commons license, can come together a little more easily, in Coasean fashion, when their interests coincide. (Search engines such as

Google can be restricted to return only Creative Commons material, thereby facilitating the identification of licensed content.) But this is not to say that the interests of consumers are perfectly represented within current copyright law, even as that law has been augmented by initiatives such as Creative Commons.

That many writers (and other content creators) choose to license their work via Creative Commons is indicative of the fact that a good deal of writing, even extensive, painstaking writing, is generated when there is no direct monetary incentive for the authors.[39] For this content, the trade-off that serves as the foundation for copyright—the cost of restricting access to material is tolerated to gain the benefit of increased incentives to produce new material—is all cost and no benefit: the material needs no enhanced incentive for it to be forthcoming. One important subset of writing (beyond fan fiction) tends to be almost entirely of this nature: research articles that appear in professional journals, such as, oh, the *Journal of Law and Economics*.[40]

Researchers who publish articles in scientific journals typically do not get paid for their articles. Instead, their salaries from universities or research centers, coupled with grants from both government and private sources, provide their livelihood and much of the unscheduled time to conduct and write up their research. These authors receive indirect career benefits, not cash on the barrelhead, from published articles, especially if the articles appear in prestigious, peer-reviewed outlets. Wherever an article appears, authors generally have incentives to see it made as widely available as possible—it is exposure and influence, not royalties, that provide the relevant (initial) coin in the research realm. Scientific authors profit from moral rights—attribution and protection against distortion—but not copyrights.

The authors of journal articles, then, gain little or nothing from copyright. Nonetheless, most journal publishers maintain the copyright to published articles and do not allow the articles to be freely available—even though free access is technologically simple and even cheaper than setting up and maintaining a gated system. The current business model of many journal publishers depends on charging for access—and the ability to charge for access depends on copyright—even though the authors of the articles would prefer that the material be in the public domain. Further, most of the crucial inputs for journal publishers, including editing and peer review along with the article itself—are provided without charge.[41]

The fact that it is now nearly costless to distribute scientific research globally has sharpened the tension between the interests of authors and traditional journal publishers. One reaction has been the "Open Access" movement. Open access involves precisely what it suggests, making research articles freely available over the web to anyone with a connection to the Internet. Both readers and scholarly authors tend to benefit from open access relative to a priced alternative—and this mutual benefit remains intact even with no legislative change to the copyright regime.[42] Thousands of scientific journals now are open access, and it has become common for universities and funders to encourage or mandate that research they sponsor be made freely available.[43]

The De Facto Liberalization of the Copyright Regime

Squeezing-the-balloon-type reasoning suggests that when the rules change, induced behavioral adjustments by individuals can counteract the intended effect of the rule amendment. Recall, however, that rules themselves comprise standards for compliant behavior, enforcement regimes to detect noncompliance, and penalties imposed upon detected wrongdoers. Technological changes that greatly reduce the costs of reproducing and distributing digital content form, in essence, a change in the rules of copyright: the lower costs imply that effective enforcement of copyright has diminished. Not surprisingly, there have been efforts to offset the effects of this implicit but major rule change, by altering the standards, by increasing penalties, and by supplementing the resources focused on enforcement or the barriers to illegal copying. Some of these actions have taken a legal and public character, and some have been private responses by content producers and distributors.

Two measures involving ramped-up private enforcement actions have been particularly prominent. The Recording Industry Association of America (RIAA), the music industry's chief trade group, sued tens of thousands of individuals that it accused of illegally downloading or sharing copyrighted digital music files. Further, music producers have attempted to develop technological measures to make it harder to copy and distribute digital works, or at least to do so without detection. This process, known as Digital Rights Management, involves encryption that impedes copying of digital files, or the tagging of files so that copyright infringement is easier to identify.

The law has helped to bolster these private efforts. In 1998, the United States adopted the Digital Millennium Copyright Act, which among other features makes it illegal to circumvent Digital Rights Management technologies; in 1999, the Digital Theft Deterrence and Copyright Damages Improvement Act increased the penalties imposed upon people convicted of copyright infringement of digital works. Higher standards, increased enforcement, augmented penalties: all three elements of rules have been reconfigured in response to the effective diminution of enforcement against copyright infringement that the digital revolution has wrought. These reactions have to some extent counteracted the significant de facto liberalization of the copyright regime caused by digital technology.

Despite the rule-tightening, most copyright violators operating in the digital world probably go undetected. But for those who are sued, the potential damages can be devastating. One litigant whom a court determined had shared 24 copyrighted songs over the file-sharing system Kazaa was ordered to pay $1.92 million—a figure that later was greatly reduced.[44] (These high payments are based on applicable statutes and are unconnected to the actual damages suffered by the copyright owners; indeed, owners might not have been damaged at all by the file-sharing.) It looks as if non-commercial copyright violations are met with a version of low probability-high penalty enforcement, accompanied by all of the problems associated with such a legal regime.

A World without Copyright

What if countermeasures are futile? That is, what if technological advances, despite enhanced enforcement efforts, fully undermine the copyright regime? Would the diminished incentives to originate content that would accompany the loss of monopoly control lead to too little creative activity—books, movies, poems, songs, and so on—or would the fact that all existing content would be in the public domain, ripe for use by others, more than compensate for the destruction of intellectual property rights?

Even without effective copyright protection, there are some forms of creator-consumer interactions which cannot easily be replicated. For instance, while digital music can be accurately and easily copied, the experience of a live concert is not so readily pirated. One of the measures that authors and musicians would adopt in a post-copyright world would be to use the freely available material—songs available on the web, say—as an advertising vehicle for live lectures or concerts that are comparatively immune from copying.[45] Selling web ads for unrelated products is a second route by which content creators can profit from open access material—much as television shows that are free to viewers raise revenues from commercials. Another measure to generate revenue for musicians might involve packaging CDs with liner notes, artwork, or other extras that, while replicable, provide the original seller an appreciable advantage relative to copiers. The digital reproduction of a song can be accomplished with essentially perfect fidelity—but the entire "music experience" often is better with the original than with a copy. Low-priced, official downloads from sites such as iTunes can compete successfully with seemingly identical unofficial versions that are obtainable on the Internet at zero nominal cost. (Informally distributed material might suffer from embedded spyware or some other digital degradation, however.) Further, material that can be freely copied and distributed is more valuable to consumers than is non-reproducible content, and some of that increased value might be captured by creators in the form of higher prices than they otherwise could charge.

The technology-induced erosion of effective copyright protection will not, by itself, undermine creative incentives—at least outside of extremely expensive undertakings, such as the production of high-quality, full-length motion pictures. For these types of costly endeavors, heightened, targeted copyright enforcement might be sufficient—along with the typical reduced or uncertain quality of pirated copies—to maintain adequate inducements for producers. (And there is some evidence that Internet-based movie piracy raises a film's box office earning power—except for blockbuster-style hits—presumably because the illicit online viewing serves as a form of advertisement.[46]) A world with lessened copyright protection will not be a world without new creative content. Further, a limited copyright world probably would stimulate derivative works, so the total amount of new content might be enhanced. Finally, overall efficiency eventually depends both on what content is available, and on the terms on which that content can be accessed by consumers. Diminished incentives to produce new content could still lead to higher social well-being, if existing content is made more readily accessible.

Radiohead and Nine Inch Nails

Two established bands, Radiohead and Nine Inch Nails, have taken the lead in embracing the digital revolution in the distribution of music. These bands have made their music available on much more generous terms for consumers than has been typical with major record labels. Radiohead, for instance, initially released its 2007 album, "In Rainbows," through Internet downloads. Further, for a few months after the album's release, consumers were offered the music on a pay-what-you-want basis: downloaders could pay nothing beyond a nominal service fee, or any positive amount that they chose. Later, more traditional formats, such as CDs, were made available for standard sale. Radiohead also offered a limited edition "discbox" for "In Rainbows" that included additional songs, a lyrics book, and other extras. A contest was established for fans to outline animated videos for "In Rainbows" songs, eventually paying four winners $10,000 each to produce the videos.[47] The sales of physical units were sufficient for "In Rainbows" to reach the top of the album charts in both the United States and the United Kingdom.[48]

Nine Inch Nails and its impresario Trent Reznor also moved from traditional record labels to independent distribution. In 2008, Nine Inch Nails released two albums for free digital download, complemented by sales of limited edition physical recordings. The music is governed by a Creative Commons license (Attribution Non-Commercial Share Alike). Reznor also made available free downloads of concert videos, which have been utilized by fans to produce a documentary film, also available for free, entitled (appropriately) *Another Version of the Truth: The Gift*.[49]

Both Radiohead and Nine Inch Nails appear to have enjoyed financial and popular success with their distribution strategies, despite (or because of) the centrality of free downloads to those strategies.[50] Of course, they were already well-known and acclaimed music brands prior to their embrace of the Internet, and their innovative marketing might have contributed to increased sales of their earlier work (and possibly future work, too, including live performances).[51] Nonetheless, relative unknowns across many creative fields also have found ways to make the provision of free content a major element of building their reputation and profits. The business model has become known as "freemium," where some content is provided for free, but additional, premium features are sold.[52] Online newspapers, including the *New York Times*, have adopted the freemium approach.

Copyright Vacuums

Some areas of human endeavor seem appropriate for copyright protection, yet nevertheless fall outside of the current legal copyright regime. These areas, which include fashion design and stand-up comedy, offer evidence of what can be expected to happen more broadly if copyright protection wanes or is eliminated.

Fashion Design

If I make a drawing of a new haute-couture dress, I have a copyright interest in the drawing. No one can reproduce my drawing without my permission. When I use the drawing to render in fabric a prototype dress, however, my rights to forestall copiers dissipate, at least in the United States: clothing manufacturers are free to make dresses employing that precise design without requiring permission from me. The same is true of couture that is lower than haute: fashion designs generally cannot be copyrighted in the United States, under the legal principle that the designs are inseparable from a useful article, the clothing itself, and such articles are not copyrightable.[53]

The economic purpose of copyright is to provide incentives to creative activity. Does the lack of copyright protection for fashion design undermine those incentives, in a socially detrimental manner? Any answer to this question requires the exploration of a counterfactual, what the fashion design industry would look like if it enjoyed standard copyright protection. Data relevant for this counterfactual exist. First, in the 1930s, a fashion industry group tried to limit copying via private measures—the group's activities later were found to be in violation of antitrust laws. Overall innovation in the US fashion industry does not appear to have been severely restricted by the decline of the industry's private anti-copying effort. Second, the European Union grants copyright protection (for three years, with an opportunity to apply for a longer term) to fashion designs. Again, fashion design creativity seems no less robust in the United States than in Europe, despite the American lack of intellectual property for fashion design. A further, implicit piece of evidence comes from recent fashion innovation. Technological progress has greatly speeded up the time required to produce close copies of new designs. This technical advance has eroded the first-mover advantage that previously offered a degree of effective intellectual property protection to fashion designers— but innovation does not seem to have been undermined substantially as that implicit protection has waned.

In overall terms, it seems as if uncontrolled copying has not had a severely detrimental impact on new designs, though perhaps there has been some marginal disincentive.[54] It is the relative absence of evidence that fashion innovation has been hindered by lack of copyright that seems most striking. This observation has been termed the "piracy paradox": unrestricted copying might be a complement to, not a substitute for, original fashion designs.[55]

Comedy

Design copying in fashion, where it is legal, is often quite open and admitted. Some manufacturers revel in their abilities to quickly copy and make available to retail outlets facsimiles of haute couture. In the case of stand-up comedy, unauthorized rewriting and retelling of jokes, along with close copying, is rarely admitted—although it is legal, or at least might not constitute a copyright violation. Does the lack of legal protection reduce incentives to innovate in the production of stand-up comedy, to the point of social detriment?

Once again, answers depend on counterfactual scenarios that generally are not clear-cut. What is obvious are the responses that comics have taken to their lack of intellectual property rights—responses that help to maintain robust incentives to develop new comedy material. In particular, a set of behavioral norms has developed that dissuades close copying and provides sanctions when the dissuasion proves wanting.[56] The sanctions include gossip and shunning and have sometimes involved violence directed at suspected joke "thieves." There appears to be no evidence that the lack of legal protection results in suboptimal investment into comic innovation, though it may deflect innovative impulses into those aspects of comedy (style, personal monologues) that are less appropriable than mere joke-telling.

Those who see a world without copyright as one that is markedly inferior to our current system can find little support in creative areas that operate without effective copyright protection.[57] Social norms can substitute for formal law to regulate unauthorized appropriation, while first-mover advantages and novel business models can provide payments to innovators even in the absence of official recognition of intellectual property.

Squeezing Newspapers

The technological advances that have undermined the effectiveness of the traditional copyright regime—and hence attracted the interested attention of book publishers, music distributors, motion picture producers, and so on—also have harmed the profitability of the newspaper industry. In the case of newspapers, it is not copyright ineffectiveness that is the main impetus for change. Rather, the Internet has increased competition and simultaneously facilitated the decoupling of products that traditionally were bundled together within a newspaper. In particular, elements of newspapers that formerly raised revenues have become separated from those branches that newspapers implicitly subsidized within the publishing firm. The subsidized component involves the production of news content, including time-consuming investigative reporting, and hence the technological changes threaten to weaken the incentives to gather news.

Increased competition from the Internet, without the unbundling, would itself have put significant pressure on local newspapers. Readers of the *Chicago Tribune*, for the first time, easily can receive world and national news expeditiously from websites of newspapers published in Boston and Philadelphia, Houston and San Francisco—newspapers that in the past were not competing for readers with the *Tribune* (though to some extent, these newspapers did compete to be the first to uncover stories of broad interest). For global reporting, Chicago residents can turn to newspapers in Britain, or, via their own language aptitudes or web-based translation applications, dozens of other countries, too. With respect to the dissemination of world and national news, the *Chicago Tribune* and other daily newspapers now operate in a much more competitive environment.

Of course, the *Chicago Tribune* can attract new, geographically distant readers via its own web offerings, too. Nevertheless, this trade-off—losing local print readers but picking up remote consumers via the web—tends to be a losing proposition for newspapers. It has proven (so far) to be hard to convert web readers into paid subscribers: to some extent, the proximate-for-remote trade-off involves exchanging paying customers for non-paying ones. The problem is worsened by the fact that local advertisers, such as major department stores, traditionally provide substantial revenues to newspapers like the *Chicago Tribune*. Those advertisers benefit from reaching local paid subscribers, but are much less likely to benefit from web readers who see Internet ads. So the willingness of these major patrons to pay for advertisements is diminished as local print readership declines. (Further, department stores themselves have not been the most stable economic partners in recent decades.)

The Internet also is the chief driver behind the unbundling of profitable elements of newspapers from costly newsgathering. Classified advertisements—for jobs, real estate, pets, dates, automobiles, and myriad other goods and services—traditionally generated reliable cash flows for daily newspapers. This form of advertising has been co-opted by the web, and much of it is dominated by websites such as craigslist that are unconnected with newspapers.

Individual firms and entire industries rise and fall, a necessary element of the creative destruction that makes economic progress possible. From that perspective, the shrinkage or closure of newspapers that occurs as Internet competitors develop is an acceptable price for continued prosperity. The main social concern, however, is that the overall production of hard news will be diminished as the newspaper industry declines—a concern based on the reasonable notion that reduced news reporting is undesirable.

As already suggested, it is indeed likely that the loss of subsidies from profitable elements of newspapers (including local business ads and classified ads) will result in diminished news gathering and reporting. The competitors who now attract the attention of web surfers who otherwise would be reading newspapers either do not generate the same revenues or do not use them to subsidize newsgathering to the same extent, or both—craigslist and eBay are two obvious cases in point. Newspaper staffs have been falling, with some traditional beats (such as religion, science, and arts) being cut back or eliminated. Between 2006 and 2013, full-time daily newspaper employment fell by about one-third.[58]

Is diminished production of hard news or investigative reporting an important concern? In a democratic society, the people are supposed to choose representatives who will do a good job, in the aggregate, of enacting policies that will promote the social welfare. Hard news keeps the electorate informed about issues, including the extent to which the government is meeting its fiduciary duties. Scaling back the press diminishes the accountability of government officials (as well as private actors such as corporations); the result to be expected and feared is that the reduced oversight will lead to behavior that serves the public interest less, and private interests (including the interests of government officials themselves) more. There is evidence that information about the workings of local government, in particular, becomes degraded when newspapers expire.[59]

The squeeze that the Internet is placing on traditional newsgathering is being countered in various ways. Newspapers are not sitting idly by as their traditional business model is undermined; rather, they are searching for alternatives. Many of these alternatives involve seeking increased revenues from web readership, either through online advertisements, sales of complementary goods, or by making some of their digital content available only via a paid subscription: the freemium model. Foundations and other benefactors are subsidizing newsgathering, analysis, and the exploration of novel approaches to financing investigative reporting.[60] Further, the technological revolution which has threatened traditional newspapers simultaneously provides new opportunities for reporting, including using social media to identify stories, live-blogging breaking news stories online, in real time,[61] and using electronic means to allow for anonymous deposits of documents; both existing newspapers and new ventures are looking to take advantage of these opportunities.

Hyperlocal News

The threat to the twentieth-century business model of daily city newspapers and local television and radio news broadcasting is spawning a host of experiments into new ways to finance newsgathering and dissemination. One element of many such experiments is a focus on "hyperlocal" news. Hyperlocal news refers to information specific to a very small geographical area, perhaps a zip code, a neighborhood, or even a specific street. Hyperlocal news generally leverages three features of current hardware and software: ubiquitous cameras and video recorders, wireless connections, and social networking capabilities. Technology has decentralized news gathering and reporting so that non-professionals, including bloggers, twitterers, cell-phone photographers, and movie and restaurant goers, can act as occasional journalists. Many people have both the interest and the ability to develop and distribute news content pertinent within small geographical regions. Further, every larger news story takes place within some locality. One of the highest returns to news reporting comes from the timeliness and relevance of information. People on the scene of breaking news are able to make use of their propinquity, by uploading photos or films, or tweeting about the situation. Major news stories, such as the Arab Spring revolutions of 2010 and beyond, and the Aurora, Colorado, theater shootings of July 2012 were brought to the world in part through social media communications by those near ground zero. At the same time that it has become possible for amateurs to effectively publicize breaking news, it has become easier to collect, through electronic search and retrieval means, existing information relevant to a small locality—to gather together all online stories, for instance, from virtually any source, that concern Maple Street in Middletown, USA.

There is some hope that hyperlocal news will offer a revenue stream that will maintain incentives for newsgathering. Consumers will be drawn to websites that can filter and direct the avalanche of information into relevant and digestible parcels. Perhaps traditional news outlets can charge for access to their web editions or generate substantial advertising revenue by providing hyperlocal news to multiple separate localities: extreme narrowcasting, as opposed to broadcasting, of content. To this point, however, the ability of hyperlocal news to become financially viable on a broad scale has yet to be established.[62]

Business reviews already have proven to be susceptible to the hyperlocal and social networking approach. In the past, information about the quality of a restaurant that you had not previously visited was fairly sparse—perhaps a few reviews in newspapers or published guides, and perhaps some word of mouth reports from friends who had patronized the restaurant. The total available information was vanishingly small when compared with the unreported experiences of the possibly thousands or tens of thousands of diners who had eaten at the restaurant. Social networking sites give many more people the ability to disseminate their opinion of a restaurant or other business to prospective customers. For instance, in cities throughout the United States, Canada, Britain, and elsewhere, reviews of local businesses can be accessed via Yelp.com. (The site is supported through business advertisements; Urban Spoon (urbanspoon.com) is another popular restaurant review site.) Millions of reviews are available, and millions of users visit the site each month—many via mobile phones, as they decide, for instance, where to have dinner. Information from Yelp and similar facilities can be spread via hyperlocal outlets and popular social networking sites such as Facebook, too.

The availability of multitudes of disparate pieces of information applies to many areas of life beyond business operations. Online sellers of goods often provide options for previous purchasers to describe their experiences. Public behavior by drivers, police officers, other public employees, and more or less anyone can be monitored, recorded, and reported upon by myriad people who have cell phone cameras or other technologies readily at hand. This increase in the effective monitoring of public behavior offers improved incentives toward better behavior—just as "How's My Driving?" signs on the back of trucks are associated with safer motoring.[63] To some extent, of course, the spread of monitoring will spur a relocation of questionable behavior into less public settings: squeezing bad behavior through increased transparency moves some of the behavior away from the oversight. Once again, however, there is no reason to believe that the benefits of better supervision will be fully offset by such countermeasures.

Deflating Subsidies

People have to decide whether to buy their shelter or to rent it. Governments around the world do not seem to be indifferent between these choices, however: they frequently implement policies designed to encourage homeownership, especially for first-time home buyers. In the United States, for instance, interest payments on mortgage loans are tax-deductible; a typical household that takes the deduction reduces its annual taxes by nearly $1,500.[64]

Consider the situation before the US tax code made an allowance for mortgage interest deductibility. Imagine that I have borrowed money to purchase a home, and that I am making significant interest payments on my loan. Subsequently, mortgage interest deductibility is enacted for the purpose of encouraging homeownership. I welcome this change—my tax bill will fall as the interest payments that I already have been making become deductible.

Nevertheless, I eventually tire of having to worry about keeping my lawn mowed (where's my neighbor Sarah?) and my plumbing in working order—I decide that I should sell my house and move back into a rented apartment. Fortunately, the deduction will be available to those who might take out a loan to buy my home, too. Does mortgage interest deductibility make homeownership more appealing to current renters? Ultimately, probably not: the purchase price of the house will rise, as potential buyers realize that they will receive years of tax breaks from their home loan. A buyer who was willing to pay $100,000 for a house if mortgage interest were not deductible will be willing to pay $100,000, plus the value of the tax break, when mortgage interest is deductible. By and large, mortgage interest deductibility does not make house buying more affordable.

If mortgage interest deductibility is not serving its purpose of providing a net subsidy to home buyers, perhaps the deduction should be repealed. But how will current homeowners feel about the loss of the deduction? They essentially paid for the deduction up front, in the form of a higher price for their home. If the tax break is eliminated, they will be worse off, either because of higher tax bills or because the price at which they can sell their home is reduced (essentially by the value the now-abolished subsidy would have had to prospective buyers). Existing homeowners, then, are unlikely to support repeal, even though the subsidy is not working as hoped. Perhaps a phased repeal, whereby the percentage of interest that can be deducted falls gradually from 100 to 0 over twenty years, would help to ease the transition.[65]

The futility-style story of mortgage interest deductibility is replicated in many other settings, where government policies aim to help a specified group.[66] (*Droit de suite*, as discussed earlier in this chapter, is one case in point: artists who sell a painting under the requirement that they receive a share of future increases in the value of their work will not earn more, on average, than they would in the absence of the mandated payments.) Those group members who receive the original subsidies might be made better off—like artists whose old paintings, previously sold without *droit de suite*, can reap windfalls if *droit de suite* is introduced retroactively for those works—but induced price changes offset the benefit for those who come later. For instance, licenses (or medallions) to operate a taxi cab are very valuable in some cities. Those who were granted licenses when the regulations were first installed received a significant gift. (This gift holds some social utility: taxis are subject to a host of regulations, and the possibility to revoke a valuable medallion adds an enforcement lever that promotes compliance with those regulations.) But firms that want to operate cabs now are not similarly subsidized, as they must pay high prices to procure a medallion from an existing taxi operator. Repeal of the licensing system, no longer effective in providing a subsidy to taxi cab owners, nevertheless is complicated by the fact that those who hold licenses—and paid for them in advance—would be harmed if the licenses become valueless. Even the issuance of additional permits will be contested by current taxi operators, who will see some diminution of the value of their medallions when the supply is increased.[67]

‖ 5 ‖

Deorum injuriae Diis curae [Injuries to the Gods Will Be Remedied By the Gods]

The Latin title of this chapter comes from the ancient Roman historian Tacitus and apparently can be translated "Injuries to the gods will be remedied by the gods."[1] In other words, if only the gods, not people, are harmed, people should not avenge the wrongdoing. The Latin phrase is applied here to various situations in which Law and Economics offers a guide for thinking about where responsibility lies, about who should bear the costs of damages that accrue from accidents, or from contract breaches, or from natural disasters, or from ... well, anything.

Low-Cost Avoider or Insurer

In chapter 2, we looked at a standard accident situation and argued that imposing strict liability upon potential injurers would give them incentives to take appropriate amounts of care. If injurers face the full costs (and benefits) of their behavior, they will, Robin-like, make decisions that promote societal well-being. If the injurer and the victim both contribute to the likelihood of an accident, however, then the situation is more complicated: strict liability imposed upon one of the parties implies no liability for the other party. One of the ill-fated pair will cavort in a risk-free zone and will behave as recklessly as he or she pleases.

Consider a situation where two people—Robin again, but this time, with Little John—are approaching each other on a narrow trail. As long as one person steps aside to let the other pass, there will be no accident—but if both plow straight ahead, there will be an almighty crash. Upon whom should the law place the duty to yield?

The Coasean bargaining perspective provides one vantage point for addressing this issue: What if the parties were able to sign an enforceable contract, in

99

advance, specifying who would step aside? They would stipulate the "efficient" welfare-maximizing behavior and use the contract price to split the surplus created by avoiding accidents and doing so in the least costly way. The question then reduces to which is the least costly way to avoid the accident, for Robin to step aside or for Little John to step aside? (Maximizing wealth, in this situation, amounts to minimizing the cost of avoiding the collision. We take it as a given that the benefit for both of them to be out and about is sufficiently large that the best way to avoid an accident does not involve one of them staying at home or taking an alternate route.) If Little John is huge (as the legend has it), and changing direction physically demanding for the pre-merry man, then it is probably best for nimble Robin to give way. Alternatively, if Robin is blind, say, then it is probably best for the giant to yield. The law should replicate the reasoning of the interested parties themselves and assign the duty to defer to the party for whom the cost of moving is lowest. (Of course, if transaction costs are zero, the legal allocation will not affect who will eventually step aside—the Coase Corollary assures us that the party who has the lowest cost of accident avoidance will end up taking the precaution. If transaction costs are not zero, however, then the legal regime can influence resource allocation, and the efficient distribution of rights is to require that the low-cost accident avoider provide the "After you.")

This result is more general: in determining where liability for an accident should fall, assigning it to the party best able to avoid the accident tends to promote efficiency: this party is the "low-cost avoider."[2] The same principle applies in contract law. Imagine that Robin agrees to manufacture and deliver some exercise equipment to Little John. Before delivery, however, Robin's factory burns down, and she cannot comply with the terms of the contract. Should the fire excuse her non-performance? Probably not, that is, Robin probably should be liable to pay expectation damages for breach to Little John. Robin is in a much better position than is Little John to prevent fires at her factory or to limit the harm from those fires that do break out. Holding her liable for contractual losses that arise as a consequence of a fire in her factory helps to provide her with incentives to take appropriate anti-fire measures.

Instead of a fire, however, what if Robin's factory is damaged by yet another pesky meteorite (from the same meteor shower that destroyed your lawn in chapter 2)? Should Robin be excused from complying with the contract terms, assuming that she possesses no practical means of protecting her factory against meteorite strikes? In this case, the issue is no longer which party is in the best position to prevent contractual noncompliance—since it is assumed that neither party can thwart this type of *force majeure* destruction—but rather, which contracting party is best situated to bear the risk of a loss? If Robin is in the exercise equipment business and has easy access to insurance from the Acme Meteorite Damage Insurance Company, then Robin should be held liable: she can easily escape risk (though not cost) by purchasing insurance, while forest-dwelling Little John is probably cut off from similar risk-transfer mechanisms.[3] Even without the existence of Acme, if Robin's company deals with hundreds of overweight outlaws every year, whereas Little John makes only this one purchase annually, Robin is in a position to self-insure: she can charge each of her customers a slightly higher price as a sort of implicit meteorite insurance premium, while indemnifying those customers against contractual losses brought about by her factory being damaged by the odd meteorite.

So the two questions to ponder when thinking about which parties should bear liability concern risk avoidance and insurance: (1) Which party is in the best position to reduce the risk of the loss arising? (2) Which party is in the best position to deal with the risk that remains even after appropriate precautionary measures have been taken? Many times these questions have the same answer—fortunately, as this clarifies the imposition of legal liability. In particular, the social pie will be maximized if the party who is the low-cost avoider and the low-cost insurer is held liable.[4] For instance, hidden product defects that can harm consumers even when the product is used appropriately should probably be the responsibility of the product manufacturer, who is best able to prevent those defects and to insure against the remaining risks. If the avoidance question and the insurance question have different answers, however, then a judgment will have to be made about which of the risk-controlling features is more important.

Products Liability

When Lance on his bicycle collided with Bart on his skateboard, we looked at the incentives that would be created by holding either Lance or Bart responsible for the ensuing damages.[5] But there are other possibilities. In particular, perhaps the manufacturer of Lance's bike should be made to pay for not providing better brakes or noisy horns to help warn unhurried fellow travelers; perhaps the maker of the skateboard is at fault for not installing lights or a flag on the back of the board to inform approaching cyclists of a sluggish and sub-sized sidewalk surfer.

If the bicycle manufacturer is forced to reimburse damages from collisions involving bikes, then the price of bicycles will rise—the damage payments will be passed on to bike buyers in the form of that higher price. Bike purchases, in essence, will come packaged with an insurance policy; the higher prices reflect the implicit premium associated with the insurance. If the insurance were perfect, then bikers would have no incentive to avoid accidents: perfect insurance (at least the Law and Economics version of perfect insurance) implies that bikers are completely indifferent about being in an accident or not. Of course, rarely would the provision of insurance be perfect, and it is best that it not be: since bike rider behavior surely can influence the probability of an accident, some liability for damages helps to provide better incentives for bikers to take care. Co-pays within health insurance plans are based on a similar principle.

Let's compare more closely two liability regimes, one in which bikers are responsible for damages from accidents, and a second where bike manufacturers are responsible. In the first case, prices for bikes are lower, but those bikers who are in accidents end up paying a lot. In the second case, the price of bikes is higher, but riders are indemnified against accidental damage. If it is the case, however, that the manner in which a bike is operated is more important for avoiding accidents than are the details of the manufacturing, then there will be more accidents if the manufacturers are held liable: the riders, not the manufacturers, are the low-cost avoiders of crashes.

If manufacturers needn't fear liability, however, what incentive do they have to provide proper (or efficient) safety features into their bikes? Competition can provide one spur—bikes without proper safety features will not sell as well, or for as much, as will bikes that incorporate those safety features that are worth more to bikers than they cost to manufacture. Further, government regulation can mandate certain safety features—though the extent to which safety ultimately will be improved depends on the pertinence of the Peltzman effect.[6]

But there are some elements of safety that bike purchasers cannot easily judge, and hence, market forces alone might not be sufficient to induce proper decision-making. Perhaps a worker at the bike manufacturing plant is inattentive on the job; as a result, one in 5,000 of the bikes he works on is equipped with brakes that don't stop the bike as effectively as intended. In the long run, with millions of bike purchases, this defect might become noticeable and purchasers would not be willing to pay as much for the potentially defective bikes—but it is asking a lot for the market to uncover that information and to reveal it to potential purchasers in a timely fashion, though a private subscription service that tests and rates bike safety might lend assistance. (Even these sorts of bike reviews might be ineffective given the rarity with which the harm materializes.) Some liability for accidents caused by the lethargic laborer's defect might provide a more reliable incentive for the manufacturer to rein in inattentiveness or to double check the quality of installed brakes.

The law of products liability developed to help solve the problem of manufacturing defects that are hard for the market expeditiously to reveal. The idea is that if the purchaser uses a product in its intended manner, and does not alter the product, and if the product contains a hidden defect that raises the probability of an accident, then the manufacturer can be held liable for damages that result from accidents. The low-cost avoider of accidents associated with hidden defects in a product is the manufacturer, not the consumer. Attaching liability to the low-cost avoider helps to ensure that safety measures that result in higher social well-being are undertaken.

The three conditions—that the product be in its original condition, that it be operated as intended, and that the defect be hidden—are all important in making it likely that the manufacturer, not the user, really is the low-cost avoider of the accident.[7] If Lance rides his bike recklessly or tries to use it to climb a tree or go down staircases, then it would seem that his behavior, and not any manufacturing defect (hidden or overt), would bear the primary responsibility for accidents.[8] Nevertheless, products liability law in the United States has evolved to the point where a form of strict liability adheres, where manufacturers can be held liable for injuries involving their products even if there is no negligence in manufacturing, and in circumstances where there is no hidden defect, where the product has been altered, or where it is being misused. The liability is not absolutely strict, however, and in some ways the lapses from "strictness" replicate a negligence regime: to be successful, plaintiffs typically have to show that the product was defective or overly risky in design, or that there was insufficient warning provided to consumers about potential risks.[9]

Comparative Negligence

The original collision between Lance and Bart took place when Bart swerved to avoid a pebble (from a meteorite?) in the roadway. So perhaps there is yet another claimant for the imposition of legal liability: the entity charged with maintaining the road. Roads strewn with debris probably make accidents more likely. It might be necessary for the road maintenance organization to bear some responsibility for accident damages, in order to provide incentives for keeping the road in good repair.

Incidentally, someone with a firm commitment to private as opposed to government ownership might suggest that if roads were privately owned, then those owners, Robin-like, would find it in their interest to engage in the optimal amount of upkeep. Perhaps surprisingly, this view is not endorsed by Adam Smith:

> The tolls for the maintenance of a high road, cannot with any safety
> be made the property of private persons. A high road, though entirely

neglected, does not become altogether impassable, though a canal does. The proprietors of the tolls upon a high road, therefore, might neglect altogether the repair of the road, and yet continue to levy very nearly the same tolls. It is proper, therefore, that the tolls for the maintenance of such a work should be put under the management of commissioners or trustees.[10]

Back to Bart and Lance. We could imagine, Coase-like, all of the interested parties gathering in advance and specifying the actions that they should take, plus penalties in the event that they breach the resulting contract, along with clauses for how damages from accidents will be distributed. Since Bart, Lance, the skateboard manufacturer, the bicycle maker, and the road maintenance organization all can increase the probability of an accident, the resulting contract should specify the standards of behavior that they should meet. Failure to meet those standards would constitute a type of negligence and could be dissuaded by the appropriate fine.

Those appropriate fines should depend on how likely it is that sub-par performance will become known in the event that it takes place. The lower the probability of detection, the higher the fine will have to be to maintain appropriate incentives. (This is a version of keeping incentives approximately the same when the probability of conviction falls by one-half, by doubling the fines that convicted parties pay.) Notice that a party can be negligent even when no accident occurs. For instance, imagine that Bart does not meet his contractually specified standard of behavior. Bart's lapse raises the probability of an accident, but this time, everyone is lucky, an accident is avoided. If Bart's negligence goes unnoticed in these fortunate cases, fines will have to be expanded when negligence is uncovered in those unlucky instances when there is an accident, to provide Bart with appropriate incentives to take optimal precautions.[11]

In the event of an accident, there still remains the issue of who has to bear the $100 of damage sustained by Bart's skateboard and the $100 of damage sustained by Lance's bike. If no one has been negligent, perhaps the damages should just remain where they first fell, split between Bart and Lance. But we cannot maintain incentives for all parties to take proper (i.e., efficient) care if we cannot use fines and bonuses, that is, if all we can do is reallocate that $200 in losses in the aftermath of an accident.[12]

Given the complexity of potential Coasean-style negotiations in an accident setting, it isn't surprising that the regulatory regime that applies to non-negotiated Bart/Lance-type encounters is pretty intricate. There will be safety regulations in place, perhaps, for all parties, including vehicle manufacturers, road maintenance organizations, and our travelers; for instance, there might be a speed limit for bikes, or a mandated helmet-wearing law intended to reduce the costs of accidents.[13] If there is an accident, under the *comparative negligence* approach that many jurisdictions employ, the liability will be shared in such a way that the parties who are deemed to be relatively more negligent shoulder a higher proportion of the damages. Along with the *ex ante* regulations, the sharing of damages in this manner helps to provide all parties with incentives to behave responsibly.[14]

Foreseeable Misuse and Attractive Nuisance

Recall that the traditional products liability doctrine would impose on manufacturers responsibility for harms only if the manufacturing defect is hidden, the product is unmodified by the consumer, and the product is operated as intended. The failure of any one of these three conditions to hold would make it significantly less likely that the low-cost avoider of harm is the manufacturer, as opposed to the consumer.[15]

But what does it mean for a product to be utilized as intended? Can a producer simply stipulate how the product is intended to be used, with any deviating uses resulting in no liability for the manufacturer? Such an approach to the meaning of "intended use" would be unsatisfactory. One could imagine, for instance, a knife manufacturer, anxious to avoid liability for accidents even in the case of negligent production, incorporating into the operating instructions an admonition that the knife is not to be used for cutting. A somewhat analogous example that currently exists concerns cotton swabs. These handy little tools often are employed for the purpose of cleaning wax out of ears—indeed, earwax removal might even be their primary use. Nevertheless, cotton swabs are sold with a warning that they are not to be placed in ear canals. (The risks of cleaning the ear canal with cotton swabs include pushing the earwax further into the canal and puncturing an eardrum.)

Instead of a warning not to place cotton swabs in ears or not to cut with a knife, might it be better—more efficient—to explain the risks of undertaking these activities and offer suggestions as to how to limit those risks? Alternatively, perhaps design changes that would make accidents less likely or eliminate the incentive to "misuse" the product would be the best approach.

In other words, some proclaimed "misuses" or consumer alterations are foreseeable and possibly even socially desirable. Manufacturers could profit considerably from sales that clearly are spurred by the potential to "misuse" the product; without any liability for accidents, they might not bother to take cost-justified safety measures or issue appropriate warnings to limit the damages that arise during nominal misuse. It might likewise be foreseeable that warnings will go unheeded.

One view of fairness might suggest that consumers should be held legally responsible for any harm they do to themselves when they ignore a warning or employ a product in a manner inconsistent with the instructions: let such reckless consumers beware. But Law and Economics uses efficiency, overall preference satisfaction, as its guide to good rules, as opposed to perceptions of fairness. For *foreseeable misuses* that, on net, are better to accept than to suppress, *caveat emptor* (let the buyer beware) need not be the legal doctrine that leads to the best outcome.

Once again, we can take a Coasean view of this matter and ask what sort of contract manufacturers and users would agree to if they negotiated over liability for harms occasioned by misuse. (The fact that manufacturers and consumers actually are in contractual relationship—or connected by a chain of contracts, from manufacturer to wholesaler to retailer to consumer, say—adds salience to the contractual approach.) Presumably such a contract would call on manufacturers to take into account foreseeable misuses—rendering them uses, not misuses—and to apply appropriate safety measures and warnings. Alternatively, if the contemplated (mis-) application of the product is excessively risky even when performed with care, then perhaps the product should be redesigned not just to dissuade but to preclude misuse. Cotton swabs, for instance, could be made significantly larger, physically preventing their misuse in cleaning ear canals. These sorts of redesigns might be the lowest cost method of avoiding accidents that are not worth risking.

In any event, a Coasean-style negotiation and its resulting contract will ensure that the manufacturing process is optimized for foreseeable uses and misuses. The product will still involve some risk, but all cost-justified measures that can be taken by the manufacturer will be specified by the contract. Failure of the manufacturer to take these measures will be a breach of contract (or constitute negligence) and subject the manufacturer to damage payments, providing the incentives for manufacturer compliance.

Consumers, too, should take cost-justified actions to control the risk and extent of injury, and the optimal contract will delineate these actions. To ensure buyer regard for the efficient contract terms, then, consumers who do not use the product properly (with respect to what an optimal contract would call for) should themselves face some liability. Consumers should not be fully insured against harms that they cause or contribute to, because such full insurance will result in too little care when utilizing products.

If, however, the extent to which accidents occur is not under the control of consumers (by and large), then manufacturers might be in the best position to provide accident insurance—requiring them to charge a higher price to all consumers (an implicit insurance premium) to fund damage payments following injuries. But whatever the "optimal" contract consists of in a specific situation, foreseeable misuses rightly enter into the picture—they cannot simply be ignored, nor can it simply be presumed that the best policy is for damages from accidents that arise from misuses to fall upon the disobedient consumer.

Incidentally, prescription medicine is one area in which a type of foreseeable misuse is common. In the United States, the Food and Drug Administration must approve a drug before it can be made available to consumers via a doctor's prescription. Drug approval is related to specific health conditions; the criterion, roughly speaking, is for the drug to pass a cost-benefit test, weighing the risks of the drug (these are the costs) against its potential benefits.[16] Once a drug is approved for a particular ailment, however, doctors have the right to prescribe that drug for any medical situation that they deem fitting for the use of the drug. Unapproved uses could be highly lucrative to pharmaceutical firms, and also, perhaps, valuable to patients. To what extent can drug manufacturers promote the writing of prescriptions for their drug aimed at unapproved uses? In late 2008, the Food and Drug Administration adopted a guideline that permits drug manufacturers to distribute to doctors copies of articles in medical journals that concern unapproved uses of drugs.[17]

Related ideas feature in the legal doctrine of *attractive nuisance*. What if you set up a clown mannequin on your property near the sidewalk and booby trap it in such a way that if a child approaches the clown, the child will fall into a deep ditch? The child will be injured, but he was trespassing. Should you, as the clown-trap owner, be liable for the damages resulting from the child's injuries? Under the doctrine of attractive nuisance, you will be liable. It was perfectly foreseeable that the clown would attract a child, and the child would be in no position to judge the risks of approaching the clown: the dangerous clown is the attractive nuisance. It need not be a clown, of course: a swimming pool or even a pile of lumber could qualify as an attractive nuisance.

Mill and the Harm Principle

In his 1859 essay *On Liberty*, John Stuart Mill asks under what circumstances society has the right to interfere with adult decision-making. Mill's answer has become known as the *harm principle*: society can intervene only into those decisions that involve a non-negligible risk of "harm to others." Firing a gun down an urban street or driving recklessly along that street are situations ripe for regulatory control. My choices of what restaurant to patronize for dinner and what color to paint my kitchen do not threaten harm to others, so from Mill's perspective, society has no right to attempt to coerce me into a specific restaurant or a specific color.

In economic terms, the harm principle states that society cannot interfere with adult decision-making unless those decisions involve non-negligible externalities. As noted in chapter 3, an externality arises when one person's decision affects someone else, but where there is no mechanism to induce the decision-maker to fully account for the spillover effect. The *e pluribus unum* function of the law (chapters 1 and 2) is about the internalization of externalities, forcing decision-makers to respond to the consequences of their choices upon others just as if those consequences fell upon the decision-maker directly. Tragedies of commonly owned assets like the oceans reflect inadequate attention to externalities—though if transaction costs are zero, people could always get together and negotiate themselves to efficient outcomes: contracts are another method of internalizing externalities.

Reckless driving or mishandling a weapon obviously present a non-negligible risk of harm to others, so governmental regulation of these activities might be called for. But what about less immediate risks or less tangible harms? Should you be allowed to insult me in public, profanely, with impunity? Should you be allowed to legally procure and use methamphetamine, if there is some risk that you will ruin your life with a meth addiction and require support from your family or from society? Speech and vices (such as alcohol and drug consumption, gambling, and prostitution) comprise the terrain in which applying Mill's harm principle becomes challenging, precisely because speech and vice typically do not pose significant risks of direct, tangible harms to others—though they might present intangible harms (I am offended by your insults) or risks of indirect harms (the addict requires social support). Much of *On Liberty* consists of Mill's attempt to apply his harm principle to the speech and vice arenas.

Can offensive speech or hate speech be prohibited under the harm principle? No: for Mill, taking offense at what someone says is not the sort of harm that can justify societal intervention. Mill's view anticipates the formulation provided by Justice Louis Brandeis concerning the proper way to respond to bad or hurtful speech: "If there be time to expose through discussion the falsehood and fallacies, to avert the evil by the processes of education, the remedy to be applied is more speech, not enforced silence."[18] Mill allows societal coercion against speech only when there is no opportunity for the salutary effect of more speech to prevent direct and tangible harm:

> An opinion that corn-dealers are starvers of the poor, or that private property is robbery, ought to be unmolested when simply circulated through the press, but may justly incur punishment when delivered orally to an excited mob assembled before the house of a corn-dealer, or when handed about among the same mob in the form of a placard.[19]

For Mill, mob violence can be prohibited by law; further, speech that presents an immediate threat of mob violence can be prohibited, too. But speech that might inflame violent passions, unconnected to an immediate threat, should be met by counter speech, not by repression—an approach that comports well with some aspects of current US law, too.[20]

Mill's view, that offended feelings are not the sort of harm that can justify regulatory interventions, conflicts somewhat with the standard economics approach. If people value not being offended by oral communications— if they would be willing to pay to avoid offense or need to be compensated to accept offense voluntarily—then offensive speech involves real harm, an externality. The efficient outcome, therefore, should internalize this externality, perhaps by taxing or prohibiting offensive speech, by requiring damage payments when offense occurs, or by encouraging Coasean-style bargaining.

But Mill allocates the property right of speech to speakers and more-or-less makes that right inalienable. Mill argues that the actual externalities, even from offensive speech, are positive, not negative:

> Let us suppose . . . that the government is entirely at one with the people, and never thinks of exerting any power of coercion [to suppress speech] unless in agreement with what it conceives to be their voice. But I deny the right of the people to exercise such coercion, either by themselves or by their government. The power itself is illegitimate. The best government has no more title to it than the worst. It is as noxious, or more noxious, when exerted in accordance with public opinion, than when in opposition to it. If all mankind minus one, were of one opinion, and only one person were of the contrary opinion, mankind would be no more justified in silencing that one person, than he, if he had the power, would be justified in silencing mankind. Were an opinion a personal possession of no value except to the owner; if to be obstructed in the enjoyment of it were simply a private injury, it would make some difference whether the injury was inflicted only on a few persons or on many. But the peculiar evil of silencing the expression of an opinion is, that it is robbing the human race; posterity as well as the existing generation; those who dissent from the opinion, still more than those who hold it. If the opinion is right, they are deprived of the opportunity of exchanging error for truth: if wrong, they lose, what is almost as great a benefit, the clearer perception and livelier impression of truth, produced by its collision with error.[21]

As with speech, so with vice, at least for Mill and harm principle adherents. Society can only intervene in the presence of direct harm, and my (or my faith's) not liking the fact that others engage in vice is not a direct harm: Deorum injuriae Diis curae (injuries to the gods will be remedied by the gods). Nor is the fact that there is some probability that a drinker or drug-taker will injure herself and require assistance an acceptable rationale for banning an activity. (The imbiber could be punished if inebriation leads to a crime or the neglect of a duty, however; people can be punished for crimes or breaching duties irrespective of the source of their delinquency.) As a result, for Mill, there would be no such thing as an illegal drug. Substances like alcohol or cocaine could be regulated and taxed by the state, but not in such a way as to make them difficult for adults to procure. Gambling and prostitution likewise could be controlled, but not banned, under Mill's application of his harm principle.[22]

The possibility of Coasean-style bargaining provides another lens on why taking offense at words or at other people's vices does not constitute a direct harm that would justify, for Mill, social coercion. I might like a world in which I can say whatever I like, and where I can censor those annoying other people who are insufficiently enlightened to agree with me fully. If we were to think about signing a contract, however, it is unlikely that I could get them to assent to establish those rules that are biased toward me. They face similar obstacles to achieving consensus over rules biased toward them. Unbiased rules—which is what we are left with if biased rules cannot be secured—come in two broad flavors: (1) rules where no one is allowed to speak freely (or to engage in their preferred vice), and (2) rules that allow everyone to speak (or to indulge in their vice of choice) irrespective of the offense that others might take. The personal gains to being able to speak and act (in the absence of physical externalities) as one pleases are so significant that it is likely that our Coasean bargainers would agree to a framework that opts for mutual liberty and not for control. (For instance, with liberty to speak we needn't constantly devote substantial attention to monitoring our talk for fear that an unguarded phrase will land us in prison.) If Mill is correct that on balance, the externalities from speech are positive, not negative, the case for mutual forbearance is stronger still.[23]

Pecuniary Externalities

When I decide to eat at Joe's Diner, I simultaneously am deciding not to eat at Moe's Diner. My pro-Joe decision hurts Moe. Isn't that a form of harm to others that should be taken into account by regulatory authorities? Why is it that if I hurl a brick through Moe's window and damage him by $50 I will get in trouble, but I can refuse to eat at his establishment (costing Moe, say, $50) without being prosecuted?

One answer is that the harm I impose on Moe by choosing to dine elsewhere is precisely countered by my aid to Joe—society as a whole is not made worse off if I go to Joe's instead of Moe's and is better off given that I prefer Joe's and I am part of society! My failure to eat at Moe's is "harm" to Moe, perhaps, but does not threaten overall efficiency—in marked contrast to the social costs involved when I commit crimes or behave recklessly. (If I ate at Moe's instead, would I have to pay Joe $50 in damages? If I ate at home, would every diner owner have a valid claim against me?)

Consider a slightly different scenario. Joe's Diner has been chugging along, but now Moe enters the lucrative diner market—some of Joe's patrons start to eat at Moe's. Not me, though—I remain loyal to Joe. Nevertheless, the fall in demand for Joe's food results in lower prices. That is, Moe's entry into the diner business has helped me, because I can eat at Joe's more cheaply. But Moe did not take my gain into account when deciding whether to open his diner. It appears that there is an externality, and perhaps social optimality requires that the state subsidize Moe's entry into the greasy spoon sector.

Once again, however, this appearance is deceiving. The lower price that I pay—a gain to me—is, from Joe's point of view, lower revenues: the benefit to me is exactly offset by Joe's loss. For us dedicated Joe-ists, the fall in meal prices brings no net social gain: we win, but Joe loses. Despite some reshuffling of costs and benefits, there is no reason to believe that society will gain by subsidizing Moe's entry, or by subsidizing a decline in Joe's prices more directly. (Indeed, the fall in demand that led to a decline in Joe's prices could have been caused not by a new diner, but by new vacation opportunities that drew people out of town—should vacations be subsidized, too?)

The external effects that occur through market-based price changes are not "real" externalities that threaten social optimality, but so-called *pecuniary externalities*. Yes, a rise in a price hurts buyers—while it simultaneously helps sellers. And a fall in price has the opposite distributional impacts. These distributional effects matter a lot for the individuals involved—just ask Joe—but social efficiency is not compromised, there is no waste associated with pecuniary externalities.

Internalizing real externalities, as when Robin has to make good any damage her reckless behavior causes for Friday, increases efficiency. The law, therefore, should look to encourage such internalization. Pecuniary externalities, alternatively, do not influence the overall size of the pie—though, of course, they do influence the size and distribution of individual slices. Therefore, there is no efficiency rationale for a public policy aimed at promoting or offsetting such externalities. There is no social harm, no diminution in overall wealth, when Moe's Diner outcompetes Joe's Diner, as bad as it is for Joe and Joe's partisans. The harm suffered at Joe's Diner, therefore, is not the sort of harm that we should force Moe to recompense.

Many price changes affect the size of the pie as well as the distribution of the slices. What if Moe's diner is successful because Moe has discovered a less expensive way to produce and serve quality meals? His lower prices attract customers and drive his competitors out of business. The competitors (including hapless Joe, alas) lose, whereas Moe's customers and Moe share some gain—customers receive their meals at a lower price, and Moe makes some profit. Much of the pecuniary gain to the buyers and Moe is offset by the losses to those erstwhile competitors—much, but not all. The fact that Moe's meals are cheaper to produce means that fewer of society's scarce resources—land, labor, and capital, to invoke the economists' traditional triad—are used up in supplying meals: the decline in the cost of production is the source of a net social gain, an increase in the size of the pie, as those released resources now can be used to produce other things that people value. Further, the lower prices will entice some new customers into the diner market, and they will be purchasing meals for less than they think the meals are worth to them—so they gain, too. (The fact that the newcomers did not find a diner meal to be worth buying at the old, higher price suggests that these gains are fairly small potatoes—as it happens, a Moe's Diner specialty.)

A potential offset to the efficiency-enhancing properties of Moe's cost-saving innovation lies (perhaps hidden) in those "released resources." These resources include workers who have lost their jobs, along with idled capital equipment. If these resources are expeditiously re-deployed and if the owners of these resources receive essentially the same (or greater) remuneration as before, then all should be well. But, of course, many unemployed workers go months and even years without finding alternative employment, and often what employment that they do find pays much less than they earned before. The new ideas and technological advances that undergird economic growth are far from Pareto improvements: many people are severely harmed when the value of their labor falls through changes in market prices. Economic growth is fueled by what has famously been termed "creative destruction."[24] It is worth keeping the destruction in mind, along with the creativity, and in seeking ways to use compensation to convert ostensibly efficiency-enhancing changes into something closer to Pareto improvements, changes where no one's welfare is substantially lowered. Unemployment insurance is one element of such a mechanism of compensation.

Assuming that those resources "freed" by Moe's novel idea are indeed expeditiously redeployed and overall welfare is enlarged, we might be worried that since Moe only receives part of the social gain from finding a cheaper way to produce meals, he will have inadequate incentives to search for such innovations. (Moe's customers also receive some of the gain.) We might respond by providing patent protection or by publicly subsidizing basic research into meal-making.

The provision of patents and unemployment insurance might be reasonable responses to general issues involving incentives to innovate and the distributional consequences of price changes. But there is no public rationale for designing policy to encourage or discourage specific pecuniary externalities, those harms or benefits imposed upon others through price changes in standard markets, such as the benefit I receive when Joe's prices fall due to a decline in demand for his meals.

Blocked Exchanges

Societies ban all sorts of exchanges: votes cannot be sold, sex cannot be sold, and human organs like kidneys cannot be sold—at least in many places. Often it is the sale itself that is the stumbling block: votes and sex can be implicitly bartered and kidneys can be donated, even in jurisdictions where direct monetary quid pro quos are not allowed. The touch of filthy lucre can defile otherwise permissible exchanges.

Why? Competitive markets generally are thought to lead to efficiency—why not allow sales of votes or sex or kidneys to increase overall satisfaction? Creating new markets, as we saw in chapter 1, is a standard economics prescription for inefficiencies, whether those inefficiencies exist in the realm of controlling pollution or decontrolling apartment rents. So why not create markets in votes or sex or kidneys? Indeed, it is less a matter of creating and more a matter of formalizing and regulating the existing markets in these "commodities," as illegality does not actually eliminate their exchange for money.

A Law and Economics approach to blocked exchanges would, as usual, put efficiency at the center of the inquiry. Perhaps the bans on money-mediated exchanges are consistent with economic efficiency—after all, such bans are widespread in both time and space. The bans might be welfare-improving if the conditions under which markets promote efficiency do not apply in these contentious realms.

First, it is voluntary exchange that is associated with increasing efficiency. A coerced "trade," such as a theft, possesses no presumption of contributing to aggregate well-being. Maybe the conditions under which sex is traded render it hard for some participants to say no safely, or hinder the policing against implicit or explicit coercion.

For a different but familiar context, consider drivers waiting at a red light at traffic intersections. These drivers are to some extent a captive audience, as the signal (and perhaps the traffic) prevents them from driving away. Should our commitment to free speech imply that beggars must be allowed to solicit drivers under these conditions? Should merchants offering ostensible services such as windshield cleaning (squeegee men, to employ the common term for these informal entrepreneurs) be allowed to ply their trade at traffic signals? The fact that drivers cannot quickly extricate themselves from a proffered exchange adds an element of coercion to red-light transactions. In the case of windshield cleaning, the coercion might go further, where the cleaning begins before the driver agrees to the service or despite indications of disagreement. There can be an implicit threat to damage the vehicle or person of a non-compliant driver, and unscrupulous individuals might try to foreground that threat. Further, the threat can materialize at the moment of choosing of the beggars or squeegee men—most of the time they can behave with decorum, but when there are few other drivers or police or other witnesses around, they can ramp up the coercive element. If regulation of such markets were costless and perfect, then permitting and regulating non-coercive begging or soliciting at traffic intersections might be a desirable policy. But given the realities of how the regulatory structure would work in practice, it is often the case that the best rule is to ban solicitations in such settings, while allowing them in environments more conducive to fully voluntary trades.

An extraordinary potential for coercion, then, provides one rationale for banning some market exchanges. Third-party effects, externalities adhering to a non-coercive exchange present another rationale. Consider rules against scalping, the resale of tickets to concerts or plays—many jurisdictions ban ticket scalping.[25] Why? The trade of tickets would seem to be win-win, like other voluntary exchanges. This improvement in overall welfare, however, requires that the only people who are affected by the resales be those who are engaged in the trade. But often other people have an interest in who purchases tickets. Some of the value of attending an event comes not from the performers, but from the audience. If almost all the tickets to a Lady Gaga concert are purchased on the secondary market by rich, old, curious accountants, then the concert itself becomes something different—and perhaps less valuable to the few young Lady Gaga fanatics mixed among the accountants. So the concert promoters might want to prevent resale, and some of the concert goers (at least some of those who already have tickets) might support that policy. (Even those accountants who attend probably prefer a concert environment that is not accountant-intensive.[26]) A direct profit motive can be in play, too: the accountants might not buy any Lady Gaga merchandise at the concert—they are not that curious! Or, the profit interest might be more indirect, with a concern about the long run viability of Lady Gaga once it becomes clear to young (would be) fans that only rich old accountants attend Lady Gaga concerts.

Universities are a lot like concerts. The value of attending a university depends to a large degree on the other consumers (i.e., students). Good universities, like popular musicians, underprice their product: at the going rate for tuition, the demand for admission and attendance exceeds the supply of slots. A "queue" develops, and universities choose among their potential customers in ways that they think promote the long-term interests of the institutions. Should an accepted student be allowed to resell his or her admission to someone else?

Voluntary exchanges that arise in the presence of imperfect information or outright fraud might not be welfare improving. One problem with ticket scalping is that purchases from unofficial sources are more susceptible to counterfeiting or other misrepresentations. This concern provides more of an argument against unregulated scalping than against ticket resale per se. Concert promoters or venues can (and sometimes do) set up or license official secondary markets that offer protections against fraud that are similar to those available in the initial market.

The point is more general: fraud, coercion, and externalities often can be more effectively dealt with in a formal, regulated market than in an informal or black market. Legal brothel prostitution tends to be much safer than illegal streetwalking;[27] legal ticket resales are less problematic than informal scalping. Formalizing and regulating an informal market often reduces the harms associated with operating in that market.[28]

There are many instances where market transactions are precluded not by law but by custom. Offering to pay for a home-cooked meal prepared by a relative, as if you were patronizing a restaurant, will result not only in refusal of the offer but astonishment at your vulgarity.[29] Widely shared social norms prevent market pricing from being directly involved in many casual interactions, such as the proverbial aid to an elderly person crossing a street.

Would it be more efficient to replace or augment these informal arrangements with formal markets? Generally not. First, markets themselves are not costless to establish.[30] Second, the conditions under which markets contribute to efficiency—non-coercion and sufficient information, for instance—might not be met in these domains. As with acquiescing to uncontrolled speech, we might all be better off if we agree that either as a "buyer" or a "seller," we will not attempt to move these informally regulated transactions into the market. Further, the goods that are exchanged via social norms can become corrupted or less valuable in the process of transferring them to an explicit market context.[31] Consider a young couple of modest means, engaged to enter into a "traditional" sort of marriage, one intended to last throughout life. What if the pending bride or groom raises the possibility of negotiating a pre-nuptial agreement that will specify the distribution of their assets should their union end not with death, but divorce? It is quite possible that such a suggestion would lower, at least in the other partner's mind, the value of the union.[32] Of course, this view might not be universal, and as divorce rates increase, or as the couples involved are in a more pecunious state, then such contracts likely will become more common: social norms can change.[33]

Kidney Markets

Tens of thousands of Americans are in serious medical need of a kidney transplant. The current supply of suitable kidneys for transplant from deceased and live donors is insufficient to cover additions to demand: the waiting list of those needing organs grows longer every year.[34] Further, the annual elongation of the queue arises despite the fact that many people are removed from the list because they perish while they wait—often from conditions that a transplant could correct.

The number of kidneys available through cadaveric donation and live uncompensated donation—the only current sources of legal organ supply—continuously fall short of the need. With the stakes literally life-and-death, there have been many suggestions for how to enhance the procurement of kidneys. One approach is to increase the supply of cadaveric organs, perhaps by encouraging people to sign organ donor cards that indicate their willingness to donate their organs in the event of their death. Those who commit to allowing the post-mortem harvesting of their organs can be guaranteed priority access to organs should they themselves, while still among the living, require a transplant—Israel implemented such a priority system in 2008.[35] Cadaveric organs also are underutilized due to a version of the Tragedy of the Anticommons. Physicians generally are unwilling to harvest organs, even from registered donors, if any family members do not approve. That is, each family member has de facto veto authority over the cadaveric organ donation of a loved one—and the request for harvesting comes at an extremely trying time. With many possible objectors, it can be difficult for physicians to secure permission to harvest organs.[36]

Contributions from live donors also can be expanded through chains of donations: if Alice's sister Barbara would like to donate a kidney to Alice, but Barbara's kidney is not a good medical match for Alice, while Carol's sister Diana also wants to donate a kidney to her sibling, but again cannot because of medical incompatibilities, then it can be arranged for Diana to donate to Alice and for Barbara to donate to Carol, if these exchanges are medically appropriate. This concept can be extended to numerous donor-donee pairs.[37] Over the course of four months in late 2011 and early 2012, a chain of thirty kidney transplants was implemented in this fashion; a similar chain of twenty-eight transplants took place over the course of five weeks in 2013.[38]

Despite clever ways of arranging multilateral exchanges and promoting donations, organ shortages remain. (Indeed, the number of kidney transplants conducted annually in the United States rose consistently throughout the 1990s and the early 2000s, but peaked in 2006; the number of transplants from live donors peaked in 2004. The waiting list for a kidney transplant in the United States lengthens every year, and in 2014, more than 100,000 patients were on the list.[39]) In most markets, shortages are overcome expeditiously by an increase in the price. The persistence and expansion of shortages for kidney transplants arise because suppliers legally cannot be compensated for providing their organs: it is against the law in the United States to sell your kidney (though some of the expenses faced by live donors can be reimbursed), whether the sale is for a live transfer or for posthumous organ removal.[40] The one country that permits live kidney providers to be compensated—Iran—has essentially eliminated its own organ shortage.

Healthy people with two kidneys who allow one of their kidneys to be transplanted generally continue to live in a healthy manner: humans can live well with one functioning kidney. The transfer of a kidney poses a few months of recuperation and recovery for living providers, though as with any operation, there is a small chance of serious complications or death.[41] People with failing kidneys typically require kidney dialysis prior to receiving a transplant—a treatment which tends to result in poor and deteriorating health conditions over time. For these people, the acquisition of one functioning kidney is life-changing or life-saving. In economic terms, the "highest valued use" of a kidney often involves transferring it from a person with two healthy kidneys to a person with no healthy kidneys. If transaction costs were low, we would expect many such transfers. The illegality of sale, however, is an attempt to raise transaction costs, to prevent such sales (though not uncompensated transfers) from taking place. Organ sales that do take place despite the law operate in a black market, one that is likely to increase the medical as well as the contractual risks relative to what would arise with legal, regulated sales.

Why the reluctance to allow sales of organs from living suppliers? The usual suspects of imperfect information, externalities, and fears of coercion or fraud might be part of the picture. People who decide to sell a kidney might overweigh the current pleasure that the cash will bring, while underestimating the medical risks of the procedure and potential future problems. Patients desperate to receive a transplant (or the loved ones of such patients) might want to encourage such misperceptions among potential sellers. The potential for co-ercion, fraud, and imperfect information is manifest—though an appropriate regulatory apparatus should be able to mitigate these problems. Much of that apparatus is already in place, as coercion, fraud, and imperfect information must be dealt with in the case of donated organs. Indeed, a family member can feel quite pressured to donate an organ to a sick relative.

Imagine that coercion, fraud, and imperfect information are adequately ad-dressed. Then who will offer to sell a kidney? While it may be that providers will come from all parts of the socioeconomic distribution, surely it will be relatively poor people who will be most likely to sell a kidney. Are they making a fully voluntary decision, or does their economic situation weigh too heavily in the balance? Are they like the famished apothecary in *Romeo and Juliet*, who agrees to illegally sell Romeo some poison (a capital crime) for a high price: "My poverty, but not my will, consents"? The issue is quite general, of course. Poor people often take jobs that are low-paid or unsafe or otherwise unappeal-ing to workers with better earning opportunities. The philosopher Michael Sandel inquires into the voluntary nature of such exchanges:

> If a desperately poor peasant sells a kidney, or a child, the choice to sell might be coerced, in effect, by the necessities of his or her situa-tion. So one familiar argument in favor of markets—that the parties freely agree to the terms of the deal—is called into question by une-qual bargaining conditions. In order to know whether a market choice is a free choice, we have to ask what inequalities in the background conditions of society undermine meaningful consent.[42]

Those committed to efficiency as a guide to good policy might agree that inequalities in society are excessive, but also ask how banning compensation for organ donations remedies the distributional problem. Are poor people helped by being forbidden to sell their organs (or by being forbidden to accept relatively unsafe jobs)?[43] And perhaps organ sales will benefit many poor pa-tients, too, by allowing them to receive a transplant that otherwise would not be forthcoming.[44]

One potential offsetting response to legal organ sales is that such sales could crowd out the supply of donated kidneys—with the possibility that the overall supply could fall once sales are legal. Of course, the compensation offered to kidney sellers could presumably continue to increase to a point where the overall quantity offered would be enhanced.[45] Nevertheless, it is quite possible that some people who would be willing to donate a kidney to a relative, say, would not be willing to do so if they believed the relative could acquire some-one else's kidney on the open market. (This change in their behavior might contribute to overall well-being, of course, as it suggests that their commitment to donation was not all that profound in the first place—maybe they were feeling coerced: My family, but not my will, consents.) The medical suitability of kidneys for transplant varies, both among donor-donee pairs and among kidneys in general. Perhaps kidneys offered for sale would be lower quality, on average, than donated kidneys.[46] But the more likely outcome is that by reducing the severity of the kidney shortage, the pressure for physicians and patients to accept rather low-quality organs would be diminished, not enhanced, through the adoption of compensated donations.[47]

As noted earlier, some people might find the transfer of body parts to be immoral or repugnant. Often this view is specific to sales: the uncompensated donation of organs might simultaneously be viewed as praiseworthy. (Alternatively, as is often the case with sex "trades," it might only be monetary compensation that raises concerns; gifts or other types of non-monetary compensation might be acceptable.[48]) Repugnance is real, and where it exists, it can operate as a meaningful constraint on the types of exchanges that are countenanced.[49] Although real, repugnance is curiously unstable. Behaviors widely viewed as repugnant years ago, such as blood transfusions or charging interest for loans, are widely accepted today. (Simultaneously, some practices that used to be common and accepted—indentured servitude, for instance—have come to be viewed with repugnance.) Visceral reactions against the notion of organ sales seem to be decreasing, and the possibility exists that many countries will look to legal, regulated organ markets in the near future.[50]

The Iranian Kidney Transplant Program

For more than two decades, Iran has permitted living providers to be compensated for making one of their kidneys available for transplant.[51] The Iranian approach has been quite successful at securing kidneys for patients who need them.

The regulatory structure is fairly complex; much of the complexity appears to be aimed at combating the potential difficulties for markets presented by coercion, fraud, and imperfect information. Further, even within Iran there is substantial regional variation in the details of the compensation program; it might be more accurate to speak of multiple kidney transplant programs in Iran.[52] Nonetheless, the general picture is that young adults who are willing to sell a kidney contact a

(Continued)

nonprofit agency. After medical screening, the agency pairs the seller with a compatible patient at or near the top of the list of those seeking kidneys. (That is, medical professionals and patients needing kidneys do not directly procure organs from strangers—though relatives often donate kidneys to sick family members, in Iran as elsewhere. There is no government advertising aimed at convincing citizens to sell their kidneys.) Eventually the putative seller and buyer are brought together, and they can negotiate terms; the guidelines suggest a price of more than $3,000, with the recipient also reimbursing the seller's costs and perhaps offering payment above the guideline. The medical costs of the transplant procedure are paid by the government.[53] The government compensates sellers directly, too, in the form of a payment of more than $1,000 and one year of health insurance coverage.[54] (The government compensation is made available to kidney donors as well as kidney sellers.) Most kidney sellers are from lower socioeconomic groups—but so are most recipients of purchased kidneys.[55]

In Iran, the average elapsed time between a patient placing herself on the list for a kidney and the transplant operation is less than six months. In the United States, the median wait time for a kidney from a stranger is some four years.[56] About 37 percent of kidney transplants in Iran involve cadaveric organs (as opposed to kidneys sourced from live providers); in the United States, the majority of transplanted kidneys come from deceased donors.[57]

The Parthenon Marbles in London

The Parthenon Marbles, also known as the Elgin Marbles, are a group of marble carvings that were removed from the Parthenon and other buildings on the Acropolis in Athens, Greece, and relocated to Britain in the early nineteenth century.[58] The individual responsible for the export of the art was the Earl of Elgin, then the British ambassador to the Ottoman Empire, which at the time included Greece. (Athens became part of the Ottoman Empire in 1458.) The marbles are displayed in the British Museum in London, where they are viewed by millions of museum-goers annually.[59] The government of Greece is pressing for the return of the ancient sculptures and has built a museum at the foot of the Acropolis that includes a dedicated display area for the Parthenon treasures, including those now in London. To this point, Britain has refused to repatriate Lord Elgin's acquisitions, though the British

Museum has suggested that it might lend the marbles to Greece in exchange for recognition of their British ownership.

One of the contentious issues surrounding the Parthenon Marbles is the extent to which their original transfer to Lord Elgin was legal. Elgin had secured written permission to take away some pieces of stone from the Parthenon—the Turkish-language original document, called a *firman*, is lost, but a putative, contemporary Italian-language version is extant. This version of the firman authorizes access to the Parthenon and even some removal of stones—perhaps loose stones found among the rubble—but it is doubtful that permission extended to the large-scale deconstruction and export of the marbles that took place.[60]

Even if we assume that Elgin possessed authorization for his actions, was that authorization freely given? British military dominance—and the Ottoman debt to the English for defeating the French in Egypt—raises questions of the degree of coercion involved in obtaining whatever consent was granted. When the representative of the world's most powerful country asks for a favor, is it a request or is it a command? Even if the authorities freely approved of Elgin's actions, are temporary Turkish overlords legitimate donors of Greek antiquities? Athens had been under Ottoman control for some three hundred and fifty years by the time of Elgin's activities, but that is a relatively short spell in the life of the Parthenon.

Britain's claim to legal control is perhaps bolstered by the more than two hundred years that the British have possessed the Marbles, under standard statute of limitations reasoning.[61] Another dimension of the dispute includes the extent to which the British and the Greeks have been responsible stewards of the Parthenon's treasures. Was the removal of the Marbles a rescue as well as an act of destruction? Both sides of this debate have their champions, and it may be the case that the quality of the evidence, now more than two hundred years old, is unable to resolve the issue of the legality or legitimacy of Elgin's actions with confidence. Neither Elgin's theft nor Elgin's act of protection can be established beyond a reasonable doubt.

Statutes of Limitations and Adverse Possession

A statute of limitations precludes court cases from being brought concerning activities that occurred long ago—where "long ago" can range from a few years to decades. Why should the search for justice be time limited? The main benefit of statutes of limitations is that they allow people to live without fear that at any moment they will be haled to court over some dated, alleged behavior. This might not be a social benefit if it means that many serious wrongdoers escape justice. But the case for temporal boundaries is bolstered by the consideration that the quality of evidence about events tends to degrade as time passes—records disappear and memories decay—and by the suspicion that a long delay in bringing charges is suggestive that there is not much of a case to answer. (A relevant amendment of Tacitus might be: If the putative injury occurred in the distant past, let the past deal with it.) When the alleged behavior is particularly egregious, however, or when there are compelling reasons for a delay in seeking justice, statutes of limitations are likely to be extended or not applicable.

Another legal doctrine, that of *adverse possession*, bears some relationship to statutes of limitations.[62] Adverse possession allows a "squatter," under certain circumstances, to acquire legal title to a property, once a number of years have passed: the ownership is involuntarily transferred from the original owner to the squatter. If someone uses your land or other property for a long period of time (perhaps ten or twenty years) without your permission, and without you objecting, then they can claim the property for themselves: it is as if property owners face a statute of limitations that restricts the amount of time they can wait before they eject a trespasser. (One of the conditions for claims of adverse possession to succeed is that the squatter's occupancy of your property has to be open: they cannot be hiding in an out-of-the-way cranny.)

Efficiency rationales for rules of adverse possession abound. As with other statutes of limitation, they protect someone who occupies a piece of property (and believes that she is the rightful owner) against the sudden appearance of a person who claims to be the actual owner based on a purchase, say, forty years ago. Even if the newly emerged claimant is speaking truthfully, adverse possession allows the current "owner" to fend off the long-dormant claim. The fact that the claim has long been dormant, and the fact that you have been in possession for a considerable time, both also suggest that you, and not the resurrected former owner, are the "higher valued possessor" of the property. If this suggestion is wrong, however, the newcomer of ancient right can negotiate to re-purchase your land.

Should the Parthenon Marbles Be Returned?

Assuming either that the original transfer of the marbles was proper, or that the passage of time provides Britain legally unassailable ownership rights, does Greece still have a case for the return of the marbles?[63] A Coasean, Law and Economics approach might involve asking where the Marbles produce the highest overall satisfaction—the "efficient" location, to use the standard terminology. If there were no impediments to moving the Marbles and to reaching and enforcing agreements, then the Marbles should be located where they bring the most overall benefits. No matter who owns the Marbles, it will always be possible for a deal to be reached that would move them to the highest valued location—precisely because it is highest valued. Everyone can get a bigger slice of pie by making the pie as large as possible.

How would we think about determining the highest valued location? What if some individual (Robin again?) owned the Marbles, had the clear legal right. In what location would that person put them? Imagine that the owner is neither British nor Greek, neither an Anglophile nor a Hellenist. Better yet, "Imagine there's no countries," or that Britain and Greece were part of the same country, say, a ramped up European Union? Where would such an uber-state locate the Marbles?

Much of the value, the preference satisfaction, that emanates from the Marbles comes from people having the opportunity to view them. If the choice were between the British Museum and an extremely remote location such as the planet Jupiter, then availability to viewers would strongly militate in favor of keeping the Marbles in Britain. While London vies with Paris for being the most visited city in Europe and is one of the most populous, Athens also attracts millions of visitors annually and is about a three-and-a-half hour plane ride from London.

The setting in which the Marbles are placed affects the "viewing experience." Being able to view the Marbles within minutes of visiting the Parthenon itself, I believe, would offer particular delights. Indeed, the Parthenon is visible from the gallery intended to hold the Elgin Marbles in the Acropolis Museum, and unlike in London, the Athens location allows the Marbles to be positioned in their original orientation.[64] Encyclopedic collections such as that housed by the British Museum, alternatively, allow for the nearly side-by-side comparison of ancient Greek art with equally venerable antiquities from many other cultures—though the Acropolis Museum also holds artifacts from multiple epochs in Athens.

Disasters can destroy cultural treasures, so there is something to be said for diversifying their location. It is by and large a good thing that paintings originating in Italy, for instance, can now be found in museums (and private collections) all over the world. The diffusion of Italian painting offers more viewing opportunities than would occur if all art of Italian provenance remained in Italy and provides insurance against catastrophes.[65] (And, of course, most paintings are created and purchased with the understanding that they are not permanently tied to one location.) Likewise, not all the art that originated in ancient Athens should now be located in Athens. Whether the marbles are better protected against catastrophe in London than they would be in Athens is not easy to say. The Parthenon and its marbles were severely damaged, sometimes as a result of warfare, over the centuries in Athens. The British safe-guarded the marbles during World War II shortly before the gallery that had contained them was destroyed by a German bomb.[66]

Accidental damage to art, as to humans, is more likely to happen in trans-port. Minimizing the number of transfers of valuable and fragile artifacts helps to preserve them. The original removal of the marbles by Elgin's agents re-sulted in significant damage to the Parthenon. One of the ships transporting the Elgin marbles to Britain sank, leading to a lengthy and costly (and success-ful) salvage operation. Restoration attempts also present the possibility for ac-cidental harm to aged art; some damage to the marbles, it seems, has occurred in London through previous ill-advised restorations.

Notice that the "most valuable location" is independent not only of who has the legal right to the Marbles but also of their current location—as long as we continue to assume that those moving and transaction costs are zero. So imag-ine that all of the statuary currently resided in Athens. Would there be much of a case for relocating half of them to London? I suspect that if someone sug-gested, "hey, I have an idea, let's take half of the extant marbles out of the Acropolis Museum and permanently move them to Britain," that people would be astonished. Even if moving half of them sounded like a good idea—perhaps on risk-spreading grounds—another European location would not likely be value maximizing. Perhaps somewhere in Asia or South America instead?

Assume (there's that old econ trick) that my suspicions are correct, that the most-valuable location for most of the Marbles is Athens, not London. That implies that there is some deal that could be made whereby the Elgin Marbles are moved to Greece, and both Greece and Britain are made better off. What would be the nature of such a deal?

People do not like to pay to repurchase property that they believe to have been stolen from them; nor do they like to part, in the absence of recompense, with valuable property that they believe they acquired honorably and cared for faithfully. An agreement that moves the Marbles to Athens, then, presumably will not have the character of a simple repurchase or a pressured gift. Rather, the deal will have to be constructed in such a way that both parties can realis-tically view themselves as having been made better off.[67] One part of that deal could be a joint commitment to a celebration and study of the Marbles and perhaps a long-term agreement of scientific, educational, and cultural ex-changes that could signal that commitment. The transfer of the Marbles could mark a great festival of British-Greek cooperation. The 200th anniversary of the British Museum's acquisition of the Marbles is coming up in 2016, so the relevant actors should get working.

My ultimate goal is not to convince you that Athens is the most valuable lo-cation for the Elgin Marbles; rather, it is, once again, to indicate how someone trained in Law and Economics might apply an efficiency approach when considering property disputes and legal questions more generally. Why should anyone think that efficiency or value maximization should play a role in determining whether a law is good? The Elgin Marbles logic applies again: because a law that does not serve efficiency can be jettisoned in such a way that at least in theory, everyone could benefit from the improved law: the larger pie allows larger slices for everyone.

Let's look at the efficiency of a broader rule with the help of the Elgin statuary. One of the concerns that the British and others face with respect to the Parthenon Marbles is that their transfer to Greece might set a precedent for returning antiquities to the modern successor states of other source areas. That is, the Elgin case could establish (or help to establish) a rule that ancient artifacts cannot legitimately be owned outside the region of their provenance. Common law itself develops in such a way, through the precedents established through the resolution of actual cases.

Is the rule that art has to stay put a good rule? No—even if Athens is the highest valued location for the Parthenon Marbles. In general, the place of origin (sometimes itself rather murky) will not be the best of all possible places for art to be located. Indeed, most art is designed to be moved. The case for Athens as the appropriate repository for the Elgin marbles relates to the site-specificity of the statuary, and to the fact that the Acropolis and the Parthenon itself still exist. Most ancient art does not possess the same site-specific features.

In the absence of strong evidence of recent theft, I do not think that there is an efficiency case, or a moral case, for antiquities to be returned under pressure to the lands of their birth. The claims of people who today live in Athens to materials fashioned in Athens (or shipped to Athens) 2,500 years ago, to my mind, are no more compelling than the claims of others.[68] Encyclopedic museums such as the British Museum are valuable institutions, and they should not be compelled to display only materials manufactured in their vicinity.[69]

So it is important to separate the case of the Elgin Marbles from a far-reaching rule that artifacts cannot be exported; the return of the marbles should create only a narrow, limited precedent. The myriad elements of the deal that would result in the transfer of the marbles—including the British-Greek cooperation and the celebration of the site-specific statuary—would help distinguish the Marbles from most other antiquities and would lessen the precedential value that might attach if the Marbles simply were returned to Greece under duress.

|| 6 ||

Humanity's Crooked Timber

Out of the crooked timber of humanity, no straight thing was
ever made.

—Immanuel Kant[1]

Economics starts from the presumption that people typically are as rational as
our Robin, and hence their choices will serve their own interests (which might
include altruistic concerns). The "internalization," *e pluribus unum* function of
law aims to ensure that a person's choices appropriately account for the interests of others, when those interests are implicated—as we saw after Friday relocated to Robin's isle.

But what if people are not rational? Then we can't be sure that they even
do a good job of serving their own interests, while our laws and policies
might not create the intended incentives. Trying to identify socially desirable outcomes, always a precarious task, becomes still more speculative in a
less-than-rational world: the "willingness to pay" heuristic by which we
judge the intensity of individual desires, and hence the relative magnitude of
those desires in the overall social calculus, seems quite arbitrary when individuals do not have stable desires. Robin's willingness to pay for push-pin is
$100 right now, but in an hour, perhaps it is $1,000, perhaps it is zero. Perhaps her announced willingness to pay for push-pin bears no relationship to
the well-being she would garner from push-pin.[2] Should we design rules to
reflect the fact that people might not be all that stable, or are otherwise less-
than-rational, and adjust our view of social optimality to reflect the inscruta-
bility of individual preferences?

In extreme cases, we should and do adjust policies to better deal with potentially irrational behavior. Those whose rationality we have strong reason to
question operate under different legal regimes than others. Children and the
insane cannot enter into legally binding contracts, for example. Special rules
are fashioned to protect these classes of people from their own bad decisions.
With protection comes control: these regimes restrict the freedom of action of

the protected classes, and the inability to enter into a binding contract can be a severe hindrance. (What bank will lend you money, for instance, if your promise to repay will not be enforceable?) Should similar, though less severe, "protections" be imposed upon everyone, on the grounds that all of us fall short of full rationality? Or perhaps there are common circumstances in which rationality is compromised, and the legal regime should recognize these circumstances and react accordingly?

Organ transplants and the consumption of mind-altering substances are two contentious arenas in which concerns regarding irrationalities greatly influence laws and policies. These arenas, along with many others, feature an array of conditions—risks of extremely negative outcomes, vivid and visceral reactions, demands upon willpower—that tend to promote less-than-rational decision-making. Later in this chapter, we will examine policies that respond to such conditions—but policies that respond without blocking all market-type exchanges for either human organs or psychoactive drugs.

Enforcing Contracts

When two sane adults sign a contract, they presumably do so because they each believe that the contractual commitment makes them better off. They recognize that events down the road might make them regret the contract—the deal is not riskless—but on average, they both expect to gain. Otherwise, why would they form the contract?

This simple logic provides a strong argument that courts should enforce almost any contract among adults. While one party might later want to be excused from performing the contract—perhaps because circumstances adverse to that party materialized—failure to enforce contracts just because one party wants out would render many or most agreements unreliable. Much of the benefit of entering a contract is that you can feel confident that the other party will perform as promised or make recompense for a failure to do so. A permissive approach to unilateral abrogation of contracts would create a significant (and often insuperable) barrier to complex, long-term endeavors, reducing the wealth of society.[3]

Nevertheless, we have already seen that many potential exchanges are ruled out as a matter of law. People cannot (legally) work for less than the legislated minimum wage or in conditions that do not meet workplace safety norms. People cannot become indentured servants, or sell themselves into slavery, or enter loan contracts involving extremely high rates of interest. The extent to which the state limits agreements suggests that the presumption that adults, as rational actors, should be given broad freedom of contract, is frequently overridden. One rationale might be (as we have seen in chapter 5) that contracts between two rational people might affect third parties, so the government might want to intervene to protect the interests of those otherwise unrepresented folks (and otherwise defenseless animals, too). Fraud and hidden coercion might be other concerns. But many of the restrictions in place seem aimed at protecting the contractors themselves, from their own imprudence or irrationality.

Lochner v. New York (1905)

Joseph Lochner was a master baker in Utica, New York: he hired employees to help him conduct his baking business.[4] In 1897 the state of New York passed a law that limited the working hours of bakery employees: workers could not be required to work more than 10 hours per day, or 60 hours per week. (The law also instituted various measures to prevent unsafe working conditions.) In 1899, Joseph Lochner violated the state law by having an employee work more than 60 hours per week. Lochner was fined $25 for the violation. In 1901, Lochner became a repeat offender, again by requiring an employee to log more than 60 hours in a week. Lochner was fined a second time, now for $50, and he elected to challenge the constitutionality of the law.

The Fourteenth Amendment to the US Constitution holds, in part, that no state shall "deprive any person of life, liberty, or property, without due process of law; nor deny to any person within its jurisdiction the equal protection of the laws." The "liberty" that the amendment speaks of might include the liberty to form employment contracts that involve working more than 10 hours per day or more than 60 hours per week. This is what Joseph Lochner argued, and the Supreme Court found the argument compelling: the New York law was held to be inconsistent with the Fourteenth Amendment's protection of individual liberty against state action.

Of course, the Fourteenth Amendment does not provide an unconditional guarantee of liberty; rather, it protects against the state depriving an individual of liberty "without due process of law." The process by which New York passed and enforced its bakeshop law was thoroughly proper. The Supreme Court chose to read the Fourteenth Amendment broadly, viewing the due process clause as providing a check not just on the methods by which laws are passed, but restricting the substantive content of laws as well. The idea that the due process clause of the 14th Amendment (and a parallel clause applying to the federal government in the Fifth Amendment) protects Americans against restrictions on some fundamental rights—going beyond the requirement that fair procedures be followed when restricting those rights—remains a part of Supreme Court jurisprudence.[5]

What does not remain from the *Lochner* decision is the idea that an expansive freedom of contract is one of the fundamental rights that cannot be abridged by the government. The labor market, as well as the economy in toto, are now much more highly regulated—and by today's standards, legally so— than would have been acceptable under the continued viability of the *Lochner* ruling. The law has not followed the majority opinion in *Lochner* as much as it has embraced a dissenting opinion authored by Justice Oliver Wendell Holmes Jr., which questioned the posited constitutional commitment to freedom of contract:

> a constitution is not intended to embody a particular economic theory, whether of paternalism and the organic relation of the citizen to the State or of *laissez faire*. It is made for people of fundamentally differing views, and the accident of our finding certain opinions natural and familiar or novel and even shocking ought not to conclude our judgment upon the question whether statutes embodying them conflict with the Constitution of the United States.[6]

Dealing with Uncertainty

Contracts help to govern the future actions of the contracting parties. But no one can be sure what will happen in the future—one of those irksome meteorites might strike—so contracting always takes place in the shadow of risk and uncertainty. Alas, it turns out that people do not seem to be all that adept at making decisions in risky environments.

A key element of any rational approach to dealing with risk is to have some handle on just how likely an outcome is, as well as how dire (or beneficial) the outcome will be should it arise. Do you have a good notion of how prone your home is to damage from a meteorite? Or from a hurricane? Or from a fire? Or from a terrorist strike? For events that happen relatively rarely, people do not possess a deep understanding of likelihoods. If they have a friend who recently suffered a meteorite strike, they will be apt to overvalue the true probability of a meteorite seeking them out; if terrorist attacks have been getting a lot of attention in the news, people will overestimate the probability that they will be victimized by terrorists.[7] If you live in a flood plain but there has not been a flood in a long time, you are likely to underestimate the possibility of flood damage. Absent a recent vivid event like a terrorist attack or a friend's victimization, people have a tendency to be excessively optimistic about their own good fortune; even someone who correctly understands the general threat of risk, therefore, might think, incorrectly, that she is relatively safe.[8]

Two approaches to managing risks are to take measures to reduce the chance that the bad event will come to pass—driving more carefully reduces the likelihood of an accident—and to insure against losses should the risk materialize. Again, for low probability events, people by and large do not address these decisions in a fully rational manner. While a moment's reflection on driving behavior might be support enough for the proposition that decisions concerning risky matters frequently are less-than-rational, consider, instead, the case of floods.[9] In many areas, as low probability events go, floods are fairly common! Nevertheless, people tend to underinsure against flooding, even when flood insurance is heavily subsidized. Flood insurance purchases do not vary much with the perceived risk (which itself can be biased relative to the objective, "true" risk)—whereas a rational person, presumably, would be more eager to buy insurance at a given price if the risk of a flood increases. People appear to view insurance as if it were a standard consumer good, so if they have not "used" it in a few years—there has not been a flood—then they stop buying insurance. Their questionable decision-making goes beyond insurance to methods of shielding themselves from harm: people excessively expose themselves to flood risk by constructing buildings too close to waterways.

Government might be able to help, perhaps by mandating flood insurance purchases by the owners of homes located in flood plains. If flood insurance premiums reflect true actuarial risks, then such a policy would have the benefit of inducing people to face the actual costs of the risks they undertake. Government also can have trouble dealing with risk, though. Certainly some public programs have contributed to problems caused by flooding, by subsidizing the reconstruction of buildings located inside flood-prone locales. Within the National Flood Insurance Program (NFIP) in the United States,

> There are about 71,000 currently insured "repetitive loss properties," which represent about only 1.2 percent of the NFIP portfolio but account for 16 percent of total claim payments between 1978 and 2008 (24 percent if one considers both current and former repetitive loss properties). About one in ten of these repetitive loss properties have received cumulative flood insurance reimbursements that have exceeded the value of the house.[10]

Another arena in which the state fares poorly in terms of dealing with risk is safety spending. Imagine that society would like to reduce the risk of death and has $100 to invest toward that end. If it can invest the $100 in such a way as to save (OK, prolong) ten lives, then surely that is better than investing the $100 in a manner that will save only five lives. The actual expenditure pattern, dollars per life saved, however, suggests that regulation-induced spending in some areas is very ineffective in terms of saving lives—that is, the money could have been spent in other ways that would have led to much greater increases in safety. In recent years, regulations in the United States aimed at controlling toxins have been much less effective, on a per-dollar basis, at saving lives than have safety regulations such as mandating that cigarette lighters be designed to make it hard for children to operate them and by requiring the installation of less damaging steering columns in automobiles.[11]

Unconscionability

You are a person of substantial means, but you have a temporary cash flow shortfall—perhaps your merchandise-laden ships currently are spread out among the seas and harbors of the world. So I lend you some money for a few months, without charging interest. We agree to insert a clause into the contract that in the event—the amazingly remote event—that you do not repay me on time, I will be entitled to cut off one pound of your flesh. Unluckily enough, your ships miscarry, and the date has arrived to undertake the action that we agreed to. You (or your friends) balk, however, and ask a court to invalidate the contract term. Should the court refuse to enforce our agreement?

The doctrine of *unconscionability* provides one legal basis for the court to refuse to enforce the pound-of-flesh clause. (The doctrine was not yet available when Shakespeare presented the Antonio-Shylock pound-of-flesh contract in *The Merchant of Venice*.) If a court finds a term in the contract to be unconscionable, it can excise or rewrite that term or invalidate the entire contract. Two conditions typically must be met for the court to make a determination that the clause is unconscionable. First, there must be some putative defect in the bargaining process, so that the resulting agreement does not look like it emerged from the considered negotiations of rational agents who had meaningful opportunities to craft things differently. An undistinguished or unintelligible contract term that is buried in fine print on page 32 of a form contract, for instance, might be viewed as not meeting the requirement that the process be fair. Compromised bargaining mechanisms are referred to as being "procedurally unconscionable."

In addition to a questionable bargaining process, a court must determine that the contract term itself appears to be wildly unfair or otherwise defective. A term that is found to shock the conscience of the court is said to be "substantively unconscionable." Again, the usual test is that for a contract (or a specific contractual term) to be voided by a court on the grounds of unconscionability, both procedural and substantive shortcomings must be evident.[12]

The case that cemented the doctrine of unconscionability in US law, *Williams v. Walker-Thomas Furniture Company*, concerned an unusual term in a consumer credit contract.[13] Over a period of several years, Ms. Williams bought many home furnishings from the Walker-Thomas Furniture Company in Washington, DC. She purchased the items on credit provided by the seller and made monthly payments to reduce her bill. She paid her debt conscientiously for a long time, but she also continued to buy more items, so that over the course of their dealings, her balance was never reduced to zero. Ms. Williams's troubles began when she purchased a stereo from Walker-Thomas, again on credit, for approximately $515. (Prior to the stereo purchase, her outstanding debt to Walker-Thomas was $164, on total purchases in excess of $1,200.) This time she was unable to make the monthly payments. Walker-Thomas sued to repossess her stereo, and to repossess all of the other items she had purchased from them over the previous five years. Walker-Thomas could do this because of a term in the credit contract that Ms. Williams signed with the furniture company, a term known as a "cross-collateralization" clause. The idea of the clause is that as long as the balance owed does not fall to zero, previously purchased items serve as collateral for later purchases, even if the total sum remitted fully covers the price of some of the earlier items. Until the balance is paid in full, all items in a stream of purchases act as security for the consumer loans made for any of the items. According to the contractual terms, once Ms. Williams defaulted, Walker-Thomas could seize all the furnishings it sold her over the previous years.

The appeals court, however, did not feel compelled to enforce the contractual terms. The opinion instead laid out the notions of procedural and substantive unconscionability, and suggested that both of these tests might be met by the cross-collateralization clause: the contractual clause itself was part of a form contract that could not be renegotiated by a store clerk (and the clause is hard to understand in any event); further, the fact that the cross-collateralization term allows a store to seize a large amount of furniture for a small amount of debt is capable of appearing shockingly inequitable.[14]

But the cross-collateralization clause has its defenders, too. If everyone is rational and understands the clause, presumably the term allows Walker-Thomas, thanks to their improved collateral, to offer credit (or the furniture purchased on credit) more cheaply than if the term did not exist. If the furniture retail market is competitive, we might think that any terms we see in contracts will be efficient because, faced with a store's inefficient contract, customers will go elsewhere to stores that do offer efficient terms and share some of the increased surplus. (Similar reasoning appears in chapter 5's discussion of product liability, where competition helps drive bike manufacturers to include those safety features that bring net benefits to bike purchasers.)

The distinct possibility that a purchaser would not have any knowledge or understanding of the cross-collateralization clause (and hence cannot use that term to discriminate among sellers when shopping) is heightened by the fact that the term itself only comes into play in the event of a default—a contingency which might not be all that probable. Consumers might underestimate (or completely disregard) the risk that they will default, in keeping with the general human tendency to ignore some unlikely events, and with the common penchant to exhibit excessive optimism about one's own prospects. The view that people tend to overestimate their luck, as well as their talent, dates back to Adam. In *The Wealth of Nations*, Adam Smith notes: "The over-weening conceit which the greater part of men have of their own abilities, is an ancient evil remarked by the philosophers and moralists of all ages. Their absurd presumption in their own good fortune, has been less taken notice of. It is, however, if possible, still more universal."[15]

The idea that competition will exert pressure for only efficient terms to appear in contracts—because firms offering inefficient terms will be undersold by firms that offer efficient contracts—requires that buyers and sellers not suffer from systematic lapses of rationality. If buyers, for instance, discount the probability of being unable to repay a loan, then firms that offer onerous (and inefficient) terms with respect to non-payment in their loan contracts will be able to offer a lower interest rate than firms that offer better terms in the event of default. Borrowers, ignoring the rules concerning missed payments, will be drawn to the low interest (but inefficient terms) contract, providing an edge in the marketplace to the lender with the onerous default rules. That is, competition can require that firms take advantage of systematic lapses of rationality on the part of their consumers: sellers who fail to take advantage will be outcompeted by those that do.[16]

Willpower Lapses

Uncertainty does not constitute the only barrier to full, Robin-like rationality. People often seem to suffer from a shortage of willpower, an inability to make those choices that they themselves believe to be in their own long-term best interests. They suffer from what the ancient Greeks called *akrasia*, when they know the better course of action but choose the worse. The lure of instant gratification can trump considered evaluation among alternatives.

Our excessive interest in instantaneous gratification is familiar to us, and we frequently adopt strategies to counter it. We (OK, I) do not keep ice cream at home, for fear that otherwise we (I) will find ourselves (myself) eating ice cream in the middle of the night. If our more considered mind intends not to smoke, we avoid situations where we will be particularly tempted to light up. Knowing our sluggish morning selves, our evening selves set up noisome alarms, and place the alarm clocks out of arms' reach of our bed. We do not go grocery shopping on an empty stomach.

Other individuals will be motivated to take advantage of our willpower lapses. They will tempt us with free ice cream samples or fan the smell of baking cookies into our path or offer initial magazine subscriptions at highly discounted rates or dazzle us in casinos with light and sound and alcohol and spectacle. Even those of us who are most cognizant of our excessive interest in indulgence might find that our private self-control strategies will be overwhelmed by the tactics of highly motivated purveyors of temptations. Of course, other profit-minded individuals might cater to our interest in self-control, by offering us dietary aids or fitness center memberships or illiquid savings accounts or discounted health insurance rates for non-smoking. We can make mistakes in both directions, simultaneously: we can eat too much ice cream, while paying a substantial monthly membership fee for a fitness center we rarely use.

Just as we adopt private policies to try to fashion a tolerable balance between indulgence and control, society might want to adopt public policies that can help people achieve such a balance. Mandatory cooling-off periods might be one such policy. If you want to buy an encyclopedia set from a door-to-door salesperson, or if you want to get married, that is fine: but any agreement to buy the encyclopedias or to walk down the aisle cannot legally take effect for 24 or 48 hours, say. In the meantime, you can back out of your original plan. If you later change your mind again, a new waiting period is established. The idea, of course, is to make sure that significant and hard-to-revoke decisions are not taken in a passing state of impaired judgment. Care must be applied in designing cooling-off policies—rules that help people to make decisions that are rational when examined by their considered selves—as these policies will not be costless. Some desires to get married immediately are quite reasonable, and a compulsory three-day wait for a marriage license will be burdensome for people possessing such desires.[17]

Marketing controls might complement cooling-off periods in terms of aiding people to be faithful stewards of their own long-term interests. High-pressure sales techniques can be banned (or countered with those obligatory waiting periods for purchases made under their influence), along with tactics intended to deceive such as bait-and-switch. Disclosure of relevant information—the annual percentage rate on a loan, perhaps, or the payback rate of a slot machine—can be mandated. Such policies can be implemented at low cost and with little or no threat to buyer autonomy, for "liberty consists in doing what one desires"[18]: helping a person implement the choices that he or she desires is consistent with a healthy, even Millian, respect for individual liberty.[19]

The Endowment Effect

Recall that the Coase Corollary says that in the absence of transaction costs, assets will move to their highest valued use independently of where the law assigns initial property rights. If it is more valuable for the Parthenon Marbles to be in Athens than in London, then they will end up in Athens, irrespective of which city is deemed to be their lawful owner or where they currently reside—if it is easy to craft agreements and if it doesn't cost much to move the stones.

One of the underlying, unstated assumptions of the Coase Corollary, however, is that the worth of an asset in different uses (or in different locations) does not change based on the law's assignment of property rights. That is, if society values the Marbles in Athens more than in London, then even if the relevant court says that Britain owns the Marbles, they are still more valuable in Athens. The assignment of ownership rights does not change the fact that society's overall wealth is larger with the Marbles in Athens.

There is some evidence that the unstated assumption is systematically violated—the value of assets in different uses varies with property rights. If I think that a coffee mug that I do not own is worth $5 (and not a penny more) to me, once I own it, I will think more highly of the mug—I will turn down offers of $5.50 for the mug. This type of phenomenon is known as the *endowment effect*—people value more highly things that they own.[20]

The endowment effect is not a sign of irrationality (although it creates some problems for traditional economic theory), but it does complicate the search for efficient laws.[21] Imagine that the ownership of the Parthenon Marbles is uncertain, and that a court is about to decide whether Britain or Greece is the lawful owner. Under Coase Corollary-type reasoning, once the court assigns the property right, the Marbles will end up where they are most valuable. Either the court initially assigns ownership to the country where the Marbles are most valuable, in which case they stay there and the alternative country will not be willing to make an offer sufficient to induce their sale and relocation, or the court will assign the Marbles to the "wrong" country, in which case the "right" country will be able to buy the Marbles in a mutually agreeable deal. But if the endowment effect is substantial, then the "right" country will end up being whatever nation the court assigns the ownership rights: once a country is declared the owner, it will raise its own subjective value of the worth of the Marbles. Offers from the other country (even if, prior to the court decision, this other country was the highest valued location) will be turned down. The court decision itself determines the highest valued location, if the endowment effect is sufficiently severe: the endowment effect acts in some ways as a large transaction cost, such that assets cannot easily be transferred away from original owners. The distribution of resources is no longer independent of the court's assignment of property rights; rather, the ultimate allocation of resources is completely controlled by the court.

Default Rules

Court-assigned ownership becomes sticky, then, if the endowment effect is significant. Such inertia tends to be much more general: people have a strong tendency to remain attached to an initial allocation. Imagine that on our first day at a new job our employer assigns us to a specific retirement plan. At that moment, or at any time in the future, we have the option of shifting away from the assigned plan to one of myriad alternatives. Years down the road, we are pretty likely to still be with that originally assigned plan—even if we would not have chosen that plan ourselves if forced to make, explicitly, the initial decision.

Defaults are usually not chosen at random, of course.[22] Presumably those who set up the default intend to pick an option that will be good for most people. So maybe blithely accepting the default is the sensible thing to do, especially if it is particularly costly to examine the other options. But the attractiveness of defaults seems to go beyond the extent that strict rationality would suggest. It applies when defaults are chosen at random, and when there are options that are substantially better.[23]

The power of default options can be harnessed by policymakers. If there is some choice that the government wants to encourage, it can make that preferential option the default: people who do nothing are assigned, automatically, the encouraged choice. If there is some behavior the government wants to discourage, it can adopt a rule that provisionally prohibits the behavior; the prohibition can be overturned if the individual makes an explicit choice to override the default setting.

Recall that one of the functions of contract law is to provide a set of default terms for contracts, rules concerning what will happen if meteorite strikes or other unlikely events cloud the setting for full performance of the contract. The default rules lower the costs of contracts, as contracting parties themselves are saved the trouble of specifying the appropriate actions to take should an unlikely contingency come to pass. Further, the parties usually can override the defaults, so there is little cost in terms of imposing inefficient contract terms on captive contractors. Or at least the cost is small, unless the default rules provided by contract law have the same sort of extraordinary staying power that accompanies defaults in other settings. And indeed, they might—default rules might create a sort of increase in transaction costs so that parties stick with the rules even in circumstances where, without the rules, they would have written different terms into the contract.[24] This extra-stickiness is not exactly inefficient, as it is perfectly sensible to adhere to the status quo when the costs of alternatives arise, even if those costs are of the psychological sort, or due to the assigned status quo itself affecting the preferences of the parties. Nonetheless, such a status quo bias suggests that the unwillingness of most contracting parties to override legal defaults does not constitute strong evidence for the efficiency of the specific default terms: it might be the fact that these terms are defaults, and not the content of the terms themselves, that drives the reluctance to override them.[25]

Organ Donations, Reprise

As we saw in chapter 5, one behavior that society generally wants to encourage is organ donation. States in the United States allow people to sign up as organ donors—in Illinois, you are presented this option when you acquire a driver's license.[26] Registration as an organ donor facilitates the post-mortem use of your organs (possibly including your corneas and body tissues) for transplants. Driver's license sign-up and other approaches to ease registering as an organ donor have been important in increasing the number of designated donors in recent years. By 2013, about 45 percent of US adults were registered as organ donors, though there is significant state-by-state variation.[27] For brain-dead patients who are not on the registry, consent of the next-of-kin (or other legal representative) is required before organ harvesting takes place.

Some countries have taken ease-of-registration one step further. In "opt-out" countries, people are presumed to be willing to serve as organ donors in the event of their death—but they can choose to remove themselves from the registry. That is, in opt-out jurisdictions, the default is that you are an organ donor; in opt-in jurisdictions like the United States, you only join the registry if you explicitly choose to do so. Singapore has doubled down on the opt-out plan: people in Singapore who choose to opt out of donation will receive lower priority should they find themselves in need of receiving an organ.[28]

Nations such as Spain and Austria that have switched from opt-in to opt-out approaches have seen large increases in the number of registered donors. (The number of organ transplants conducted, however, does not seem to be as mutable as the number of registered donors; nonetheless, on average, an increase in registered donors is associated with an increase in transplants.[29]) As in many other situations, default options in organ donation tend to have considerable staying power.

While opt-out systems can swell the rolls of potential donors, they suffer (in some people's eyes—including mine—) from creating the impression that our very bodies are the property of society or the state, even though we can reclaim them by a simple opt-out procedure. A middle ground of sorts can avoid this impression, while still serving to encourage registration. This middle ground crafts the default as the necessity to make an explicit choice—perhaps as a requirement (or near requirement) for receiving a driver's license.[30] Under this system, license applicants are asked if they want to register as an organ donor—yes or no. The answer that they give will then determine their status. In this way, no one is added to the organ-donor list simply from a failure to make an explicit choice. On the other hand, people might resent being asked on a regular basis to consider their demise and to make (or re-make) a decision concerning the disposition of their organs; autonomous individuals might prefer letting others make these decisions.[31]

Selling Kidneys

Creative default rules, valuable as they might be, would not be sufficient in the United States to stem the ever-increasing tide of end stage renal disease (ESRD) patients in need of a working kidney.[32] Alternatively, as mentioned in chapter 5, compensated donations of kidneys from living people—that is, a form of kidney sales—could shrink the waiting time for kidneys and reduce the toll imposed upon those ESRD patients who die while waiting for an appropriate organ for transplant. (Even for patients who survive long enough to receive a kidney transplant, the extended time on dialysis is itself debilitating, and longer dialysis times reduce the effectiveness of transplants once received.[33]) But how can kidney sales be permitted without stimulating rash or irrational decisions to sell a kidney by people facing stressful economic circumstances? Can we ensure that, unlike Romeo's druggist, a kidney seller's rational will is not overcome by his or her poverty?

Note that many of the concerns about imprudence or irrationality apply with as much force to decisions to donate a kidney without compensation as they do to decisions to sell. Decades of experience with live kidney donations, even to unrelated and indeed unknown recipients, have allowed procedures to evolve that safeguard the interests of donors. (People who donate a kidney to a specific individual, usually a family member, are referred to as "living directed" donors. People who simply donate a kidney to whoever is a medically fit recipient—a donation "to the waiting list"—are referred to as "non-directed" or "undirected" or "anonymous" donors.[34] Through paired donations, a living directed donor might end up donating a kidney to someone other than his or her intended recipient in the first instance, but nonetheless donates with the interest of that directed recipient in mind.) Independent Living Donor Advocates, for instance, are affiliated with transplant centers; the job of these advocates is to protect the welfare of donors. Would-be donors, including donors related to the intended recipient, already are carefully screened to try to ensure that social or family pressure is not unduly coercive, and they receive information about the potential negative consequences associated with kidney donation. All of these procedures could be used in essentially the same form for compensated donations.

More generally, the established organ procurement and allocation protocols need not be altered when compensation to donors is introduced. The only "buyer" would be the existing organ procurement organization—each geographical region has only one such organization for deceased donors, there is no interregional competition. Living directed (and undirected) donors currently can choose among numerous transplant centers, but it would make sense (given that compensation becomes available) to channel their initial inquiry through the organ procurement organization as well.[35] A person who is thinking about donating a kidney would approach the local organ procurement organization, and medical and psychological screening would commence. Recipients need not know the identity of their kidney donor, nor even know if the donation was compensated or not.[36]

The main new feature that compensation brings to the kidney donation decision is the possibility—and it is only a possibility—that irrationalities are intensified when money is part of the mix. The form, magnitude, and timing of compensation can be constructed in such a way, however, to limit the pertinence of this possibility.

An ongoing healthcare subsidy, perhaps involving health and life insurance, can be an extremely valuable form of compensation for donors.[37] The fact that little of that value is received immediately, however, helps to protect against excessive present-bias leading to rash decisions to donate. People who are not otherwise disposed to donate a kidney, but who are temporarily strapped for cash, will not suddenly be drawn to donation because of future healthcare subsidies. There is a possibility that people who sense that they are not healthy, and hence will need considerable healthcare in the future, will try to donate a kidney to secure funding for their projected demand. So careful medical screening, which already is involved in live organ donation, will remain an important element of the donation process, to ensure that only medically appropriate individuals donate.

The provision of healthcare assistance to kidney donors possesses an attractive reciprocal, health-in-return-for-health quality. Further, this assistance might be, in itself, a sufficient inducement to donation to eliminate the waiting period for receipt of a kidney. But it might not be sufficient, in which case there is something to be said for allowing some monetary recompense to donors, too. Monetary payments, however, might spur people like Romeo's famished apothecary to imprudence.

One automatic safeguard against unconsidered donation decisions is the time delay for medical examination and testing that is requisite between indicating a desire to donate a kidney and the transplant operation. This delay would typically last many weeks, though in the case of current undirected donations, it can be extended for months to allow donors multiple opportunities to reconsider.[38] Monetary payments, as with healthcare subsidies, can be backloaded still further and spread out over many years. This timing of payments, again, can make donation unattractive to those whose only motivation is monetary and also presents the scientific benefit of easing long-term follow-up on the medical and psychological health of donors. (That is, being available for continuing medical surveillance and care could be a soft condition for the expeditious receipt of future payments.)

What amount of monetary compensation, beyond healthcare benefits, might be appropriate for kidney donors and be sufficient to eliminate long wait times for kidneys? Well, it is hard to know, though estimates range from $15,000 to more than $100,000. Beard and Leitzel (2014) suggest a total monetary component of $50,000 for donors, with half of that sum backloaded over a five-year period, in addition to health care benefits. The costs of dialysis for ESRD patients are so high that even with payments to donors of more than $100,000, healthcare expenditures will fall when compensation leads to more transplants. The overall social benefits are much greater still, as thousands of people who otherwise would die while waiting for a kidney will have their lives prolonged, while the quality of their lives also improves when they are free of dialysis.

The existing black market in kidney transplants, which necessarily forms in an unregulated environment, is unhealthy or worse. But the depravities of this market, which is spurred by the ban on compensating kidney donors (and is a signal of the desperation of the recipients), are not a reliable guide to what a regulated kidney market would look like, any more than Capone's Chicago is a reliable guide to liquor distribution today. As noted in chapter 5, fraud and coercion typically are better handled in a legal, regulated market than in an underground market. Other concerns with introducing compensation, such as an unseemly commodification of the human body, are quite speculative and probably also better handled in a legal than an illegal regime.[39] The thousands of people who die each year for want of a working kidney are not speculative, they are quite real and quite suffering, and they represent an enormous human cost imposed by the ban on payments to donors. Even if kidney compensation will lead to a worse situation than the status quo, the anguish that accompanies the ban on compensation provides a strong rationale to at least experiment with regulated forms of compensation, to learn if those speculated problems unavoidably arise in practice, and in a magnitude sufficient to outweigh thousands of unnecessary deaths per year.[40]

Vice, Rationality, and Defaults

The traditional vices such as excessive indulgence in alcohol, nicotine, opiates, stimulants, gambling, and some sexual behaviors provide an immense field in which human decision-making is suspect. Addiction and fully considered, rational choice do not seem to be all that closely paired.[41] Nonetheless, the vast majority of decisions to drink or gamble or engage in some other vice do not indicate any lapse from rationality. Further, many manifestations of vice are (to use the terminology of Jeremy Bentham and John Stuart Mill) *self-regarding*— they do not cause any considerable harms to others.

The questionable rationality of addictive behavior, along with the self-control issues faced by many non-addicts in vice-related decisions, suggests that public policy might want to counter excessive vice consumption—even in those forms of vice that do not involve significant externalities. One way to provide this counter is through a prohibition; this is the method we now employ against the sale, purchase, and possession of drugs such as marijuana, cocaine, and opium. The evidence from decades of experience indicates that prohibition, at least in any form similar to the current drug bans, results in huge numbers of arrests annually (currently more than 1.5 million arrests, with more than 80 percent being for mere possession of illicit drugs), significant rates of imprisonment, an impetus to police corruption, and a host of other highly undesirable outcomes.[42] Another way to curb excessive vice consumption is through a legal market, one that adopts regulatory safeguards that push against widespread vice involvement, and against overindulgence on the part of those who are legal vice consumers. Applied to the currently illegal drugs, creative use of policy defaults minimizes coercion, and relative to prohibition, offers a much superior method of countering excessive drug use.

Chapter 5 introduced the legal doctrine of attractive nuisance, via the rather unsettling example of a booby-trapped clown mannequin that tempts children to trespass. Homeowners who maintain such attractive nuisances cannot escape liability when a child succumbs to temptation and is harmed.

Traditional vice behaviors such as alcohol or opium or gambling consumption can be as tempting to some adults as clowns or swimming pools are for some children.[43] Concern with the potentially excessive allure of vice underlies drug prohibition: criminal penalties augment the otherwise insufficient disincentive to use drugs. This added deterrence is purchased at the cost of punishing, sometimes severely, those who remain undeterred—punishment imposed despite the fact that drug consumption per se does not involve significant externalities.

The penalties inflicted on those who supply the drugs are even more severe, of course. That the current prohibition will produce such suppliers is perfectly foreseeable, even if they are less sympathetic victims of the war on drugs than are consumers. Nor is it clear that harsh penalties for suppliers are consistent with justice, much less with overall well-being. Adam Smith made the case in *The Wealth of Nations*:

> An injudicious tax [or prohibition!] offers a great temptation to smuggling. But the penalties of smuggling must rise in proportion to the temptation. The law, contrary to all the ordinary principles of justice, first creates the temptation, and then punishes those who yield to it; and it commonly enhances the punishment too in proportion to the very circumstance which ought certainly to alleviate it, the temptation to commit the crime.[44]

Are drug sellers deserving of harsh treatment? Again, Adam Smith comments on a smuggler: "a person, who, though no doubt highly blameable for violating the laws of his country, is frequently incapable of violating those of natural justice, and would have been, in every respect, an excellent citizen, had not the laws of his country made that a crime which nature never meant to be so."[45]

That is, drug prohibition establishes a sort of attractive nuisance for adults. Our drug laws take advantage of human temptations, like a booby-trapped clown or swimming pool. If we were all like rational Robin, the deterrence provided by prohibition might work tolerably well—though at the cost of eliminating all the non-problematic drug consumption that people enjoy. (And if all children were fully informed and rational, they would avoid clowns placed on private property marked off by clear "No Trespassing" signs.) But given what we know about the allure of mind-altering substances, and the realities of black market operation and policing, prohibition is a recipe for punishing many people—people whose only fault is engaging in an officially unapproved act that does not generate, directly, any social harms.[46] Indeed, in many instances, even in the face of the prohibition, the unapproved act does not generate any indirect harm, either, beyond (perhaps) the law breaking per se.

Vice prohibitions for adults involve a seemingly self-contradictory view of rationality. Addiction and self-control shortcomings, lapses from rationality, present the main case for vice prohibition. The punishments applied to those who might evade the prohibition are defended because those punishments provide deterrence against vice participation. But raising the price of an activity works as a disincentive to participation for people who respond "rationally" to changes in costs and benefits. That is, the prohibition that is justified because of irrational choices is only effective for those whose choices to be law-abiding, even in the vice arena, are made in a rational manner!

Re-legalizing Drugs

As suggested, prohibition is not the only way to counter overindulgence in drugs. Alternative policies, ones that are likely to be much less costly and much more humane, can replace prohibition, without saturating society with piles of mind-altering drugs and hordes of mindless drug users.[47] The shared feature of such policies is that they offer some assistance to those who are susceptible to addiction, without imposing in a significant way upon the majority of consumers whose rationality with respect to drug use is not particularly suspect.[48]

A non-prohibitory regulatory regime that features two levels of defaults can bolster individual willpower and fight drug addiction. The first level involves consumer licensing, where adults who elect to consume drugs apply for a buyer's license.[49] That is, adults must affirmatively opt in to become legal drug users: the default is abstinence. The second level of default concerns the terms under which drugs are made available to license holders. These default terms are chosen conservatively, with an eye to limiting the potential for use to cascade from occasional to compulsive; license holders who want more liberal access will have to opt out of the second level of defaults, at some cost. The defaults are designed to dissuade intemperate drug use, without employing the coercive, punitive tactics of prohibition. To implement the licensing system, sellers will have to be licensed and regulated, or, as is sometimes the case with alcohol sales, the government could be the sole legal supplier.

Consider the case of heroin. The reputation that heroin has developed should be sufficient to persuade most adults not to pursue a license to purchase the drug. (Most current non-users of heroin probably do not view the prohibition as necessary for them to abstain!) Even those who are intrigued by the possibility of experimenting with opiates will generally look for something softer, just as most drinkers do not imbibe the highest concentration ethanol potions that are available. Indeed, prior to the ban, typical opiate consumers used opium itself, often by ingesting it in liquid form. Prohibition tended to shift undeterred users toward the more potent heroin, and often toward injecting it.[50] So in a re-legalized regime, it can be expected that most of those who pursue the consumption of opiates will look for relatively dilute preparations, such as opium tea.

What steps must a would-be adult heroin consumer take to acquire a license to consume, to opt into legal heroin use? First, a buyer's license must be acquired. I imagine that there will be a general opiate license, though users could specify what particular opiates or opioids they desire to purchase, along with the route of administration, as the appropriate drug preparation and safety information will depend on the mode of ingesting. The license fees would be calibrated so that the choice of more potent opiates, and more dangerous administrative modalities, would be accompanied by higher fees. Legal heroin access, therefore, would be more expensive than opium access, and the right to purchase doses for injecting would involve a fee premium, too.

Acquisition of a heroin buyer's license requires more steps than simply being of age and paying the requisite fees. Users must pass a short test, indicating that they understand the risks of heroin use, the regulations concerning time, place, and manner of consumption, and appropriate responses to accidental overdoses. (Heroin consumers might be required to obtain an "antidote" for overdose, too; the drug naloxone, for instance, is an opiate blocker that is an effective temporary treatment for heroin overdose.) Perhaps a meeting with a drug counselor will be required (or at least available) as well, to try to identify potential problems with compulsive use and provide information on treatment or desistance strategies. A license might last for two years, with renewals again involving discussions with a counselor about drug-related problems.

The second set of defaults would concern dosage, mode of ingestion, purchase waiting periods, and per-dose pricing. Again, these defaults would be conservative, aimed at preventing occasional users from transitioning into addicts. Users who would like to consume more than the default amount could do so, but that license option would involve a surcharge, and perhaps the per-dosage prices would be higher, too. Default quantities could be set for weekly, monthly, and annual consumption. For instance, one default setting might be five heroin doses per month, though the size of a dose could be chosen by users, too. (The tolerance developed by experienced users increases the dosage necessary to have the intended effect.) These defaults would be consistent with occasional, perhaps weekly use, but not more regular use. Purchasers could opt for higher amounts, but there would be legal maxima that could not be exceeded, to help ensure against diversion of the legal supply into the secondary market. Alternatively, users who would like to choose personal limits more constraining than the defaults could do so, and with some encouragement in the way of lower pricing.

Impulsive use would be countered, in part, by a requirement that license holders order their purchases in advance, perhaps three days in advance. Once again, they could choose longer advance purchase periods, if they so desire, and perhaps, for low frequency purchasers, with a concomitantly reduced fee.

Just as many adults would stick with the abstinence, no-license default, many license holders would abide by the default settings for purchase frequencies and other dimensions of use. People who fall into full-blown addiction would be encouraged to join a treatment regimen—perhaps involving safe injecting sites and other already proven treatment strategies[51]—that would be separate from the standard licensing system, for which they would be ineligible.

Many ardent drug and alcohol users would like to cut back or quit, but they are not ready to do so immediately. The regulatory system could help to implement such individual plans for the future, by allowing license holders to pre-commit to lower purchase quantities, or even abstinence, beginning at some future date. The commitment to stricter limits or abstinence could even be temporary, such as in fulfilling a "no consumption during January" pledge.

The sketch of a legal heroin market provided here is just that, a sketch, and many details are omitted. Further, elements of the proposed regulatory system might be entirely wrongheaded. And earlier in this chapter, a legal kidney market was sketched, with some elements that may well be mistaken. These policy alternatives are worth considering—and worth trying out—not because they are flawless, but because the existing policies are extremely costly—costs that are not speculative but are quite concrete and involve thousands of deaths annually (from both the prohibition on compensated kidney donations and from the prohibition on the manufacture, sale, and possession of illicit drugs).[52]

An Option to Commit to Opting Out: Self-Exclusion

Gambling jurisdictions around the globe have demonstrated the viability (and popularity) of a regime that is intermediate between an opt-in (licensing) and an opt-out (automatic adult eligibility) default: self-exclusion programs. Everyone who meets the minimum age is eligible to gamble and to whatever extent they choose: this part is just a standard opt-out system, where adults do not need a license to gamble. Self-exclusion programs, however, allow individuals not only to opt out, but those programs remove, for some time (perhaps one year or five years), the possibility of opting back in. A person who (voluntarily) places himself on a self-exclusion list will not be allowed into casinos, nor keep any considerable winnings if he evades the exclusion and manages to gamble anyway. For people who face severe self-control problems, a self-exclusion program can be a significant boon.

Without self-exclusion (or buyer licensing), opting out of vice consumption requires recurrent decisions to desist. The willpower to continue to abstain often proves wanting in those whose rationality with respect to vice decision-making is most suspect. With a self-exclusion program, however, the opt-out can occur at one moment and maintain a degree of enforceability for long periods of time. The new, voluntarily chosen default economizes on willpower and has shown itself to be a valuable tool in curbing pathological gambling.[53]

Preventive and Punitory Measures, Again

In chapter 3 we looked at the regulatory use of before-the-fact (*ex ante*) controls and after-the-fact (*ex post*) punishments. Drug prohibition is a massive *ex ante*, preventive control, one that does not distinguish between those drug uses (the majority) that are benign and those that impose significant costs on misguided consumers or on society more generally. As with firearms or automobiles, the better able we are to target effective controls *ex post* at the problematic drug uses, the less need we have for broad, preventive controls. (In some sense the case for *ex ante* gun or automobile controls is much stronger than for *ex ante* drug controls, in that misuse of a gun or car can impose immense, direct costs upon others, while the direct costs of drug misuse fall upon the user.)

What *ex post* controls are available for problematic drug use? Those who commit crimes such as assault or theft while under the influence of drugs can be dealt with through the standard criminal legal system; drug-impaired driving can be handled similarly. That is, for the currently illegal drugs, the rules concerning misuse that we have in place for alcohol can be adapted.

We can go further, however, to keep people away from their drug of choice when their drug habit is harming other people or when they decide that it is harming themselves. In either case, policy can make available the withdrawal, temporarily or permanently, of their eligibility to continue to use the drug. Buyer licenses can be revoked, or people can be added to exclusion lists for drugs or activities (like gambling) that typically do not require a buyer's license.[54]

License revocation or a mandated exclusion might prevent a person from purchasing a drug through official channels, but not necessarily prevent a person from using a drug once obtained. The potential to require testing for the presence of the drug (including alcohol) offers one route to enforcement of a no-consumption mandate, whether voluntarily undertaken or imposed by a court. In recent years, some jurisdictions (including Hawaii and South Dakota) have instituted frequent testing programs for alcohol or drug-involved offenders. The programs feature short (a few days in jail, for example) but more-or-less immediate sanctions when a drug test is missed or failed. Note how this briskness in punishment creates additional deterrence by taking advantage of present bias, our interest in advancing pleasure and postponing cost. Using the forbidden drug no longer brings present pleasure and future pain (the standard profile of imprudent drug use); rather, the quick sanctions convert the present pleasure into (almost) present pain.

The drug-testing regimes in Hawaii and South Dakota have shown great success in keeping alcohol and drug using offenders away from their problem drug.[55] Further, these programs have succeeded in a relatively low-cost fashion, with decreases in overall jail time, for instance. They demonstrate the efficacy of *ex post*, punitive measures, to regulate the behavior of problematic drug users. This efficacy further reduces the rationale for the blunt and costly *ex ante*, preventive control represented by drug prohibition.

A Happy Ending?

Much of this chapter has been devoted to rationality shortfalls: difficulties in dealing with risky choices, limited stores of willpower, excessive attachment to the status quo, and so on. The foundation of economic efficiency analysis, willingness-to-pay, itself seems to be more of a shifting sand than a rock; Tom Sawyer's ability to convince his friends to pay him for the opportunity to whitewash a fence was an early literary example of the more general phenomenon of the manipulability of willingness-to-pay.[56] These common departures from full rationality hold implications for what sorts of public policies might be desirable but also magnify the concerns with whether economic efficiency offers a usable standard for assessing the quality of rules.

Is efficiency worthy of the central role that it plays in Law and Economics? According to philosopher Michael Sandel: "Efficiency only matters insofar as it makes society better off. But what counts as better off? The answer depends on some conception of the general welfare or the public good."[57] An economic purist might simply equate efficiency with the public good, and leave it at that. Jeremy Bentham offers a different guide, identifying the greatest happiness as the ideal gauge of general welfare.

In chapter 1, it was noted that Bentham's overall happiness is a "close analogue" to economic efficiency. Nonetheless, there is a sizable gap between happiness and efficiency. Willingness-to-pay underlies the Law and Economics version of efficiency, but there is no reason for either the ability or the willingness to pay to closely track happiness. In totaling up happiness, every individual counts the same;[58] in aggregating the size of the economic pie, those with more resources count more. It might be "efficient" for a gang of wealthy bullies to torment a poor man, but such sadism would not increase, in Bentham's view, the social surplus of pleasure over pain (as we have seen in Bentham's general opposition to retribution as a rationale for punishing criminals).

Recent decades have witnessed an upsurge of research into the measurement, nature, and causes of happiness. Perhaps Bentham's notion that laws should be designed to serve the greatest happiness has become more "implementable," to the extent that social science (along with neuroscience) has made it possible for people to agree about what laws best will serve happiness. The advantage of the happiness standard (relative to efficiency) is augmented by the many systematic departures from standard economic rationality that people exhibit—including those shortcomings in handling uncertainty, lapses in willpower, excessive procrastination, and unwarranted commitment both to default settings and to addictive drugs that undermine well-being.

As for measuring happiness, the standard method involves asking people to rate their own happiness. (Other methods including observing smiles, asking people to rate their friends' happiness, and even using brain scans to see what stimulates neurochemical pleasure channels.) Queries about happiness first must deal with the fundamental issue of what people think happiness means when they respond to surveys.[59] For some people at some times, happiness is connected to "positive affect," a general good feeling and an abundance of smile-inducing moments. (Avoidance of bad moods, "negative affect," is a related but by no means identical contributor to this version of happiness.) At different moments or for other people, happiness refers to a longer term phenomenon concerning not so much pleasure or mood as general satisfaction with one's life. People who report favorable assessments of their overall life satisfaction might nevertheless not seem, even to themselves, as very happy on a day-to-day basis.

Alternative ways of asking questions about happiness can push people toward either a positive affect or a life satisfaction assessment. Small temporary events such as good or bad weather also impact assessments of happiness—even assessments of overall, long-term life satisfaction.[60] When generated through self-reports, happiness seems to be as manipulable as willingness-to-pay. Further, retrospective views of the happiness of an event can be quite different from what was experienced at the time. The happiness that lives in memory, for instance, is closely tied to the very best of all the moments experienced in the course of some desirable event (such as a vacation), as well as to the quality of the conclusion; other factors, such as the duration of the event, are rather inconsequential in retrospect, though of paramount import when the event is taking place.[61]

Occurrences that promote our happiness (or unhappiness) in the here and now tend to diminish in significance rather quickly over time: acclimation is common, for both positive and negative happenings, though adjustment to the new normal seems to be a stronger factor for positive than for negative events.[62] There are common exceptions to complete adjustment: marital success can boost happiness over the long-term and a spell of unemployment undermines long-term well-being.[63] Nevertheless, for the most part, today's good or ill fortune, even if it is of a long-standing nature—a promotion at work or the death of a colleague—will have very little influence on one's happiness down the road. (Centuries ago, our stalwart Adam Smith noted this phenomenon, which now is called the "hedonic treadmill": "in every permanent situation, where there is no expectation of change, the mind of every man, in a longer or shorter time, returns to its natural and usual state of tranquillity."[64]) People do not seem fully to anticipate this acclimation, this pull toward a sort of set point for happiness—a set point, incidentally, that owes much to an individual's genetic make-up[65]—when they make decisions that alter the probabilities of good or bad events arising.[66]

Does money buy happiness? Richer people do report higher levels of life satisfaction on average, and richer countries tend to be happier than poorer countries. Nonetheless, it is far from apparent that rising incomes over time in the United States (and recently, in China) have led to greater well-being, and it may be that money only promotes happiness for people who are not financially well off; at some point, further increases in income might not induce more happiness.[67]

Adam Smith claimed that people typically misunderstand the (limited) value of wealth. When we are young and healthy, we think that the rich are happy, or at least possess the means to happiness. This view is a socially useful "deception," according to Smith, as it rouses people to be industrious. But when we are old or in poor health, we see more clearly:

> Power and riches appear then to be, what they are, enormous and op-erose machines contrived to produce a few trifling conveniencies to the body, consisting of springs the most nice and delicate, which must be kept in order with the most anxious attention, and which in spite of all our care are ready every moment to burst into pieces, and to crush in their ruins their unfortunate possessor.... They keep off the summer shower, not the winter storm.[68]

Nonetheless, a "poor man's son, whom heaven in its anger has visited with ambition," is enchanted with the notion of riches. The enchantment fades with old age, when "he begins at last to find that wealth and greatness are mere trinkets of frivolous utility, no more adapted for procuring ease of body or tranquillity of mind than the tweezer-cases of the lover of toys; and like them too, more troublesome to the person who carries them about with him than all the advantages they can afford him are commodious."[69] With respect to contentment, the pursuit of riches not only is futile, it is perverse: for Adam Smith, the Peltzman effect is more than complete in the realm of income.

Our forecasts of what will bring us happiness are inaccurate in realms other than income. For many addicts, for instance, there seems to be a profound disconnect between their desire to consume their drug of choice and the hedonic payoff that their drug use brings.[70] But even non-addicts making ordinary decisions regularly (and probably unintentionally) sacrifice happiness. Students who choose a college dorm room sometimes have to decide between living in a small suite with a private bedroom and a semi-private bath or, the old standard of a shared room plus a very unprivate bath. All else equal, students flock to the rooms with modern comforts and privacy. But which arrangement is likely to lead to happiness in college? It seems that the factory-like dorms of yesteryear, while less popular, are better at fomenting the social relationships that are the source of collegiate contentment.[71]

Putting aside the possibility, even the likelihood, that we do not really understand what will make us happy or give us long-term satisfaction,[72] when presented with a choice between two alternatives, will people choose the option that they perceive as yielding them the higher happiness, the higher surplus, à la Bentham, of pleasure over pain? Generally, yes, but not always.[73] People often knowingly make choices that do not maximize their long-term satisfaction; departures from hedonic maximization seem to occur frequently in circumstances in which the chosen option contributes more to, for instance, an individual's sense of purpose, or family well-being, or feelings of control, or social status.[74] Further, people do not regard these decisions as mistakes. Why should societal welfare be equated to a happiness standard that tolerably rational individuals reject as the decision criterion in their own lives?

If we were to adopt aggregate happiness as the touchstone for choosing among potential laws, the effects would be profound.[75] We might look to subsidize the consumption of those "goods," such as socializing, happy marriages, plentiful exercise and sleep, and the avoidance of long commutes to work, that are not subject to rapid hedonic depreciation. We might tax or look to alter those goods or activities that are both causes of unhappiness and are hard to adapt to: unemployment and exposure to noise, for instance.

Specific features of the legal system also might undergo substantial change if happiness is the goal.[76] Imagine that you suffer serious harm in an accident as a result of someone else's reckless behavior, and you are left with permanent physical disabilities. By the time the resulting tort suit reaches a jury, a year has passed since the damage was incurred. Happiness research suggests that by and large, you will have adapted to your new permanent condition; you are no less happy at the time of the court case than you were prior to the accident. If the jury is instructed to award damages to restore you to your pre-accident happiness state, then you should not receive any payments. Knowing this in advance, you would not sue, presumably, unless you thought the trial would be conducted expeditiously, in which case your adaptation to your new condition would be less than complete, and hence you would be worthy, from a happiness standpoint, of receiving some recompense.[77]

But such a judicial process would be unsatisfactory, of course, even if it is the case that the "victim" is no worse off in terms of happiness pre- and post-accident. Indeed, even if the jury is instructed to compensate you for the happiness shortfalls you suffered until the full hedonic adaptation kicked in, the process would remain unsatisfactory. Hedonic adaptation does not mean that a few months down the road people are indifferent about having sustained serious permanent injuries; rather, even if they are no less happy on a day-to-day basis, they still are willing to pay considerable sums if by doing so, they could undo the effects of the injury.[78] We do not view situations as fully equivalent just because they result in identical amounts of personal happiness. An accident law system based on happiness restoration would be less satisfactory—and probably result in less happiness!—than a system that compensates for actual, but non-hedonic, damages.

The legal system already contributes to happiness through at least two channels: first, it helps to guide behavior into socially valuable directions, largely by deterring acts that impose significant costs on other people. (Violent crime in a neighborhood is quite costly in terms of reducing happiness.[79]) Second, law provides a forum in which people can have their grievances heard and their side of the story articulated.[80] This forum itself is valuable and happiness-promoting, even to a plaintiff or a defendant who loses his or her case. People care about procedures, and not just about case outcomes.[81]

As with economic efficiency, happiness offers an important input into determining which rules contribute the most to societal well-being. Neither concept provides the last word on identifying good laws. Part of the problem is that the mapping between rules and efficiency, or the mapping between rules and happiness, is highly uncertain. But even were these connections clear, the nuances of social flourishing go beyond what efficiency and happiness offer. There are more things in heaven and earth than are dreamt of in Law and Economics, even when that Law and Economics is augmented with an improved understanding of human happiness.

Conclusion

The rational choice and efficiency approach that economics brings to the study of law can be applied to property law and contract law, criminal law and accident law. We have seen such applications in this book, amidst brief stops at the British Museum and Iranian kidney markets, Radiohead concerts and Nabokov novels.

To motivate my university students to exercise their developing Law and Economics talents, I assign homework questions that ask for analyses of issues for which they lack any background. (OK, I generally lack any background in these issues, too.) I am not claiming that ignorance is a desirable condition for an analyst, but I am trying to show students that the Law and Economics lens can be applied, and profitably, even in the absence of detailed knowledge. Indeed, providing such a shortcut is more or less the point of employing economics, Keynes's "technique of thinking, which allows its possessor to draw correct conclusions." So my students have discussed what should be the property rights regime governing the moon and Antarctica, or what the liability rule should be when a homework assignment goes missing.

Let's try it here, using the venerable example of the Eggshell skull rule.[1] This rule applies in accident situations (among other settings). The cases where this rule is applicable tend to be quite tragic, where a minor misstep leads to catastrophic damages, such as a broken skull (as the name of the rule suggests). These situations are unsettling (at least for me) to dwell upon. My response, perhaps an ill-conceived one, is to adopt a sort of cartoonish attitude here, where these catastrophes are treated in a lighthearted manner (because in the next frame of the cartoon, all will be well). In fact, the victim here will be a cartoon figure, Feeble, not a person at all. He'll be fine when all is said and done.

Let's say you are swinging your elbows a bit too exuberantly, even negligently. Imagine that one of your elbows strikes a passerby—Feeble—a glancing blow on the head. For most victims of your elbow, the strike might barely have been noticeable. But Feeble possesses the dreaded eggshell skull, which promptly, uh, cracks, resulting in significant medical bills for the ill-starred cartoon character. The Eggshell skull rule holds you and your negligent elbow responsible for those medical bills, even though you did not intend any harm and even though the harm that occurred went way beyond what was reasonably foreseeable. You (as well as Feeble) were more unlucky than negligent, but you are still liable, according to the Eggshell skull rule: you take the victims of your negligence as you find them, even if you could not have expected to find them in such a Feeble state. The question I want to address is: Do you think that the Eggshell skull rule is consistent with economic efficiency? Why or why not? Those who see some normative power in economic efficiency might package the question in another form: Is the Eggshell skull rule a good law or a bad law?

Let's give it a go. Sometimes your habitual elbow negligence or recklessness doesn't do much harm, because you don't hit anyone hard or you happen to hit a person who is virtually impervious to pain or injury. Presumably you will not have to pay damages in these cases—even for those victims who feel some pain, they will not find it worthwhile to spend time and money pursuing you with a court case. But sometimes you strike Feeble or a rough Feeble-equivalent. We need to internalize the costs of the damage you impose upon those with eggshell skulls, to ensure that your incentives for controlled elbow-swinging are appropriate (socially optimal), that you take the right amount of care given the distribution of skull thicknesses out in public. There will always be people (or cartoon people, like Feeble) who are especially vulnerable, and your behavior, efficient behavior, should reflect that fact. So *e pluribus unum* seems to support the Eggshell skull rule, especially when the existence of extremely vulnerable people is combined with your effective immunity (judgment-proofness) against recompensing the minor harms inflicted upon those who are not particularly vulnerable.

But perhaps the existence of folks like Feeble isn't within anyone's contemplation of society's skull-thickness distribution. Perhaps you are choosing how to walk not under a situation of risk (with a potentially known distribution of skull thicknesses) but of uncertainty (where the pattern of skull hardiness is unknowable), and where a reasonable before-the-fact estimate of the probability of meeting an eggshell skull is zero.[2] Under these circumstances, there is less reason to believe that the Eggshell skull rule comports with efficiency. (Maybe your victim Feeble is an alien being who just beamed in from his flying saucer before making his unfortunate acquaintance with your elbow.) Even here the Eggshell skull rule should apply going forward (though perhaps not to the instant case), so that future arm-swingers will respond appropriately to the new information that there are some mighty thin skulls out there. (Thick skulls, we all know about.) If we need to hold the initial defendant liable to secure the precedent for the best future rule, well, that is no less unfair to the injurer than it is to let the blameless victim Feeble bear all of the damage himself.

We might also want to ask about who is the low-cost avoider of damage to eggshell skulls; in other words, maybe Feeble is not so blameless after all. Rather than put everyone on notice that they must constantly monitor their arm swings lest they encounter an eggshell skull, perhaps the low-cost avoider is the person with an eggshell skull. Feeble can stay at home, or wear a helmet in public. Even the standard-skulled should not be encouraged to promiscu- ously place their heads in the proximity of every pedestrian's elbow; fully in- demnifying these head owners against the risks of head bashes might fuel their own recklessness. Still, aggressive arm-swinging is a potential problem for every passerby, not just the Feebles of this world, so perhaps some sort of com- parative negligence rule would be best, where victims who did not take reason- able precautions would not be fully compensated for damages stemming from a whack by a negligent arm-swinger. Particularly vulnerable people—those Feeble-like eggshell skulls—could be held to a higher standard of reasonable care, at least assuming that they themselves know of (or should know of) their own at-risk condition.

A further issue, once we have identified the relatively inexpensive methods of avoiding the accidents, is to see if one party is in a better position than the other to deal with the remaining risk of an injury. Perhaps arm swingers are not too concerned with risk, while noggin possessors dislike risk quite a bit; in that case, the efficient allocation of risk argues for making arm swingers liable, for shifting risk away from those who are most averse to it. If both parties suffer similarly from the effects of risk, then we might look to see who has the best access to insurance—maybe the United Federation of Purposeful Walkers offers an attractively priced and easily available insurance plan to its members that reimburses accident losses. This relative ease of insuring the remaining risk would, once again, suggest that liability for accidents fall upon the arm swingers.

We could imagine Coasean bargaining, where everyone, arm swingers and skull owners alike, sits down together and works out the best rules. My guess is that indeed, we would want both parties to face at least partial liability if their precaution is less than optimal, while the standard of care imposed upon the arm swingers reflects the fact that there are some particularly at-risk skulls out there.

Fortunately, the point of the Eggshell skull exercise is not to identify the indubitably correct regulatory regime, but to indicate the Law and Economics approach to thinking about the problem. In the background is efficiency, the idea that we might want to choose the rule that will best satisfy preferences, the rule that will produce the largest social pie. We encounter this goal in the Eggshell skull analysis when we ask about low-cost avoiders, reasonable levels of care, and relatively inexpensive risk-bearers. We meet it again when we think about the outcome from Coasean bargaining, where the possibility of transfers, side payments among individuals, lends every participant an interest in finding rules that produce the largest pie. Everyone, arm swingers and skull owners alike, enjoys a big piece of pie.

Once again, what has been left out of this Law and Economics-style discussion is any direct talk of justice or of rights. Is this a feature or a bug? What could have been a lengthy discussion focused on the relative morality of the behavior of the parties has been replaced with an inquiry into what rule will best satisfy human preferences going forward. We might even be able to achieve unanimous agreement with this approach, and we might not inflame partisan feelings: in the future, almost everyone will sometimes play the role of arm swinger or of head owner, helping to promote a disinterested (or interested on both sides, symmetrically) stance. Law and Economics, two disciplines known for being contentious, in combination could generate complete agreement over difficult issues—or is that so much pie in the sky?

Well, that's it, this tour of the Law and Economics landscape has run its course. Familiarity with the Law and Economics terrain might lead to contempt, and little interest in further tours. But if you have traveled this far, you probably find some of the sights to be interesting. Perhaps you are adjusting your way of looking at public policies, or altering your views on the Parthenon marbles or the sale of kidneys.

Even if the preceding tour is not influencing your thinking directly, you now own some knowledge of Law and Economics. Do you recall (from chapter 6) the endowment effect, the notion that people tend to overvalue assets that they own relative to identical assets that they don't own? Maybe the endowment effect applies more broadly, not just to assets, but to those ideas and opinions which we possess. Herein lies a trap, the possibility that we will so overvalue "our" ideas that we will not trade them away, even for better ones.[3] Knowledge can turn us into one of those thick skulls we have heard so much about.

If you care about the correctness of your opinions, you should welcome opposing views, as only by considering the conflicting arguments can you gauge the extent to which your current opinions are justifiable. John Stuart Mill made this point with some frequency—it is a major theme in *On Liberty*—and also embodied it in his life, by showing an inordinate capacity for adjusting his opinions (though not his principles) and displaying kindness to those with whom he disagreed. According to Mill, we should view our intellectual opponents as our allies, people attempting to ascend the same hill that we are struggling up, though they are climbing from the opposite side.[4] People who disagree with us provide us, at no charge, the means to improve our own opinions, or improve our understanding of why those opinions we already hold are worthy of our stewardship. If there were no dissenters, if everyone agreed with us, we would need to subsidize the production of challengers, to ensure an adequate supply of such invaluable services.[5]

Intelligence is hard to define, and it is easy to conflate it with the accumulation of knowledge. But anyone who stops learning, whether it be at the age of 18, or 22, or 64, or later, will see assessments of his or her intelligence decline, even if the stock of knowledge remains intact (which it will not, for what constitutes knowledge tends to change with time, too, and rather quickly at that).[6] That is, to paraphrase John Stuart Mill's godson, Bertrand Russell, intelligence is more about being open and receptive to new knowledge than it is to possessing a large quantity of knowledge.[7] So beware the ideas that you possess, even the Law and Economics ideas, lest you end up serving them instead of them serving you.

On the other hand, I might be wrong . . .

GLOSSARY

The precise definitions of legal terms can be quite exacting, and cases can turn on very fine distinctions. The descriptions of terms provided in this Glossary do not constitute anything like precise definitions; they are intended only to provide some flavor of the terms, not the full legal dining experience.

Adverse possession   A common law doctrine that allows squatters to eventually claim legitimate ownership of a piece of property. If people occupy a piece of land owned by someone else for a number of years (ten or fifteen, say, though the number varies across jurisdictions), and the original owner has not raised any objections, then the squatters can receive legal title to the property, and keep out all others, including the original owner. For ownership to vest via adverse possession, the occupation must be continuous and open (no hiding), and "adverse" to the interests of the original owner (that is, the occupiers are not standard renters who have a lease with the owner, for instance), as well as long-standing.

Anticommons   A piece of property or a field of inquiry where many parties have the opportunity to veto access or use. Whereas a "commons" involves access freely available to everyone, an anticommons possesses myriad barriers to access, generally in the form of numerous owners of legal rights, each of whom can prevent unauthorized uses.

Attractive nuisance   A piece of property or a feature that is likely to arouse the interest of children, but that holds some risk that children drawn to the property might be harmed; a swimming pool is a standard example. The owner who is not careful about controlling access to such a piece of property could be held liable if children injure themselves while engaging with the property, even if the children are trespassers.

Berne Convention for the Protection of Literary and Artistic Works   An international agreement dating to 1886 that standardizes some of the terms of rights granted to writers and artists, including copyright protection and moral rights. Among the provisions of the Convention is that member nations must not discriminate against foreign authors in terms of copyright protection.

Civil law   When used in opposition to "common law," civil law refers to written rules and statutes, such as those that appear in the Napoleonic Code. In Law and Economics, the phrase "civil law" is used for systems of rules that do not change as an automatic consequence of judicial decisions.

Coase Corollary   One version of what I call the Coase Corollary (and many others call the Coase Theorem) is "in the absence of transaction costs, resource allocation is independent of the distribution of property rights." The idea is that no matter what the starting point for negotiations, it will be in everyone's interest to move to the efficient outcome, with the surplus made available from moving to efficiency somehow shared among the contracting parties in such a manner that the change makes everyone better off. For the Coase Corollary to apply, it also must be the case that the efficient distribution of resources itself does not depend on how income is distributed among the contracting parties.

Coase Theorem   If there are no costs involved when people get together to craft and enforce (possibly quite intricate) agreements, then economic efficiency is assured: any agreement that did not lead to an efficient outcome would be replaced by some efficient contract, because it would be in the interests of the contracting parties to identify a more efficient contract and to somehow share the bounty of moving from the inefficient to the efficient situation. So one version of the Coase Theorem is "in the absence of transaction costs, efficient outcomes will be achieved." Many commentators, however, offer a version of the Coase Theorem that in this book is referred to as the Coase Corollary.

Common law   The law that is developed out of previous court decisions, through a system of respect for precedent, or *stare decisis*; hence, common law rules might not even be recorded in statute books. A common law jurisdiction is one in which laws can be made by judicial decisions, provided those decisions are rendered by a court at a sufficiently high level. In the United States, federal constitutional law develops as a sort of common law, with Supreme Court decisions playing the central role. In Law and Economics, common law often is used as synonymous with "case law," as opposed to "civil law" or "statutory law."

Commons   Traditionally, a part of a town or manor estate where all local residents held certain limited use rights, such as walking or firewood collecting or grazing livestock. More generally, an asset to which everyone has access (though again, perhaps there are some limits to that access), such as the ocean or cultural productions, say. The potential for overuse of the commons leads to a **Tragedy of the Commons.**

Comparative negligence   Sometimes when a person is injured in an accident, neither the "injurer" nor the "victim" were behaving with reasonable regard for safety. In a legal regime of comparative negligence, the damages suffered by the victim will be shared between the two parties. The larger share of damages will be paid by the party whose departure from reasonable care was relatively greater, and that share will increase as the relative extent of negligence grows.

Dibs   A system of allocating "property rights" where the first to stake a claim receives "ownership." In the case of sitting in the front passenger seat in an automobile, the staking of the claim might involve an oral declaration ("I call dibs on the front"). In the case of parking along snow-covered streets, dibs are claimed by placing some sort of barrier, trash cans or old chairs, say, into the empty spot.

Droit de suite   A French phrase that means, roughly, right of continuation, but refers to resale rights for artists or their heirs. Resale rights allow artists who sold paintings or other works to receive royalties when the work is later resold.

Efficient breach   Contracts generally are not completed the moment they are signed; rather, parties commit to certain actions via the contract, although those actions might not be taken until well into the future. In the meantime, circumstances might change, such that the contractually specified actions no longer are desirable (or efficient) when the time to act arrives. Parties must decide whether to fulfill their contractual promises, or to fail to comply with the contractual terms (that is, to breach the contract). Sometimes it is better from the point of view of overall well-being that a contract not be complied with. If parties choose not to comply under such circumstances, and only under such circumstances, then the decisions not to comply are efficient breach decisions. The expectations damage measure typically helps to induce efficient breach decisions.

Endowment effect   The notion that people place a higher value on a good when they feel that they own it than they would place on an otherwise identical good that they do not own. A significant endowment effect makes people reluctant to trade away or otherwise part with items that they own. Assignments of initial property rights, then, might have considerable staying power, even if those assignments had little to recommend them (perhaps they were chosen randomly, even) in the first place.

Ex ante Before the fact or event. *Ex ante* regulations (or, preventive controls) such as the licensing of drivers apply prior to any accidents or other misbehavior or mischance. *Ex ante* regulations might be coupled with *ex post* regulations (punitory controls) that apply after there has been an accident. The "event" in question might involve the acquisition of information. I might agree to sell my lottery ticket to you for $1 before we know if it is a winner or not (*ex ante*), but *ex post*, after we know if it is a winning one or not, either you will not be willing to pay $1 (when it is a losing ticket) or I will not be willing to sell it to you for $1 (when it is a winning ticket).

Expectation damages A contracting party's "expectation" is how well off she would be if the contract is fulfilled. If the other party, however, fails to meet the contractual terms, that expectation will not be realized. Courts typically require non-compliant parties to make damage payments, some amount of recompense, to their contracting partners. There are various measures courts use to determine how much recompense should be made, but in the United States, the standard "damage measure" is expectation damages: these are payments that protect a contracting party's expectation, and hence offer a sort of perfect insurance for a contacting party, in that either the contract is complied with and the expectation is achieved, or the contract is breached and damages are paid, and once again the expectation is achieved, albeit indirectly.

Ex post After the fact. *Ex post* regulations apply after an accident has occurred, or after a crime has been committed, or after relevant information has been revealed.

Externality A consequence of an action that falls upon another person who is not a party to any agreement concerning the action. Externalities can be negative—when your neighbors make lots of noise, you suffer a negative externality—or they can be positive: when your neighbors establish and maintain a lovely garden that you can see, you enjoy a positive externality. Economists expect that when rational people face all of the consequences (positive and negative) of their decisions, then the decisions that they make will serve the social good. If externalities are present, however, individuals do not bear all the consequences of their actions, so there is no reason to expect that individual choices will serve the common good.

Fair use An element of US copyright law that allows people to copy part or all of a copyrighted text without permission from the copyright owner. (This allowance does not preclude being sued for copyright violations, but it provides an affirmative defense against the charges.) Book reviews, even quite negative ones, often contain brief quotations from the book under review, without seeking the permission of the book's author. These quotations, along with many other instances of copying, constitute a fair use.

Force majeure A major event outside the control of contracting parties that renders it impossible for a contractual promise to be fulfilled. A hurricane or the outbreak of a war that shuts down commercial shipping might be instances of *force majeure*. A *force majeure* term in a contract allows promises that cannot be fulfilled because of such major events to be unfilled or fulfilled with a delay, without the promise breaker having to pay any damages to his or her contract partner.

Foreseeable misuse The literal meaning applies. A product might be employed by a consumer in a manner that is not consistent with its intended use—possibly increasing the risk of a product-related injury. Though unintended, this "misuse" might not be very surprising, that is, the manufacturer and others might (or should) recognize that people will be tempted to employ the product in such an unapproved manner.

Frustration of purpose A contract law doctrine that allows someone who has made a contractual promise to be released from that promise (without having to pay damages to the contract partner) if the underlying rationale for the agreement has been undermined by rather unexpected events that have taken place between the time the contract was signed and the time the promise was to be fulfilled. If the contracting parties are uncomfortable with this doctrine as it might apply to their specific circumstances, they can opt out of the doctrine by explicitly indicating in the contract their preferred resolution to such rationale-destroying events.

Harm principle   The name that subsequent commentators have given to John Stuart Mill's approach (in *On Liberty*) to answering the question of when it is legitimate for society to interfere forcibly with the choices made by adults. Mill believes that it is a violation of personal liberty for society to use coercion to direct any adult decisions that do not threaten a serious risk of harms to others. In other words, if adults choose to engage in very risky undertakings, society cannot stop them, unless the risks fall (involuntarily) upon someone other than the decision-maker.

Impossibility   A contract law doctrine that allows someone who has made a contractual promise to be released from that promise (without having to pay damages to the contract partner) if the performance of the promise has (rather unexpectedly) become unattainable or extremely costly. As with the doctrine of frustration of purpose, if the contracting parties are uncomfortable with the impossibility doctrine as it might apply to their specific circumstances, they can opt out by explicitly indicating in the contract their preferred resolution when promise fulfillment becomes well-nigh impossible.

Incapacitation effect   The inability of convicted criminals who are incarcerated to commit any crimes against the general population during their prison terms. The extent to which crime rates fall solely because crime-prone convicts are isolated is called the incapacitation effect of prison. Prison also might reduce crime through other channels, in particular, by providing a threat that deters potential offenders from engaging in crime.

Judgment-proof   Incapable of being held accountable for damages that your behavior inflicts upon others, perhaps because of lack of means or mental illness or being a young child.

Moral right (or *droit d'auteur*)   The right to be acknowledged as the author or creator of a work, or to disown authorship if the work is presented in a distorted fashion. Also, moral rights for valuable artistic productions include the right not to have your work intentionally altered in such a manner as to harm your reputation.

Negligence   Insufficient caution. In an accident setting, where a victim has suffered damages, the injurer is negligent if the injurer was not sufficiently cautious, if the injurer did not take reasonable care. If the legal regime that applies to accidents is a negligence regime (as opposed, say, to a regime of strict liability), then the injurer will be required to pay for the victim's damages only in the case where the injurer has been negligent.

Non-excludable   A property of some goods (or services) such that provision of the good for one person implies that other people are automatically supplied with the good, too. National defense or the illumination from a lighthouse are examples of non-excludable goods.

Non-rival   A property of some goods (or services) such that one person's consumption of the good does not preclude someone else's simultaneous consumption of the same good; national defense is a non-rival good, whereas a kumquat is a rival good.

Pareto efficient (or **Pareto optimal**)   A state of affairs—an allocation of society's resources among the population, say, or a set of public policies—that cannot be improved upon. The sense in which no improvement is possible is that, starting from a Pareto efficient situation, any alteration would make at least one person worse off. If a society is not in a Pareto efficient situation, then a Pareto improvement is available. If a society is in a Pareto efficient situation—the more common situation—there might be a case for a change, but that change will not receive unanimous support.

Pareto improvement   A movement from one state of affairs—an allocation of society's resources among the population, say, or a public policy—to an alternative state of affairs with the result that some people are made better off and no one is made worse off. A Pareto improving move would receive unanimous support, presumably, or at least no one would feel particularly motivated to campaign against it. The move captures a sort of free lunch, and as economists are wont to point out, it is very hard to find free lunches, or Pareto improvements, lying about. If a society does happen to stumble upon a free lunch, however, it should pick it up. Judging reforms solely by whether they provide a Pareto improvement is a recipe for rejecting almost any reforms, given the difficulty of identifying Pareto improvements, reforms that would not attract a single opponent.

Pecuniary externality Impacts on would-be buyers and sellers that are mediated through the market. For instance, if I spend my money at United Airlines instead of American Airlines, I help United but, in some sense, harm American. My patronage might even cause prices at United to rise for other customers, and my lack of patronage might cause prices at American to fall. Unlike standard externalities, pecuniary externalities do not involve a diminution in efficiency, in the aggregate size of the pie. By operating through the marketplace, the third party effects of my behavior do not bring any social waste.

Preventive controls John Stuart Mill's terminology for *ex ante* regulations, as used in *On Liberty* (Mill ([1859] 1978)). Preventive controls are imposed on people (for instance, automobile drivers) even before any untoward, driver-related activity takes place. Mandatory drivers' licenses and insurance requirements are examples of preventive controls.

Public goods Goods or services that display at least some degree of non-rivalry and non-excludability; national defense and the illumination provided by lighthouses are standard examples of public goods. Public goods present a challenge for standard competitive markets, because any individual might be reluctant to actually purchase (or contribute toward purchasing) public goods: if others purchase those goods, the (non-excludable) individual will receive the benefit of the good, despite not contributing.

Punitory controls John Stuart Mill's terminology for *ex post* regulations. Punitory controls consist of punishments imposed upon those people who break the law (perhaps by driving an automobile in a reckless fashion or with homicidal intent).

Rivalry The notion that for goods such as houses or apples or desks, "consumption" by one person means that other people cannot consume the exact same good. These types of goods can be distinguished from goods such as sunlight or clean air or a nice day at a park or at the beach, where one person's consumption does not preclude someone else's simultaneous consumption.

Standard of care (or **reasonable care**) The legally imposed minimum amount of caution that represents non-negligent behavior. If accidents are governed by a legal regime of negligence, injurers will not have to compensate accident victims for the accident as long as the injurer behaved with sufficient (or more than sufficient) caution. The legally relevant level of sufficient caution is the standard of care, or represents reasonable care. Under a negligence regime, an injurer who does not meet the standard of care will have to compensate accident victims for their injuries. (Alternatively, a strict liability legal regime does not require that a standard of care be established, as injurers are liable for damages irrespective of their choice of care within a strict liability setting.)

Stare decisis Standing by the decision. A judicial system that features *stare decisis* is one in which the precedents set by the decisions in earlier court cases hold significant influence on how later, similar cases are decided. This respect for precedent puts a barrier in the way of large swings in the law and helps to reduce uncertainty about how future actions will be judged. One cost of the legal inertia instituted by a system of *stare decisis* is that bad laws might prove to be fairly immune to change. But as Thomas Jefferson noted, maybe that cost is tolerable: "I am certainly not an advocate for frequent and untried changes in laws and constitutions. I think moderate imperfections had better be borne with; because, when once known, we accommodate ourselves to them, and find practical means of correcting their ill effects" (quoted in Hunt 1996, p. 313).

Strict liability A legal regime that requires an injurer who causes an accident to recompense the victims, irrespective of the degree of caution displayed by the injurer's behavior. The "strict" element is that these damages must be paid even if the injurer was being exceedingly careful, if the behavior of the injurer was perfectly prudent and even praiseworthy. An alternative regime is one of "negligence," where injurers must recompense victims only if the injurer's actions were unreasonably careless.

Tort A wrong that the victim can seek redress for by pursuing a lawsuit against the putative inflictor of that wrong. Someone who accidentally (or sometimes intentionally) harms you may well be guilty of a tort against you. For the most part, torts involve civil, not criminal cases, so the guilty party will not be imprisoned, but might be ordered to pay damages or take other steps to remedy the wrong.

Tragedy of the Anticommons Underuse of a valuable asset because control rights are so dispersed that it is hard for all owners of these rights to agree to a specific use of the asset. As a result, the value of the asset in practice will be greatly diminished or eliminated. If a new store in a town could not open without unanimous approval of the town's residents, then even very valuable stores would, tragically, have a hard time collecting permission to open.

Tragedy of the Commons Overuse of a valuable asset because open or unlimited access allows many people to capture some of the value. In the process, their combined behavior can undermine the value of the asset. Thus, when buffalo in the United States became quite valuable in the nineteenth century, and anyone could hunt them and sell their skins, buffalo were hunted to the brink of extinction. (Taylor (2011) offers an eye-opening, sophisticated analysis of the near-extinction of buffalo in North America.) Unregulated ocean fisheries can come to similar bad ends.

Transaction costs Those costs that accompany attempts to bargain, to agree to terms, and to specify and enforce those terms. Typically, we would expect that transaction costs rise as the number of transacting parties increases, but even with two parties, transaction costs can be high enough as to preclude successful negotiations.

Trespass An intentional incursion on someone's property. A trespass is a tort.

Unconscionability A contract law doctrine that allows courts to negate or rewrite contracts that the courts feel involve terms that are shockingly one-sided. Normally courts will only rule a contract (or a subset of the contract terms) to be unconscionable if there is a perceived defect in the fairness of the original bargaining process (procedural unconscionability) along with the shockingly unfair terms (substantive unconscionability).

NOTES

Introduction

1. For background on *The Original of Laura*, see Dmitri Nabokov's introduction to Nabokov (2008) and Robert McCrum, "The Final Twist in Nabokov's Untold Story," *The Observer*, Oct. 24, 2009, at http://www.theguardian.com/books/2009/oct/25/nabokov-original-of-laura-mccrum.
2. Rae (1895, p. 434). History records famous writers, including Virgil and Kafka, whose express wishes to have some of their work destroyed posthumously were ignored.
3. Sax (2001) and Strahilevitz (2005), which inform this example, offer incisive analyses of appropriate rules for property destruction, but come to markedly different conclusions. The issue of property destruction is revisited in chapter 3.
4. This quote comes from Keynes's brief introduction to Henderson (1922, p. v).

Chapter 1

1. Bentham ([1823] 1907), chapter 13, §I, I.
2. Bentham (1830, p. 266).
3. Quoted in Marmoy (1958, p. 80); see also "Auto-Icon," UCL Bentham Project, at http://www.ucl.ac.uk/Bentham-Project/who/autoicon.
4. One of the "fundamental theorems of welfare economics" indicates that in a pristine world free of various types of distortions, perfectly competitive markets result in Pareto efficient outcomes; see, e.g., Besanko and Braeutigam (2008, pp. 638–640).
5. If Thursday is an alternative firewood supplier to Wednesday, then Thursday's interests might be hurt when Robin agrees to trade her berries with Wednesday and not with Thursday. Market competition, often praised for efficiency, does involve losers as well as winners. See the discussion of pecuniary externalities in chapter 4.
6. The notion that winners could compensate losers from a shift to a new situation, strictly speaking, only captures one element of the aggregate wealth test. The other component is that the losers cannot bribe the winners to induce them to stay with the status quo. For a discussion of this and related measures of welfare in Law and Economics, see Parisi (2004).
7. In what follows I will typically use the term "efficient" as equivalent to usages such as "maximizes the size of the pie," or "maximizes overall well-being," or similar wording using a synonym for "well-being," such as "satisfaction" or "wealth." Note that "wealth" in this sense refers to preference satisfaction, not to the value of assets. Sometimes I will apply the adjective "social" as opposed to "overall" or "aggregate" or "total," even at times when it is redundant, as in the phrase "social efficiency."
8. Smith ([1776] 1976), Book 1, chapter 7. A "coach and six" is perhaps as antiquated as push-pin. The "six" refers to six horses, those that provide the motive force for the coach that wealthy people of Smith's time would travel in.

9. Individual valuations might be inconstant or manipulable; see, e.g., Ariely, Loewenstein, and Prelec (2006). For other concerns about willingness-to-pay, see the section "The Endowment Effect" in chapter 6, along with Ellerman (2009) and Adler (2009).

10. Boadway (1974) indicates some of the limits of the willingness-to-pay criterion. Alternative methods of determining the social good in a world of heterogeneous individuals suffer from serious shortcomings, too: this is the message of a famous economics result, Arrow's Impossibility Theorem; for a succinct explanation of the Impossibility Theorem in a voting context, see Maskin (2009).

11. The appearance of a Pareto improvement might be deceptive, of course, and the fact that legal force is employed for the taking—as opposed to a voluntary sale—suggests that we should be skeptical of unsubstantiated claims that property losers have been fully compensated.

12. See *Pennsylvania Coal Co. v. Mahon*, 260 U.S. 393 (1922) and *Lucas v. South Carolina Coastal Council*, 505 U.S. 1003 (1992). For some historical background, see Banner (2011, pp. 46–69). Note that the property owner (along with competing bidders) might have anticipated the possibility of future regulation lowering the value of her property, and therefore the owner paid less to acquire her property right in the first place. If this is the case, the compensation for the regulation was, in an average sense, already "paid" when the property was purchased. Another relevant legal factor in whether compensation will be provided is whether the regulation addresses some sort of negative spillover from a specific use of the property; in this case, property owners never had the right to produce those spillovers, so compensation need not be provided when the use is forbidden by regulation; see Merrill and Smith (2010, pp. 199–200).

13. See chapter 2 of Posner (2014). The precise rendering of one encapsulation of Judge Posner's view is that "much of the common law can be interpreted as aimed at maximizing the wealth of society" (Posner 2014, p. 32).

14. Posner (2014, p. 101).

15. For a related dynamic process that promotes efficiency in the common law, see Rubin (1977).

16. Rubin (2008) provides a nice discussion of this issue; see also La Porta, Lopez-de-Silanes, and Shleifer (2008).

17. Coase (1960).

18. This version of the Coase Theorem might not be the most popular formulation. Many commentators identify the Coase Theorem with what is called the "Coase Corollary" (discussed later).

19. Usher (1998, p. 9) and Farrell (1987, pp. 113–114).

20. Professor Coase (1988, pp. 13–16) himself expressed some exasperation with the academic focus on a world of zero transaction costs, as he was offering it only as a baseline— his concern was more with the real world, where transaction costs are endemic.

21. Whalen, Carlton, Heter, and Richard (2008).

22. Ronald Coase (1937) also is a pioneer in the study of the costs of market exchange.

23. Wolkoff (1990).

24. The economist Arthur Okun (1975) likened the tendency for redistributive policies to lose some resources in the course of redistribution to transporting water with a leaky bucket. See also the "Deflating Subsidies" section of chapter 4.

25. Stigler (1988, pp. 74ff). The Coase Corollary is not a corollary in the strict logical sense, in that it does not follow from the Coase Theorem alone. Rather, the Coase Corollary additionally requires that both parties' willingness-to-pay for changes in the output of smoke is unaffected by the assignment of the property right.

26. Farnsworth (1999). Information asymmetries are a form of transaction cost that can be a severe hindrance even in bilateral bargaining situations; see, e.g., Farrell (1987). One common instance is when a strike shuts down a business for an extended period of time. Labor and management eventually come to an agreement that ends the strike, though both sides would have been better off if they had made the exact same agreement earlier, prior to the shutdown.

27. But "fairness" is not much of an argument in a Law and Economics analysis! The fairness concern here also implicates efficiency issues. First, the fact that people have chosen to wait for a long time indicates that they have a fairly serious interest in getting a visa; indeed, they have revealed a substantial willingness-to-pay (in terms of time) for the visa. The newcomer has claimed to have a high willingness-to-pay, but her behavior so far has not revealed that willingness. Based on the information at hand, it is likely that the efficient distribution of the right to enter belongs to people who have been waiting, and not to the newcomer. Second, what will happen if it becomes clear that the way to get to the front of a line in an embassy queue is to produce a credible tale of woe? Among other things, the standard of what constitutes credibility in a tale will be likely to rise.

28. See Heller (1998, 2008).

29. See Heller (2008, pp. 27–29); Banner (2008) contains an extensive treatment of the history of the evolution of overflight rules.

30. On patent thickets, see Shapiro (2001). Industries enmeshed in patent thickets might suffer from a second sort of hold-out problem: any single firm might be unwilling to undertake a legal challenge to the validity of a patent—even a weak and probably invalid patent—when many other firms that operate within the industry would receive the bulk of the benefits from a ruling that the patent is invalid; see Harhoff, von Graevenitz, and Wagner (2014).

31. And such contracts would have to be permitted by the actual sovereign.

32. See, e.g., Epstein (1979, pp. 60–64). Rights to sunlight are becoming more valuable as solar energy becomes more more cost-effective, and hence development of the property rules to sunlight is taking on more importance; see Bronin (2009).

33. Calabresi and Melamed (1972).

34. A standard sequence would be that someone infringes your property right, and you take them to court. If the court agrees that they did indeed infringe, an injunction will be issued forbidding future trespassing, and the trespasser will be required to pay damages for the past incursion.

35. Calabresi and Melamed (1972) originated this analysis.

36. Accidents are examined again in chapters 2, 3, and 5. One of the shortcomings of a liability rule is that it requires courts to determine the appropriate amount of damages, whereas with a property rule, the owner herself can determine how much she needs to be compensated to permit an incursion. Generally we would expect that owners are better able to gauge the value of their property rights than are courts, and hence, if transaction costs are low, we should encourage the would-be "infringer" to bargain with the property owner.

37. Note that the anticommons problem applies to any land assembly deal involving numerous property owners, whether or not the deal involves a government (as opposed to a private) project.

38. *eBay Inc. et al. v. MercExchange, L.L.C.*, 547 U.S. 388 (2006). Patents are addressed in more depth in chapter 3.

Chapter 2

1. See "2 Years for Law School?" by Colleen Flaherty, *Inside Higher Ed*, August 26, 2013; at http://www.insidehighered.com/news/2013/08/26/president-obama-calls-cutting-year-law-school.

2. "A tort is a wrong. To commit a tort is to do wrong to another" (Goldberg and Zipursky 2010a, p. 1). Accidents frequently involve torts; negligence, battery, defamation, and products liability all fall (at least partially) within the ambit of tort law.

3. DuVivier (2014, p. 393).

4. See the Bureau of Land Management's webpage, "Rockhounding on Public Land," at http://www.blm.gov/or/programs/minerals/noncollectables.php.

5. Although here, the relevant contact law doctrine would be *impossibility*, which applies in some instances when an unexpected event has rendered the contractually specified actions to become essentially impossible.

6. Holmes ([1881] 1991, p. 301).
7. Holmes (1897, p. 462).
8. See Graham and Peirce (1984).
9. Another circumstance that might lead to full indemnification occurs if Robin is well-placed to serve as an insurance company, so that Friday chooses to purchase accident coverage from Robin.
10. And just as a fully insured accident victim takes too little effort to avoid an accident, a fully protected (through expectation damages) contracting partner will treat compliance with a contract as a sure thing and make inordinate expenditures in complementary investments that only are valuable when the contract actually is complied with. The efficient breach brought about by expectation damages simultaneously induces socially excessive spending on such complementary investments, unless the law caps the protection of such investments—which it does; see Leitzel (1989).
11. Intentionally invading someone's property without permission is a trespass, but private necessity is a defense against charges of trespassing; nonetheless, damage done to the property by a necessary incursion generally must be recompensed.
12. See, e.g., Polinsky and Shavell (1989).
13. See, e.g., Shavell (2004, pp. 531–539).
14. Levitt (1998). The size of the incapacitation effect is almost startling high. It appears that the average person in prison would commit many, many crimes were he at large; see the discussion and estimates in Levitt (1996). For recent evidence on deterrence and incapacitation effects from Italy, see Drago, Galbiati, and Vertova (2009) and Barbarino and Mastrobuon (2014).
15. See Wiseman (2014).
16. Durose, Cooper, and Snyder (2014); this information is based on data from thirty states for prisoners released in 2005.
17. Or perhaps offer the best hopes for avoiding highly undesirable consequences: the improved future well-being that is aimed at by adopting a new rule might accept a lower average level of satisfaction (compared to what would result from some alternative rule) for decreased chances of truly awful outcomes.
18. For recent assessments of retribution, see the edited volume Tonry (2011b); the first chapter, Tonry (2011a), was a particularly helpful source for me in preparing this section.
19. For a skeptical look at retribution from a Law and Economics perspective, see Kaplow and Shavell (2002, pp. 294–317).
20. Bentham ([1823] 1907), chapter 13, §I, II, n. 1.
21. Russell ([1954] 1992, p. 98) and Russell (1951, pp. 80–81).
22. While Russell himself has no interest in ensuring criminals receive their "just rewards," his thought experiment does not rule out that other members of society are committed to retribution. Because they are misinformed about the true state of affairs, their demand for retribution can appear to be satisfied without actually imprisoning convicted offenders.
23. This is a version of what is known as Blackstone's ratio; see Volokh (1997).
24. Note how the usual requirement that a guilty verdict returned by a jury be unanimous sets up a sort of intentional Tragedy of the Anticommons—any single juror, acting alone, can veto a verdict of guilty. This requirement is symmetric, in that "not guilty" verdicts, too, generally require unanimity, but defendants are punished only via guilty verdicts.
25. Becker (1968).
26. Kaplow (2011).

Chapter 3

1. McChesney (2001) and Epstein (2001). Incidentally, the effort involved in clearing a parking space can be considerable, even with moderate snow. Road plows push snow out of the center of the street toward the curbs; in the process, parked cars can become snow-entombed. Snow shoveling-related orthopedic injuries and (thankfully to a lesser extent) heart attacks are frequent; see Watson, Shields, and Smith (2011).

2. Ellickson (1991).

3. On copyrights, see chapter 4. Motion pictures, music, and other creative works also qualify for copyright protection. The use of the term "monopoly" to refer to the control rights given to patent (or copyright) owners is traditional but misleading. It does not imply that the patent owner possesses any market power; indeed, the vast majority of patents earn no licensing or royalty fees. The control right conferred by a patent is more analogous to property rights in physical assets—you can exclude others from using your property—than it is to market power. See Landes and Posner (2003, p. 374).

4. This analysis points to the more general consideration that the standard anti-monopoly disposition of economists should be at best provisional, given that a monopoly can serve some societal interests that might more than make up for the static inefficiency.

5. See, e.g., Moser (2012).

6. Bessen and Meurer (2008–2009). For more evidence on the relatively small impact of patent protection on innovation, see Lerner (2009), Mokyr (2009), and Sakakibara and Branstetter (2001).

7. Whether patent thickets in actuality dissuade entry into some technological fields was an open question for a while, but now the evidence is rather firmly in the affirmative; see Hall et al. (2013).

8. Kremer (2004).

9. World Trade Organization rules permit countries, under certain circumstances, to produce or obtain patented pharmaceuticals without the consent of the patent holder—though these "compulsory licenses" are still supposed to involve adequate remuneration to the patent holder; see http://www.wto.org/english/tratop_e/trips_e/public_health_faq_e.htm.

10. See http://www.gavi.org/funding/pneumococcal-amc/.

11. Kremer (2004).

12. See the pneumococcal vaccine support webpage, at http://www.gavi.org/support/nvs/pneumococcal/.

13. See the section "Low Probability, High Punishment Regimes" later in the chapter for a discussion of attempting to improve deterrence by ratcheting up penalties for crimes.

14. Mill ([1859] 1978, pp. 95–96). This discussion draws upon chapter 5 of Leitzel (2003).

15. Viscusi (1984); see also chapter 4.

16. Mill ([1859] 1978, p. 95).

17. The discussion in this section draws upon chapter 8 of Leitzel (2003).

18. Not all gun criminals are strongly motivated to acquire and employ firearms. One study of juvenile offenders in Atlanta found that many of them acquired their weapons in a haphazard fashion, without a firm intention to become armed; Ash et al. (1996).

19. Vizzard (2000).

20. Mill ([1859] 1978, p. 96); Mill's comment was made in the context of regulating sales of poisons.

21. Mill ([1848] 1909), V.11.23, at http://www.econlib.org/library/Mill/mlP73.html#Bk.V,Ch.XI. Mill expresses similar sentiments in his 1835 essay on Adam Sedgwick, reprinted in vol. 10 (Mill 2006) of Mill's collected works: "To rear up minds with aspirations and faculties above the herd, capable of leading on their countrymen to greater achievements in virtue, intelligence, and social well-being; to do this, and likewise so to educate the leisured classes of the community generally, that they may participate as far as possible in the qualities of these superior spirits, and be prepared to appreciate them, and follow in their steps—these are purposes, requiring institutions of education placed above dependence on the immediate pleasure of that very multitude whom they are designed to elevate [internal note omitted]."

22. Mill ([1861] 2006, p. 212).

23. If you think that wealthy people speeding with impunity while dropping $100 bills out their window as they damage other cars does not conduce to social well-being, you might be right. Their behavior renders the crashes intentional, not accidental, and hence the

property rights in your car should probably be protected by a property rule—the speeders need your permission before damaging your car—and not by a liability rule. (Recall the discussion of property rules versus liability rules in chapter 1.)

24. Becker (1968).
25. Stigler (1970); Bentham ([1823] 1907, XIV.14–18) noted this point, too. Low probability/high punishment regimes are examined again in chapter 4.
26. And if jail sentences are part of the punishment, low probability regimes might be undesirable because most offenders will not be caught and imprisoned; hence, the incapacitation rationale for punishment via jail is poorly served by enforcement systems that feature a low probability of conviction.
27. Those fully committed to a Law and Economics-style analysis perhaps would suggest that the perceived unfairness itself emanates from underlying inefficiencies.
28. Strahilevitz (2005).
29. There is a similar suggestion in Strahilevitz (2005); see also Sax (2001). (The discussion here on property destruction draws deeply on these two sources.) Strahilevitz's proposal relates to the remainder value of an asset after the owner is deceased; a provision in a will calling for destruction of sufficiently valuable property would be ignored unless an auction were held (before the owner is deceased) to determine the market value of the remainder interest. The property owner then could accept the high bid, so that the asset would not be destroyed upon his or her death, or reject it, in which case the provision in the will would be carried out.
30. See Krutilla (1967).
31. Strahilevitz (2005, pp. 817–821).
32. See Buccafusco and Sprigman (2011) and Norton, Mochon, and Ariely (2012).
33. In reality, there are no chapter divisions in *The Original of Laura*, and it is still under copyright.
34. Article 6*bis*, paragraph 1; the text of the Berne Convention is available from the World Intellectual Property Organization, at http://www.wipo.int/treaties/en/ip/berne/trtdocs_wo001.html.
35. 17 U.S.C. §106A; see Rosenblatt (1998).
36. See Ben Quinn, "Man Who Defaced Tate Modern's Rothko Canvas Says He's Added Value," *The Guardian*, October 7, 2012, at http://www.theguardian.com/artanddesign/2012/oct/08/defaced-tate-modern-rothko.
37. Vladimir Umanets, "I Regret Vandalising a Rothko, but I Remain Committed to Yellowism," *The Guardian*, May 15, 2014; at http://www.theguardian.com/commentisfree/2014/may/15/vandalising-rothko-yellowism-black-on-maroon-tate-modern.
38. Mark Brown, "Tate Modern Unveils Painstakingly Restored Rothko," *The Guardian*, May 13, 2014; at http://www.theguardian.com/artanddesign/2014/may/13/tate-modern-unveils-restored-mark-rothko-black-on-maroon.
39. See Umberto Bacchi, "Ecce Homo Fresco Painter Who Turned Jesus into 'Hairy Monkey' Signs Lucrative Royalties Deal," *International Business Times*, August 22, 2013; at http://www.ibtimes.co.uk/articles/500845/20130822/ecce-homo-spain-painting-christ-monkey-cecilia.htm. More than two years after the restoration, the fresco continues to generate considerable interest, sparking further creative efforts in music, cinema, and opera; see Cecilia Giménez, "A dos años, el Ecce Homo se convirtió en un gran negocio," *El Pais*, August 16, 2014, at http://www.elpais.com.uy/vida-actual/ecce-homo-convirtio-gran-negocio.html.
40. Bacchi, "Ecce Homo Fresco Painter Who Turned Jesus into 'Hairy Monkey' Signs Lucrative Royalties Deal."
41. Nozick (1974).
42. From the section "The Incommodities of Such a War," in chapter 13 of Hobbes (1651).
43. Recall the many qualifications that should make us wary of too quickly associating this approach to efficiency with social well-being, however. Those qualifications include the dependence of willingness-to-pay upon the existing distribution of wealth, and the questionable existence or stability of individual preferences that generate unambiguous measures of willingness-to-pay.

Chapter 4

1. A central insight associated with the Austrian school of economics is that the dispersion of information makes it impossible for any person or bureaucracy to know what behavior is socially optimal, while the price mechanism does a serviceable job at aggregating that information in ways that tend to induce behavior that at least tends toward social benefit; see Hayek (1945).
2. This discussion draws upon Leitzel (2003, pp. 65–70). The even more extreme argument is that the offsetting effects will overwhelm the intended effect, resulting in a perverse outcome; see Hirschman (1991).
3. And cars generally have become much safer, as suggested by a striking video of a laboratory crash between a 2009 and a 1959 Chevrolet; see http://www.consumerreports.org/cro/video-hub/cars/safety/2009-chevy-malibu-vs-1959-bel-air-crash-test/17188412001/41311737001/. I originally learned of this video—along, undoubtedly, with many of the other sources noted throughout the text—from the blog Marginal Revolution (http://marginalrevolution.com/) operated by Tyler Cohen and Alex Tabarrok; many of the posts on Marginal Revolution are related to the field of Law and Economics.
4. From Table FI-200 in *Highway Statistics 2011*; at http://www.fhwa.dot.gov/policy information/statistics/2011/fi200.cfm.
5. The idea of a spike emanating from a steering wheel as a demonstration of the Peltzman effect sometimes is attributed to economist Gordon Tullock; see the April 24, 2009, post on the blog Offsetting Behaviour at http://offsettingbehaviour.blogspot.com/2009/04/in-which-masthead-is-explained-and.html. The Offsetting Behaviour blog features a drawing of a steering wheel with a spike coming out of it.
6. The idea that increased energy efficiency will spark more energy consumption is known as the "rebound effect"; see, e.g., Borenstein (2013).
7. Jacobsen and van Benthem (2013).
8. Or maybe not. The incentives to inform others of your invention might be greater when you have a patent than when the invention is in the public domain. If it is hard for potential users to retrieve the information in the absence of patent-owner marketing, then maybe patents increase the effective availability of inventions, even as they increase the nominal price of utilizing the invention.
9. Perhaps technology already has developed to the point where driverless cars are quite safe. As early as 2010, a driverless van drove from Milan to Shanghai without incident; see http://edition.cnn.com/2010/TECH/innovation/10/27/driverless.car/index.html?iref=allsearch.
10. The discussion in this paragraph draws upon Adler (2008).
11. And if that forewarning is available before they purchase their land, then they will pay less for the land—in effect, the lower price compensates the owners in advance for the diminution in value from future regulatory actions.
12. Langpap and Kerkvliet (2012).
13. Bardach (1989) provides the tripartite division of rules into standards of behavior, enforcement, and sanctions.
14. Philipson and Posner (1996).
15. See, e.g., Amnesty International (n.d.).
16. Adam Smith ([1776] 1976, vol. 2, pp. 372–373) mentions variations on the window tax.
17. See Table 1 (http://goo.gl/7RRsW2) of the summary statistics (http://www.iucnredlist.org/about/summary-statistics) of the IUCN Red List of Threatened Species.
18. See the World Wildlife Fund's species list, at http://www.worldwildlife.org/species/directory.
19. Estimates of the number of species extinctions per year are extremely wide-ranging; 200 is at the very low end of the range. See, e.g., the World Wildlife Fund's Biodiversity webpage, at http://wwf.panda.org/about_our_earth/biodiversity/biodiversity/.
20. One standard approach to species conservation is to restrict hunting or fishing to a specified "season." This approach can be subject to extreme Peltzman-style effects, where the benefit from reducing the temporal dimension of hunting is offset by an increase in the intensity of effort devoted to hunting; see, e.g., Adler and Stewart (2012).

21. Existence value is defined as resulting just from the bare knowledge that an asset exists, not from an ability to visit that asset. It might be more precise to refer to the sightseeing safari model as one that monetizes visitation value. As long as the animal does not go extinct, it also presents a valuable option for people who do not take a sightseeing safari, in that such a safari remains a viable choice for them in the future. Maintaining the existence value also preserves, at least to some extent, this option value.

22. This possibility is explored in a story on the television show 60 Minutes, "Can Hunting Endangered Animals Save the Species?" January 29, 2012, at http://www.cbsnews.com/video/watch/?id=7396832n. See also Nicola Harley, "Eat Ponies To Save Them—Says Charity," The Telegraph, September 24, 2014, at http://www.telegraph.co.uk/news/11119194/Eat-ponies-to-save-them-says-charity.html.

23. Singer (2002) and Francione (2004).

24. From n. 122 in chapter 17 of An Introduction to the Principles of Morals and Legislation; Bentham ([1823] 1907). In an 1852 essay, John Stuart Mill (2006, pp. 185–187) offers support for Bentham's position on the moral status of non-human sentient beings.

25. See Article 14ter of the Berne Convention, at http://www.wipo.int/treaties/en/ip/berne/trtdocs_wo001.html#P188_36636.

26. The California version applies a royalty only if the resale price exceeds the original sale price.

27. A careful empirical examination of the effects of droit de suite in the United Kingdom found no evidence suggesting offsetting effects in general, though some evidence that younger artists saw lowered initial prices following the introduction of droit de suite; see Banternghansa and Graddy (2011).

28. Other potential induced behavior changes from mandatory droit de suite mimic responses we have seen to gun controls, endangered species protections, and even meteorite ownership regimes. In particular, droit de suite applied only to some locations or to some subset of art might see art sales move to other locations or focus on uncovered works. If the sales are diverted to informal markets effectively (and sometimes legislatively) out of the ambit of droit de suite, then information about the location and provenance of art might be degraded. See Abigail R. Esman, "The Droit de Suite Dilemma (And Why It's Just a Bad Idea)," Forbes, December 21, 2011, at http://www.forbes.com/sites/abigailesman/2011/12/21/the-droit-de-suite-dilemma/. For a critique of recent attempts to expand droit de suite in the United States, see Rub (2014).

29. The food stamp system in the United States worked something like this prior to 1979; now, families are given food stamps in an amount equal to the difference between their ability to pay and the cost of a frugal, nutritious diet; see Hoynes and Schanzenbach (2009, p. 119).

30. Ben-Shalom, Moffitt, and Scholz (2012).

31. But transferable stamps need not be fully equivalent to a cash handout. Because most recipients of food stamps in the United States receive stamps in amounts that are far from their total food spending, we would expect that they would respond to the stamps pretty much the same as they would to receiving an equivalent amount of cash. Nonetheless, it appears that the provision of stamps results in more food purchases than the cash equivalent. One possibility is that the household member who makes the decisions about food stamp-related purchases is not the same person who controls most spending decisions; see Hoynes and Schanzenbach (2009, p. 134).

32. Kaplow and Shavell (1994); but see Usher (2009). If transaction costs are precisely zero, there is no efficiency cost associated with aiming the allocation of property rights at the poor, or at anyone else.

33. Friedman (1993); the borrower-lender example discussed later derives its flavor from this source.

34. But the presumption is rebuttable; see chapter 6. Agarwal et al. (2014) find that regulations limiting various fees charged by credit card companies had, at least in the first years of operation, no offsetting responses in other elements (including interest rates) of the credit agreement, but saved consumers billions of dollars.

35. Posner (2003, p. 42). A parallel exists in the realm of letters of recommendation. Many recommendation forms allow the person being recommended to waive his or her right to view the contents of the letter. Sometimes people are reluctant to waive this right, but as

their decision generally will be known to the recipient of the letter as well as to the recommender, one result of not waiving the right is that positive letters are apt to be discounted.

36. For Kutiman's work, see https://www.youtube.com/user/kutiman; for DJ Earworm's videos, go to https://www.youtube.com/user/djearworm.

37. This issue is addressed in depth by Landes and Posner (2003, pp. 108–115).

38. See http://creativecommons.org/licenses/by-nc-sa/4.0/.

39. Wattpad (http://www.wattpad.com/home) is a sizable online depository of fiction writing—some of it fan fiction that could be suppressed by the copyright holder to the source content—that generally employs Creative Commons licensing: more than 300,000 Wattpad authors have made work available via Creative Commons licenses; see http://blog.wattpad.com/wattpad-updates-to-creative-commons-4-0/.

40. Suber (2012, pp. 2–4). The Suber book, titled *Open Access*, more generally serves as a key source for the discussion of open access that appears here.

41. Suber (2012, p. 37).

42. Suber (2012, pp. 15–17, 21).

43. The Directory of Open Access Journals (http://doaj.org/) keeps track of the number of articles and journals that are open access.

44. The court-ordered damages have fluctuated—as of July 2014, they stand at $222,000—and the case is yet to be fully resolved; see Donna Tam, "Supreme Court Won't Hear Jammie Thomas' File-Sharing Case," CNET.com, March 18, 2013, at http://www.cnet.com/news/supreme-court-wont-hear-jammie-thomas-file-sharing-case/. Another file-sharing case involves jury-determined damages of $675,000; see "Joel Tenenbaum's $675,000 Music Downloading Fine Upheld," *Huffington Post*, June 25, 2013, at http://www.huffingtonpost.com/2013/06/25/joel-tenenbaum-music-fine-downloading_n_3500076.html.

45. Varian (2005, pp. 134–136) offers a long list of business models that might compensate creative artists in a world without copyright.

46. Peukert, Claussen, and Kretschmer (2013). Legal digital sales might not fare as well as in the face of piracy (Danaher and Smith 2013); but see Smith and Telang (2010).

47. The contest announcement can be viewed at http://www.youtube.com/watch?v=XssPkPFNbic.

48. See Paul Sexton, "Radiohead Scores Fifth U.K. No. 1 Album," *Billboard*, January 7, 2008, at http://www.billboard.com/articles/news/1046899/radiohead-scores-fifth-uk-no-1-album, and Jonathan Cohen, "Radiohead Nudges Blige from Atop Album Chart," *Billboard*, January 9, 2008, at http://www.billboard.com/articles/news/1046867/radiohead-nudges-blige-from-atop-album-chart.

49. The movie is available at https://www.youtube.com/playlist?list=PL0652B79BAF05635F.

50. See the Creative Commons case studies of Nine Inch Nails at http://wiki.creativecommons.org/Nine_Inch_Nails_Ghosts_I-IV and http://wiki.creativecommons.org/Nine_Inch_Nails_The_Slip. Trent Reznor has expressed disappointment at the relatively small percentage of music fans willing to purchase the $5 version of one digital album collaboration that had a "free" alternative; see Greg Sandoval, "Trent Reznor: Why Won't People Pay $5?" Cnet.com, January 10, 2008, at http://news.cnet.com/8301-10784_3-9847788-7.html. The analysis of Bourreau, Dogan, and Hong (2014) suggests that Radiohead's temporary pay-what-you-want approach was more profitable than the traditional alternative, while Nine Inch Nail's free downloads limited the sales of paid downloads, potentially leading to relatively lower overall revenue.

51. Hendricks and Sorensen (2009) analyze increased sales due to informational spillovers from new music to older works by the same artists.

52. An alternative characterization of the free download strategies of Radiohead and Nine Inch Nails is that these strategies license an official version of piracy, at least for a subset of their products. Some implementations of Open Access for academic articles constitute a freemium model, where the ungated version of the article is not the final, fully edited, published version.

53. There are some exceptions to the general rule. For instance, separate decorative items such as a patch might be copyrightable, and fabric patterns (a specific tartan, perhaps) can be copyrighted or protected by trademark.

54. Picker (2007).
55. Raustiala and Sprigman (2006). Nevertheless, the fact that some designers support copyright for fashion suggests that they view copies as unwelcome competitors to their products. Even if designers are harmed by a lack of copyright, overall efficiency might still be served if the gains to consumers exceed the losses to designers.
56. Oliar and Sprigman (2008). Such social norms (and the associated shaming of copiers) exist in fashion design, too; see Scafidi (2006, p. 123).
57. Beyond fashion design and stand-up comedy, typography and cuisine are other areas where a lack of copyright does not seem to have resulted in an appreciable lack of innovation. See Fry (2009) and Fauchart and von Hippel (2008).
58. Rick Edmonds, "Newspaper Industry Lost Another 1,300 Full-Time Editorial Professionals in 2013," Poynter.org, July 29, 2014, at http://www.poynter.org/news/mediawire/259877/newspaper-industry-lost-another-1300-full-time-editorial-professionals-in-2013/.
59. Schulhofer-Wohl and Garrido (2009). The provision of web-based journalistic-type endeavors by non-professionals does not appear to fully offset the declining oversight of local government from traditional newspapers, at least outside of large cities; see Fico et al. (2013, pp. 165–166).
60. Notable developments along these lines include the rollout in 2014 of three online news endeavors: First Look Media (https://firstlook.org/) featuring investigative reporter Glenn Greenwald; Vox (http://www.vox.com/) with Ezra Klein; and Five Thirty Eight (http://fivethirtyeight.com/) with Nate Silver. The fact that these ventures are closely tied with eminent individual journalists or analysts is itself striking, as this generally is not the case with traditional newspapers, for instance.
61. People who consume news while at work find live-blog reading to be particularly attractive; see Thurman and Walters (2013).
62. See Rem Rieder, "Tough Struggle for Patch, Hyperlocal News," USA Today, August 14, 2013, at http://www.usatoday.com/story/money/columnist/rieder/2013/08/14/aol-patch--hyperlocal-news-struggles/2652337/. One once-promising hyperlocal news pioneer, EveryBlock (everyblock.com), established by a 2006 grant from the Knight Foundation (a nonprofit that funds projects related to journalism), closed suddenly in February 2013. EveryBlock allowed users in more than a dozen US cities to search for information by zip code or address. The stories included public records pertaining to the locality, such as crime and accident reports and real estate listings, as well as restaurant reviews, school reviews, and notices of forthcoming events. (EveryBlock partnered with the traditional media in 2009 when it was purchased by msnbc.com, the website associated with NBC News.) In January 2014, some eleven months after it went dark, EveryBlock in Chicago was recalled to life.
63. Strahilivetz (2006).
64. Stansel and Randazzo (2011).
65. As with other potential regulatory changes that could affect property values, it is possible that the fading of deductibility already is foreseen to some extent, so that current homeowners paid less for their houses than they would have if they were certain that deductibility would continue.
66. Tullock (1975) analyzes the general phenomenon and addresses taxi cab licensing in particular. Note also the parallel with the court ruling on balloon payments that aims to help disaffected borrowers, discussed near the beginning of this chapter.
67. As with music distribution and newspapers, the traditional business model of taxicabs is being squeezed by technological change, which facilitates smart-phone mediated ride-sharing outside of the formal taxi system.

Chapter 5

1. I discovered the phrase not from Tacitus directly, but from John Stuart Mill, *On Liberty* ([1859] 1978, p. 88).
2. This sort of analysis was pioneered by Calabresi (1970).

3. Note that the cost of this insurance, though originally paid by Robin, is likely to be passed along in the form of higher prices to exercise equipment purchasers such as Little John. (In a perfectly competitive market, producer costs have to be passed along for the industry to remain viable because the producers have no room to accept lower profits.)

4. Time for another Bentham shout out: Jeremy Bentham coined the word "maximize"; see the webpage "Neologisms of Jeremy Bentham," part of the UCL Bentham Project, at http://www.ucl.ac.uk/Bentham-Project/tools/neologisms.

5. In doing so, we noted the informational advantage of the "passer" over the "passed"; this advantage probably implies that the "passer" is the low-cost avoider of these sorts of accidents because the passer more readily understands when the vehicles will be in close proximity.

6. See chapter 4. More generally, there is a Coase-like result lurking in the background, given that the bike market is competitive. If the buyers and sellers can easily shift their respective shares of their joint pie through price changes, and the risks are understood by all parties, then prices will always adjust so that the buyers pay the production costs of the bike along with an implicit payment for whatever amount of accident insurance that the products liability regime plus the contract with the seller provides them. Both the buyers and sellers, in these circumstances, are indifferent about what approach is taken by the law toward products liability.

7. Epstein (2005).

8. There is no shortage of extreme bicycling behavior documented on the Internet, of course; e.g., see http://www.youtube.com/watch?v=zNNYy1wkTJM.

9. See Goldberg and Zipursky (2010a, pp. 284–303).

10. Smith ([1776] 1976, vol. 2, pp. 247–248).

11. Graham and Peirce (1984).

12. That is, the contract that instills the right incentives for all parties to take proper action might call for payments (including fines) in the event of accidents that, in total, could far exceed $200. The proposition that it will not be possible for all parties to be provided with appropriate incentives simply by redistributing the $200 loss that accompanies the accident draws from Holmstrom (1982).

13. Laws requiring helmets for bicycle riders induce an interesting sort of offsetting effect: fewer bike trips are made, so overall health suffers; see Sieg (2014).

14. This is not to say that choices will be fully socially efficient, or that comparative negligence (plus some regulation) dominates other liability regimes. The desirability of shared damages relative to alternative regimes has been extensively (though perhaps not conclusively) analyzed, especially with respect to litigation costs; see, e.g., De Mot (2013) and Dari-Mattiacci and Hendriks (2013).

15. Epstein (2005).

16. See the FDA's webpage "How FDA Evaluates Regulated Products: Drugs," at http://www.fda.gov/AboutFDA/Transparency/Basics/ucm269834.htm.

17. See Lisa Richwine, "FDA Lets Drugmakers Advise Doctors on Unapproved Uses," Reuters.com, January 12, 2009, at http://www.reuters.com/article/idUSTRE50C0QK20090113. In 2012, Abbott Laboratories settled charges of wrongly promoting unapproved uses of one of its drugs for $1.6 billion; see http://www.justice.gov/opa/pr/abbott-labs-pay-15-billion-resolve-criminal-civil-investigations-label-promotion-depakote.

18. *Whitney v. California*, 274 U.S. 357 (1927).

19. Mill ([1859] 1978, p. 53).

20. *Brandenburg v. Ohio*, 395 U.S. 444 (1969).

21. Mill ([1859] 1978, p. 16).

22. Chapter 1 of Leitzel (2008) is devoted to Mill's harm principle in the vice arena.

23. See Epstein (2009, pp. 23–26) for a discussion related both to this paragraph and the next section. Frank (2008, pp. 1782–1783) offers other reasons to prefer free speech to a more constrained environment, including the ability to adapt to free speech in a manner that lowers the costs.

24. Schumpeter ([1950] 2008). For a recent analysis suggesting that the destruction associated with creation has increased in recent years, see Komlos (2014).

25. For economic approaches to ticket scalping, see Happel and Jennings (1995) and Leslie and Sorensen (2009).

26. Personally, I admire accountants and would be honored to join them in attendance at a concert.
27. See, e.g., Brents and Hausbeck (2005). In December 2013, the Supreme Court of Canada struck down prostitution-related prohibitions, primarily because of the increased risks that such prohibitions pose for prostitutes. The decision in *Canada (Attorney General) v. Bedford*, 2013 SCC 72, can be accessed at http://scc-csc.lexum.com/scc-csc/scc-csc/en/item/13389/index.do.
28. See the section "Replacing a Prohibition with a Tax" in Leitzel (2008, pp. 159–161).
29. Chapter 4 in Ariely (2009, pp. 75–102) is a fun and informative guide to market versus social norms and uses the example of an offer to pay for a family meal; the subtitle of the chapter is "Why We Are Happy to Do Things, but Not When We Are Paid to Do Them." Walzer (1983) develops a more general, philosophical approach to the limits of market exchange, where I first came across the terminology "blocked exchange."
30. Coase (1937).
31. The potential for markets to corrupt some goods is a main theme of the influential book by Michael Sandel (2012), *What Money Can't Buy: The Moral Limits of Markets*.
32. See, e.g., Mahar (2003).
33. And the norms are changing. A 2010 story in *USA Today* indicated that "only 3% of folks with a spouse or fiancée have a prenuptial agreement, but that's up significantly from the 1% reported when Harris conducted a similar study in April 2002." From Laura Petrecca, "Prenuptial Agreements: Unromantic, but Important," *USA Today*, March 11, 2010, at http://www.usatoday.com/money/perfi/basics/2010-03-08-prenups08_CV_N.htm. Even in quite overt market exchanges involving personal services such as child care or home health care, for instance, the market nature tends to be somewhat shrouded, presumably in the belief that some qualitative dimensions of the relationship deteriorate when the monetary dimension takes on prominence.
34. I will discuss only kidneys, but live donations of (parts of) livers, bone marrow, and other body products or parts also are possible. Many of the same issues related to bans on compensated donations apply to these "organs" as well.
35. See Kessler and Roth (2012), and the Frequently Asked Questions section for the Israeli system at http://www.kartisadi.org.il/eng/qna.html.
36. Beard, Kaserman, and Osterkamp (2013).
37. Such a concatenation of transplants is called "Kidney Paired Donation"; see Wallis et al. (2011). The transplant operations tend to take place within rather narrow time frames in part to limit the possibility that a second-moving donor (whose friend or relative, the original target of the donation, has already received a transplant) might change her mind—though perhaps legally binding contracts could offer a degree of commitment, too. (A person who changes her mind about donating a kidney, even if she signed a contract calling for donation, will not be required to donate, of course. Such a person could be asked to make some monetary recompense for the breach, but this might be a situation where social norms, and not the law, should be employed to manage exchanges.) The import of near-simultaneity in linked transplant operations can be lowered by the existence of altruistic donors who are willing to provide a kidney to strangers; see the March 2009 Press Release from the Alliance for Paired Donation at http://kuznets.fas.harvard.edu/~aroth/papers/Rees%20et%20al%20APD%20press%20release.March2009.pdf.
38. See Kevin Sack, "60 Lives, 30 Kidneys, All Linked," *New York Times*, February 19, 2012, at http://www.nytimes.com/2012/02/19/health/lives-forever-linked-through-kidney-transplant-chain-124.html, and Janet Christenbury, "Second Largest Kidney Swap in History Includes Emory Transplant Center," Emory News center, at http://news.emory.edu/stories/2013/06/euh_second_largest_kidney_swap_in_history/campus.html.
39. These data can be retrieved from the Organ Procurement and Transplantation Network at http://optn.transplant.hrsa.gov/latestData/viewDataReports.asp.
40. 42 USC § 274e.
41. See, e.g., the discussion and references in Matas and Ibrahim (2013), and MacConmara and Newell (2014, p. 107).
42. Sandel (2013, p. 123).

43. Rippon (2014) argues that the mere provision of a legal option to sell a kidney makes poor people worse off, in part because a failure to sell would send a (negative) signal to society that a failure to donate currently does not send. (A failure to donate to a relative might send a negative signal in the current system, however.) See also the responses to Rippon's argument, including Dworkin (2014) and Radcliffe-Richards (2014). An economics model of the potential for harm arising from the provision of a tempting new option appears in Gul and Pesendorfer (2001).

44. Many features of the current transplant regime seem to disadvantage patients with lower socioeconomic status; see, e.g., Axelrod, Dzebisashvili, Schnitzler, et al. (2010).

45. Though see Frey and Oberholzer-Gee (1997).

46. Titmuss (1970) develops the case that legal blood sales can bring in lower quality blood supplies, while crowding out donations of higher quality blood; see also Mellström and Johannesson (2008). A recent research review by Lacetera, Macis, and Slonim (2013) found essentially no field-based evidence that incentives harmed either the quantity or quality of donated blood, at least in developed countries. The inducements offered for blood donations are secured by potential donors simply by presenting for donation, not by donating itself—would-be donors screened out for medical reasons still receive the compensation—thus limiting any incentive to dissemble about one's medical condition with an eye toward receiving the compensation.

47. The potential surplus of compensated donors in Iran allows the non-profit agencies that arrange the donor-recipient matches to be somewhat choosy about acceptable donors; see Fry-Revere (2014, pp. 122–123).

48. Costa-Font, Jofre-Bonet, and Yen (2011).

49. Roth (2007) provides an excellent analysis of the constraints that repugnance places on market design; the mentions of indentured servitude and high interest loans are drawn from this source, too.

50. See Mahoney (2009), and the "Selling Kidneys" section of chapter 6.

51. Information on the Iranian kidney procurement program is drawn primarily from Hippen (2008), Fatemi (2012), and Fry-Revere (2014).

52. Fry-Revere (2014, p. 187).

53. Tayebi Khosroshahi (2012).

54. Fry-Revere (2014, p. 212) indicates that average payments to Iranian kidney sellers, measured at official exchange rates, are approximately $5,000. But using exchange rates that reflect purchasing power parity, along with accounting for non-monetary compensation, suggests that the total inducements to sellers are worth approximately $45,000.

55. Tayebi Khosroshahi (2012).

56. See Chart KI 1.11 in Organ Procurement and Transplantation Network and Scientific Registry of Transplant Recipients (2014).

57. The Iranian data are drawn from the IRODaT database maintained by Transplant Procurement Management, at http://www.irodat.org/; the US data can be found at Graph KI 4.1 in Organ Procurement and Transplantation Network and Scientific Registry of Transplant Recipients (2012).

58. "Parthenon Marbles" can refer to all the statuary that was once part of the Parthenon, and hence the Elgin Marbles would constitute but a subset of the Parthenon Marbles (along with Elgin's collections from other Acropolis sites, as well as ancient sculptures Elgin acquired elsewhere). As with many contentious issues, terminology has become correlated with policy position: people who tend to support British retention of the marbles are more likely to use the term "Elgin marbles" than are those who support the return of the marbles to Athens.

59. The British Museum's position on the Parthenon Marbles can be found at http://www.britishmuseum.org/the_museum/news_and_press_releases/statements/the_parthenon_sculptures.aspx, while the Greek view is at http://www.greece.org/parthenon/marbles/.

60. See, e.g., Hitchens (2008, p. 70) and Cook (1997, pp. 70–79).

61. See the "Statutes of Limitations and Adverse Possession" section.

62. The discussion of adverse possession provided here draws heavily upon Merrill and Smith (2010, pp. 34–38).

63. Incidentally, as there were objections to Elgin's actions almost since they first took place, it can be argued that the "case" for the return of the marbles was initiated two centuries ago, before any relevant statute of limitations or term of adverse possession had run.

64. In particular, the frieze on the Parthenon was mounted on the upper exterior of a structure in the shape of rectangular box (the cella, the interior part of the Parthenon); in the British Museum, the frieze elements are positioned as if on the inside of a box. The original orientation of the frieze, along with the original compass directions of all of the sculptures, is maintained at the Acropolis Museum.

65. This statement is not, of course, an endorsement of all the methods through which paintings of Italian origin dispersed throughout the globe.

66. Jeremy Bentham's clothed remains are located just a couple blocks from the British Museum; Jeremy, too, was moved for safekeeping during the war. See Marmoy (1958, p. 85).

67. See the "Who Owns Meteorites?" section of chapter 2: London and Athens should take their cue from Willamette and New York!

68. Again, the aesthetic case for returning the Parthenon Marbles primarily derives from their site-specificity, not their Greek origin. Modern governments, including unsavory ones, sometimes try to bolster their own legitimacy by tying their regime to some perceived, ancient golden age, and campaign for the return of artifacts from the region that have diffused across the globe over the centuries.

69. Cuno (2008) makes a detailed argument for this position.

Chapter 6

1. The title of this chapter is meant to signal that the assumption of rationality that has been maintained through most of the book now will be relaxed. The phrase "crooked timber" dates from a Kant writing of 1784, though its popularity in this loosely translated English-language version of Kant's sentence is due to its use to provide a title for Berlin ([1990] 2013); for more, see both page 50 and the unnumbered page opposite the title page of Berlin ([1990] 2013), as well as Scott Horton, "Kant—The Crooked Wood of Humankind," *Harper's Blog*, May 30, 2009, at http://harpers.org/blog/2009/05/kant-the-crooked-wood-of-humankind/. Crooked Timber is the name of a popular academically oriented cultural and political blog, available at http://crookedtimber.org/.

2. Sunstein (2007).

3. Hobbes (1651) again:

> If a Covenant be made, wherein neither of the parties performe presently, but trust one another; in the condition of meer Nature, (which is a condition of Warre of every man against every man,) upon any reasonable suspition, it is Voyd; But if there be a common Power set over them bothe, with right and force sufficient to compell performance; it is not Voyd. For he that performeth first, has no assurance the other will performe after; because the bonds of words are too weak to bridle mens ambition, avarice, anger, and other Passions, without the feare of some coerceive Power; which in the condition of meer Nature, where all men are equall, and judges of the justnesse of their own fears cannot possibly be supposed. And therefore he which performeth first, does but betray himselfe to his enemy; contrary to the Right (he can never abandon) of defending his life, and means of living.
>
> But in a civil estate, where there is a Power set up to constrain those that would otherwise violate their faith, that feare is no more reasonable; and for that cause, he which by the Covenant is to perform first, is obliged so to do.

This quote is from the "Covenants Of Mutuall Trust, When Invalid" section of chapter 14 of *Leviathan*. Versions of both of the Hobbes quotes used in this book were first brought to my attention in Kronman (1985).

4. *Lochner v. New York*, 198 U.S. 45 (1905). This section draws on Kens (1998) and Irons (1999, pp. 254–258).

5. "Substantive due process" is the oxymoronic phrase that applies to this feature of US constitutional law.

6. *Lochner v. New York*, 198 U.S. 45 (1905), Justice Holmes dissent.

7. Sunstein and Zeckhauser (2011).

8. Weinstein (1989).

9. See Kunreuther and Pauly (2006) and Kousky and Kunreuther (2009).

10. Michel-Kerjan (2010, p. 180), internal citations omitted.

11. Morrall (2003). Some safety measures that seem ineffective at saving lives might still be worthwhile in reducing non-fatal injuries.

12. The terminology of "procedural" and "substantive" unconscionability comes from Leff (1967).

13. *Williams v. Walker-Thomas Furniture Company*, 350 F.2d 445 (D.C. Cir. 1965); Korobkin (2003) serves as a source for much of the discussion of this case and unconscionability more generally.

14. The appellate court opinion did not itself employ the terminology "substantive unconscionability" or "procedural unconscionability," nor did it point to the non-negotiable form contract as the element that indicates procedural unconscionability. Rather, the court's opinion noted that unconscionability could be found given "an absence of meaningful choice on the part of one of the parties together with contract terms which are unreasonably favorable to the other party" (*Williams v. Walker-Thomas Furniture Company*, 350 F.2d 445 [D.C. Cir. 1965]).

15. Smith ([1776] 1976, p. 120).

16. Korobkin (2003).

17. Lee (2013) analyzes the impact in Korea of establishing a mandatory cooling-off period between the filing of a request to divorce and the granting of the divorce, and finds that the policy reduces the number of divorces, but not the number of couples who file for divorce. It appears that a cooling-off period of a few weeks is sufficient for some couples to rescind their intention to divorce.

18. Mill ([1859] 1978, ch. 5). Mandated disclosure is far from a panacea for shortfalls in rationality, however; see Loewenstein, Cain, and Sah (2011) and Ben-Shahar and Schneider (2014).

19. What if Millian liberty foreseeably leads to terrible outcomes for the free decision-maker? Should we be committed to personal autonomy under these circumstances? For a thought-provoking defense of coercive interventions, see Conly (2013).

20. Kahneman, Knetsch, and Thaler (1990) report experimental tests of the endowment effect, including ones involving coffee mugs; but see also Plott and Zeiler (2007). For more recent investigation into the endowment effect, see, e.g., Heffetz and List (2014) and Marzilli Ericson and Fuster (2014).

21. Alternatively, endowment effects might be said to simplify the search for efficient laws, discussed later, but only by rendering the exercise nugatory.

22. Thaler and Sunstein (2008) provide useful analysis and examples of the power of default choices.

23. See chapter 10 of Thaler and Sunstein (2008, pp. 159–182).

24. Marcin and Nicklisch (2014).

25. Recall from chapter 5 the discussion of how bringing up a pre-nuptial agreement might sour relations between a prospective bride and groom, by focusing attention on the possibility of the marriage dissolving. Perhaps contracts between firms have an element of a marriage, in that suggesting that a default rule be altered signals that one of the parties is thinking about future disputes and their potential for court resolution; see the discussion in Posner (2014, pp. 98–99).

26. The efforts in Illinois to publicize and ease organ donor registration can be seen at http://www.lifegoeson.com/.

27. See Donate Life America's 2013 National Donor Designation Report Card at http://donatelife.net/wp-content/uploads/2013/07/DLA_ReportCardFinal_2013.pdf.

28. See the Human Organ Transplant Act webpage from Live On at http://www.liveon.sg/content/moh_liveon/en/organdonation/hota.html.

29. Abadie and Gay (2006).
30. Thaler and Sunstein (2008, p. 180).
31. Sunstein (2014).
32. Cook and Krawiec (2014).
33. Patzer and Knechtle (2014, p. 677) and Helänterä et al. (2014).
34. Anonymous donations are rare in the United States, with less than 1,000 occurring between 1999 and 2010; see Brethel-Haurwitz and Marsh (2014, p. 764).
35. The long chains of transplants that arise through kidney paired exchanges also work best when even medically matching donor/recipient pairs are brought into a wider system; see Wallis et al. (2011).
36. Beard and Leitzel (2014) provide more details. Already some forms of expense reimbursement, including lost wages, can legally be provided to organ donors.
37. The value of the health care subsidy to a donor depends upon the alternative personal cost of health care, which itself depends on many factors, including public policies—and health care policies are changing considerably in the United States. For most people, however, it is likely that free future health insurance will remain a very valuable form of compensation.
38. One Swedish transplant center, for instance, uses a three-month cooling-off period for would-be non-related donors; see Lennerling, Fehrman-Ekholm, and Nordén (2008).
39. Legal, regulated markets in many other body parts, including hair, eggs, sperm, and cadavers, have been controversial in the past but are legal and not particularly contentious today.
40. This section is drawn from Beard and Leitzel (2014).
41. But see Becker and Murphy (1988) and Leitzel (2008, pp. 38–44).
42. For the arrest data, see the "Crime, Arrests, and US Law Enforcement" webpage maintained by DrugWarFacts.org, at http://www.drugwarfacts.org/cms/crime#sthash.NV gzSwFR.dpbs. For more on the various effects of drug prohibition, see chapter 4 in Leitzel (2008, pp. 93–139).
43. This section draws upon my guest post "Attractive Nuisance and Drug Laws" for the Overlawyered blog on July 24, 2004; see http://overlawyered.com/2004/07/attractive-nuisance-and-drug-laws/. That post subsequently was developed in Leitzel (2008, p. 119).
44. Smith ([1776] 1976, vol. 2, pp. 351–352, footnote omitted).
45. Smith ([1776] 1976, vol. 2, p. 429).
46. The discussion of drug prohibition offered here is very limited; in particular, a fuller accounting for externalities and the effects on children from various approaches to vice regulation is required. The intent here is to highlight just one important (and, I believe, neglected) part of the problem; see more at Leitzel (2008, pp. 93–139).
47. Society is quite saturated with currently legal mind-altering drugs, of course, including alcohol, caffeine, nicotine, and prescription painkillers and anti-anxiety and anti-depression medications.
48. This approach has been developed and applied to a wide variety of issues in *Nudge*, by Thaler and Sunstein (2008); see also chapter 3 of Leitzel (2008).
49. This approach has been suggested for alcohol by Kleiman (2007); a fuller discussion appears in Kleiman (1993).Thanks to Mark Kleiman for providing some very helpful comments just before this book went to press, though only a subset of his suggestions could be incorporated into the final version.
50. The enforcement of prohibition reduces the effective price of more potent forms relative to softer varieties; among other issues, more potent drug forms allow the same number of doses to be delivered in a smaller volume, and hence renders them easier to smuggle than bulkier alternatives. US national alcohol Prohibition, for instance, shifted consumption away from beer and toward spirits; the situation was reversed following repeal. See Levine and Reinarman (1991) and Kaplan (1983, pp. 7, 64–65).
51. Hyshka, Bubela, and Wild (2013).
52. This section is drawn from Leitzel (2013).
53. On the effectiveness of self-exclusion, see the relevant posts on my Self-exclusion blog, at http://selfexclusion.blogspot.com/search/label/Effectiveness.

54. John Stuart Mill (1859, pp. 96–97) viewed his "harm to others" standard to be consistent with an imposed personal prohibition on those whose previous drug use had put others at risk: "Drunkenness, for example, in ordinary cases, is not a fit subject for legislative interference; but I should deem it perfectly legitimate that a person, who had once been convicted of any act of violence to others under the influence of drink, should be placed under a special legal restriction, personal to himself; that if he were afterwards found drunk, he should be liable to a penalty, and that if when in that state he committed another offence, the punishment to which he would be liable for that other offence should be increased in severity. The making himself drunk, in a person whom drunkenness excites to do harm to others, is a crime against others."

55. See Hawken (2010), Kilmer et al. (2013), and Kilmer and Humphreys (2013).

56. The Tom Sawyer episode and the manipulability of willingness-to-pay form the subject of Ariely, Loewenstein, and Prelec (2006).

57. Sandel (2013, p. 122).

58. In his essay, *Utilitarianism*, John Stuart Mill ([1861] 2006, p. 257) explicates the greatest happiness principle with reference to what Mill terms "Bentham's dictum" that "everybody to count for one, nobody for more than one." As noted in chapter 4, Bentham and Mill thought that sentient, nonhuman beings also qualified for inclusion within the greatest happiness principle. Perhaps humans and other beings who are uncommonly sensitive to pleasure and pain hold disproportionate influence under the happiness principle.

59. Huang (2010, pp. 407–409).

60. Levinson (2013).

61. See chapter 35 in Kahneman (2011). The dominance in memory of the peak moment and the quality of the ending is known as the "peak-end rule." Performers who try to exit the stage on a high note understand at least the end part of the peak-end rule.

62. Lyubomirsky (2011).

63. Bok (2010, pp. 17–18, 21).

64. Smith (1759, p. 149). For many other Smithian anticipations of what became behavioral economics, see Ashraf, Camerer, and Loewenstein (2005). The term "hedonic treadmill" originates with Brickman and Campbell (1971).

65. Bok (2010, pp. 52–53).

66. Gilbert (2007).

67. Kahneman (2011, ch. 37); Kahneman suggests that in the United States, additions to income no longer contribute to improved happiness once annual household income reaches $75,000. For a flavor of the debate about the relationship between income and happiness, see Sacks, Stevenson, and Wolfers (2012) and Easterlin (2013).

68. Smith ([1759] 1982, pp. 182–183).

69. Smith ([1759] 1982, pp. 181–182).

70. Robinson and Berridge (1993, 2001).

71. Chambliss and Takacs (2014, pp. 25–26).

72. The inability to forecast what will make us happy is a major theme of Gilbert (2007).

73. This point echoes a criticism of Bentham made in 1833 by John Stuart Mill (2006, p. 6) and elaborated upon by Mill (2006, pp. 94–100) in 1838.

74. Benjamin et al. (2012).

75. See, e.g., Frank (2008), Frey (2008), and Loewenstein and Ubel (2008).

76. See the discussion in Huang (2010, p. 415).

77. The result of no damage payments would undermine incentives for potential injurers to behave safely, of course, but that outcome might comport with efficiency, given that no hedonic damage took place. If there is a few months of happiness diminution before adaptation is complete, then forcing injurers to compensate for that shortfall accomplishes the usual *e pluribus unum* task of the tort system.

78. Loewenstein and Ubel (2008).

79. Krekel and Poprawe (2014).

80. Goldberg and Zipursky (2010b).

81. Frey (2008).

Conclusion

1. See Goldberg and Zipursky (2010a, pp. 347–350).
2. This distinction between risk and uncertainty comes from University of Chicago economist Frank Knight ([1921] 2006).
3. A common cognitive shortcoming is "confirmation bias," in which people seek out, and give preponderate weight to, opinions that concur with the ones they currently hold, while conflicting ideas are met with a higher degree of skepticism. One legal setting in which confirmation bias can present serious problems concerns the gathering and interpretation of evidence. Once a culprit or a scenario takes precedence in the minds of officials or witnesses, further investigations might be aimed less at an objective understanding of the case than at promoting the current theory; see, e.g., Kassin, Dror, and Kukucka (2013).
4. This is a paraphrase of a remark that Mill made to Kate Amberley; it is quoted in Packe (1954, p. 436). Kate Amberley was Bertrand Russell's mother.
5. Mill ([1859] 1978, p. 43).
6. Arbesman (2012).
7. Russell (1926, pp. 73–78).

REFERENCES

Abadie, Alberto, and Sebastien Gay. "The Impact of Presumed Consent Legislation on Cadaveric Organ Donation: A Cross-country Study." *Journal of Health Economics* 25 (2006): 599–620.

Adler, Jonathan H. "Perverse Incentives and the Endangered Species Act." Resources for the Future, Weekly Policy Commentary, Aug. 4, 2008. http://www.rff.org/Publications/WPC/Pages/08_08_04_Adler_Endangered_Species.aspx.

Adler, Jonathan H., and Nathaniel Stewart. "The Magic of the Market: The Advantages of Catch-Share Fishing." *Milken Institute Review*, Fourth Quarter, 2012, 42–51.

Adler, Matthew D. "Bounded Rationality and Legal Scholarship." In *Theoretical Foundations of Law and Economics*, edited by Mark D. White, 137–162. Cambridge: Cambridge University Press, 2009.

Agarwal, Sumit, et al. "Regulating Consumer Financial Products: Evidence from Credit Cards." April 2014. http://ssrn.com/abstract=2330942.

Amnesty International. "The Death Penalty in Canada: Twenty Years of Abolition." no date. http://www.amnesty.ca/deathpenalty/canada.php.

Arbesman, Samuel. *The Half-Life of Facts: Why Everything We Know Has an Expiration Date.* New York: Current, 2012.

Ariely, Dan. *Predictably Irrational.* Rev. edn. New York: Harper Perennial, 2009.

Ariely, Dan, George Loewenstein, and Drazen Prelec. "Tom Sawyer and the Construction of Value." *Journal of Economic Behavior and Organization* 60 (2006): 1–10.

Ash, P., A. L. Kellermann, D. Fuqua-Whitley, and A. Johnson. "Gun Acquisition and Use by Juvenile Offenders." *Journal of the American Medical Association* 275 (1996): 1754–1758.

Ashraf, Nava, Colin F. Camerer, and George Loewenstein. "Adam Smith, Behavioral Economist." *Journal of Economic Perspectives* 19, no. 3 (Summer 2005): 131–145.

Axelrod, David A., Nino Dzebisashvili, Mark A. Schnitzler, et al. "The Interplay of Socioeconomic Status, Distance to Center, and Interdonor Service Area Travel on Kidney Transplant Access and Outcomes." *Clinical Journal of the American Society of Nephrology* 5, no. 12 (December 2010): 2276–2288.

Banner, Stuart. *American Property: A History of How, Why and What We Own.* Cambridge, MA: Harvard University Press, 2011.

Banner, Stuart. *Who Owns the Sky? The Struggle to Control Airspace from the Wright Brothers On.* Cambridge, MA: Harvard University Press, 2008.

Banternghansa, Chanont, and Kathryn Graddy. "The Impact of the *Droit de Suite* in the UK: An Empirical Analysis." *Journal of Cultural Economics* 35 (2011): 81–100.

Barbarino, Alessandro, and Giovanni Mastrobuon. "The Incapacitation Effect of Incarceration: Evidence from Several Italian Collective Pardons." *American Economic Journal: Economic Policy* 6, no. 1 (2014): 1–37.

Bardach, Eugene. "Social Regulation as a Generic Policy Instrument." In *Beyond Privatization: The Tools of Government Action*, edited by Lester M. Salamon and Michael S. Lund, 197–230. Washington, DC: Urban Institute Press, 1989.

Beard, T. Randolph, David L. Kaserman, and Rigmar Osterkamp. *The Global Organ Shortage: Economic Causes, Human Consequences, Policy Responses.* Stanford, CA: Stanford University Press, 2013.

Beard, T. Randolph, and Jim Leitzel. "Designing a Compensated Kidney Donation System." *Law and Contemporary Problems* 77, no. 3 (2014): 253–287.

Becker, Gary S. "Crime and Punishment: An Economic Approach." *Journal of Political Economy* 76, no. 2 (Mar.-Apr. 1968): 169–217.

Becker, Gary S., and Kevin M. Murphy. "A Theory of Rational Addiction." *Journal of Political Economy* 96, no. 4 (Aug. 1988): 675–700.

Benjamin, Daniel J., Ori Heffetz, Miles S. Kimball, and Alex Rees-Jones. "What Do You Think Would Make You Happier? What Do You Think You Would Choose?" *American Economic Review* 102, no. 5 (2012): 2083–2110.

Ben-Shahar, Omri, and Carl E. Schneider. *More Than You Wanted to Know: The Failure of Mandated Disclosure.* Princeton: Princeton University Press, 2014.

Ben-Shalom, Yonatan, Robert Moffitt, and John Karl Scholz. "An Assessment of the Effectiveness of Antipoverty Programs in the United States." In *The Oxford Handbook of the Economics of Poverty*, edited by Philip N. Jefferson, 709–749. New York: Oxford University Press, 2012.

Bentham, Jeremy. *An Introduction to the Principles of Morals and Legislation.* London: Clarendon Press, 1907. Reprint of the 1823 edn. http://www.econlib.org/library/Bentham/bnthPML.html.

Bentham, Jeremy. *The Rationale of Reward.* London: Robert Heward, 1830. http://books.google.com/books?id=6igN9srLgg8C.

Berlin, Isaiah. *The Crooked Timber of Humanity: Chapters in the History of Ideas.* 2d edn. Edited by Henry Hardy. Princeton: Princeton University Press, 2013 [original UK first edition, 1990].

Besanko, David, and Ronald R. Braeutigam. *Microeconomics.* 3d edn. Hoboken, NJ: John Wiley and Sons, Inc., 2008.

Bessen, James, and Michael J. Meurer. "Of Patents and Property." *Regulation* (Winter 2008/2009): 18–26.

Boadway, Robin W. "The Welfare Foundations of Cost-Benefit Analysis." *Economic Journal* 84, no. 336 (Dec. 1974): 926–939.

Bok, Derek. *The Politics of Happiness: What Government Can Learn from the New Research on Well-Being.* Princeton: Princeton University Press, 2010.

Borenstein, Severin. "A Microeconomic Framework for Evaluating Energy Efficiency Rebound and Some Implications." National Bureau of Economic Research Working Paper 19044, May 2013.

Bourreau, Marc, Pinnar Dogan, and Sounman Hong. "Making Money by Giving It for Free: Radiohead's Pre-Release Strategy for *In Rainbows*." Faculty Research Working Paper Series, Harvard Kennedy School, July 2014.

Brents, Barbara G., and Kathryn Hausbeck. "Violence and Legalized Brothel Prostitution in Nevada: Examining Safety, Risk, and Prostitution Policy." *Journal of Interpersonal Violence* 20, no. 3 (Mar. 2005): 270–295.

Brethel-Haurwitz, Kristin M., and Abigail A. Marsh. "Geographical Differences in Subjective Well-Being Predict Extraordinary Altruism." *Psychological Science* 25 (2014): 762–771.

Brickman, P., and D. T. Campbell. "Hedonic Relativism and Planning the Good Society." In *Adaptation Level Theory: A Symposium*, edited by M. H. Appley, 287–302. New York: Academic Press, 1971.

Bronin, Sara C. "Solar Rights." *Boston University Law Review* 89 (2009): 1217–1265.

Buccafusco, Christopher J., and Christopher Sprigman. "The Creativity Effect." *University of Chicago Law Review* 78 (2011): 31–52.

Calabresi, Guido. *The Costs of Accidents: A Legal and Economic Analysis*. New Haven: Yale University Press, 1970.

Calabresi, Guido, and A. Douglas Melamed. "Property Rules, Liability Rules, and Inalienability: One View of the Cathedral." *Harvard Law Review* 85, no. 6 (Apr. 1972): 1089–1128.

Chambliss, Daniel F., and Christopher G. Takacs. *How College Works*. Cambridge, MA: Harvard University Press, 2014.

Coase, R. H. *The Firm, the Market, and the Law*. Chicago: University of Chicago Press, 1988.

Coase, Ronald. "The Nature of the Firm." *Economica* 4, no. 16 (1937): 386–405.

Coase, Ronald. "The Problem of Social Cost." *Journal of Law and Economics* 3 (Oct. 1960): 1–44.

Conly, Sarah. *Against Autonomy: Justifying Coercive Paternalism*. Cambridge: Cambridge University Press, 2013.

Cook, B. F. *The Elgin Marbles*. London: British Museum Press, 1997.

Cook, Philip J., and Kimberly D. Krawiec. "A Primer on Kidney Transplantation: Anatomy of the Shortage." *Law and Contemporary Problems* 77, no. 3 (2014): 1–23.

Costa-Font, Joan, Mireia Jofre-Bonet, and Steven T. Yen. "Not All Incentives Wash Out the Warm Glow: The Case of Blood Donation Revisited." CESifo Working Paper Series No. 3527, July 2011. http://ssrn.com/abstract=1895302.

Cuno, James. *Who Owns Antiquity? Museums and the Battle over Our Ancient Heritage*. Princeton: Princeton University Press, 2008.

Danaher, Brett, and Michael D. Smith. "Gone in 60 Seconds: The Impact of the Megaupload Shutdown on Movie Sales." Sept. 2013. http://ssrn.com/abstract=2229349.

Dari-Mattiacci, Giuseppe, and Eva S. Hendriks. "Relative Fault and Efficient Negligence: Comparative Negligence Explained." *Review of Law and Economics* 9, no. 1 (June 2013): 1–40.

De Mot, Jef. "Comparative versus Contributory Negligence: A Comparison of the Litigation Expenditures." *International Review of Law and Economics* 33 (Mar. 2013): 54–61.

Drago, Francesco, Roberto Galbiati, and Pietro Vertova. "The Deterrent Effects of Prison: Evidence from a Natural Experiment." *Journal of Political Economy* 117, no. 2 (2009): 257–280.

Durose, Matthew R., Alexia D. Cooper, and Howard N. Snyder. "Recidivism of Prisoners Released in 30 States in 2005: Patterns from 2005 to 2010." U.S. Department of Justice, Office of Justice Programs, Bureau of Justice Statistics, NCJ 244205, Apr. 2014.

DuVivier, K. K. "Sins of the Father." *Texas A&M Real Property Law Journal* 1, no. 3 (2014): 391–423.

Dworkin, Gerald. "Organ Sales and Paternalism." *Journal of Medical Ethics* 40, no. 3 (2014): 151–152.

Easterlin, Richard A. "Happiness, Growth, and Public Policy." *Economic Inquiry* 51, no. 1 (Jan. 2013): 1–15.

Ellerman, David. "Numeraire Illusion: The Final Demise of the Kaldor-Hicks Principle." In *Theoretical Foundations of Law and Economics*, edited by Mark D. White, 96–118. Cambridge: Cambridge University Press, 2009.

Ellickson, Robert C. *Order Without Law: How Neighbors Settle Disputes*. Cambridge, MA: Harvard University Press, 1991.

Epstein, Richard A. "The Allocation of the Commons: Parking and Stopping on the Commons." John M. Olin Law & Economics Working Paper No. 134, University of Chicago. Aug. 2001. http://ssrn.com/abstract=282512.

Epstein, Richard A. "Heller's Gridlock Economy in Perspective: Why There Is Too Little, Not Too Much, Private Property." John M. Olin Law & Economics Working Paper No. 495, University of Chicago. Nov. 2009. http://ssrn.com/abstract=1505626.

Epstein, Richard A. "Nuisance Law: Corrective Justice and its Utilitarian Constraints." *Journal of Legal Studies* 8, no. 1 (Jan. 1979): 49–102.

Epstein, Richard A. "A Short History of Product Liability Law." PointofLaw.com, Nov. 10, 2005. http://www.pointoflaw.com/products/overview.php.

Farnsworth, Ward. "Do Parties to Nuisance Cases Bargain After Judgment? A Glimpse Inside the Cathedral." *University of Chicago Law Review* 66, no. 2 (Spring 1999): 373–436.

Farrell, Joseph. "Information and the Coase Theorem." *Journal of Economic Perspectives* 1, no. 2 (Autumn 1987): 113–129.

Fatemi, Farshad. "The Regulated Market for Kidneys in Iran." In *Auctions, Market Mechanisms, and Their Applications*, edited by Peter Coles, Sanmay Das, Sébastien Lahaie, and Boles Szymanski, 62–75. Berlin: Springer, 2012.

Fauchart, Emmanuelle, and Eric von Hippel. "Norms-Based Intellectual Property Systems: The Case of French Chefs." *Organization Science* 19, no. 2 (2008): 187–201.

Fico, Frederick, Stephen Lacy, Steven S. Wildman, Thomas Baldwin, Daniel Bergan, and Paul Zube. "Citizen Journalism Sites as Information Substitutes and Complements for United States Newspaper Coverage of Local Governments." *Digital Journalism* 1, no. 1 (2013): 152–168.

Francione, Gary L. "Animals—Property or Persons?" In *Animal Rights: Current Debates and New Directions*, edited by Cass R. Sunstein and Martha C. Nussbaum, 108–142. New York: Oxford University Press, 2004.

Frank, Robert H. "Should Public Policy Respond to Positional Externalities?" *Journal of Public Economics* 92, nos. 8–9 (Aug. 2008): 1777–1786.

Frey, Bruno S. "Happiness Policies." In *Happiness: A Revolution in Economics*, 151–175. Cambridge, MA: MIT Press, 2008.

Frey, Bruno S., and Oberholzer-Gee, Felix. "The Cost of Price Incentives: An Empirical Analysis of Motivation Crowding-Out." *American Economic Review* 87, no. 4 (1997): 746–755.

Friedman, David D. "Law and Economics." *The Concise Encyclopedia of Economics*, 1993. Library of Economics and Liberty. http://www.econlib.org/library/Enc1/LawandEconomics.html.

Fry, Blake. "Why Typefaces Proliferate Without Copyright Protection," May 15, 2009. http://ssrn.com/abstract=1443491.

Fry-Revere, Sigrid. *The Kidney Sellers: A Journey of Discovery in Iran*. Durham, NC: Carolina Academic Press, 2014.

Gilbert, Daniel. *Stumbling on Happiness*. New York: Vintage Books, 2007.

Goldberg, John C. P., and Benjamin C. Zipursky. *Torts*. New York: Oxford University Press, 2010a.

Goldberg, John C. P., and Benjamin C. Zipursky. "Torts as Wrongs." *Texas Law Review* 88, no. 5 (Apr. 2010b): 917–986.

Graham, Daniel A., and Ellen R. Peirce. "Contingent Damages for Products Liability." *Journal of Legal Studies* 13, no. 3 (Aug. 1984): 441–468.

Gul, Faruk, and Wolfgang Pesendorfer. "Temptation and Self-Control." *Econometrica* 69, no. 6 (Nov. 2001): 1403–1435.

Hall, Bronwyn H., et al., "A Study of Patent Thickets." Intellectual Property Office (UK), July 30, 2013. http://ssrn.com/abstract=2467992.

Happel, Stephen K., and Marianne M. Jennings. "The Folly of Anti-Scalping Laws." *Cato Journal* 15 (Spring/Summer 1995): 65–80. http://www.cato.org/pubs/journal/cj15n1-4.html.

Hardin, Garrett. "The Tragedy of the Commons." *Science* 162, no. 3859 (Dec. 13, 1968): 1243–1248. http://www.sciencemag.org/cgi/content/full/162/3859/1243.

Harhoff, Dietmar, Georg von Graevenitz, and Stefan Wagner. "Conflict Resolution, Public Goods and Patent Thickets." CGR Working Paper 49, Queen Mary University of London, May 2014.

Hawken, Angela. "HOPE for Probation: How Hawaii Improved Behavior with High-Probability, Low-Severity Sanctions." *Journal of Global Drug Policy and Practice* 4, no. 3 (2010).

Hayek, F. A. "The Use of Knowledge in Society." *American Economic Review* 35, no. 4 (1945): 519–530.

Heffetz, Ori, and John A. List. "Is the Endowment Effect an Expectations Effect?" *Journal of the European Economic Association* 12, no. 5 (Oct. 2014): 1396–1422.

Helanterä, Ilkka, Kaija Salmela, Lauri Kyllönen, et al. "Pretransplant Dialysis Duration and Risk of Death after Kidney Transplantation in the Current Era." *Transplantation* 98, no. 4 (Aug. 2014): 458–464.

Heller, Michael. *The Gridlock Economy*. New York: Basic Books, 2008.

Heller, Michael A. "The Tragedy of the Anti-Commons: Property in the Transition from Marx to Markets." *Harvard Law Review* 111 (1998): 621–688.

Henderson, Hubert D. *Supply and Demand*. New York: Harcourt, Brace and Company, 1922.

Hendricks, Ken, and Alan Sorensen. "Information and the Skewness of Music Sales." *Journal of Political Economy* 117, no. 2 (2009): 324–369.

Highway Statistics 2011. Federal Highway Administration, US Department of Transportation. http://www.fhwa.dot.gov/policyinformation/statistics/2011/.

Hippen, Benjamin E. "Organ Sales and Moral Travails: Lessons from the Living Kidney Vendor Program in Iran." *Cato Institute Series in Policy Analysis*, no. 614 (Mar. 20, 2008).

Hirschman, Albert O. *The Rhetoric of Reaction: Perversity, Futility, Jeopardy*. Cambridge, MA: Harvard University Press, 1991.

Hitchens, Christopher. *The Parthenon Marbles*. London: Verso, 2008.

Hobbes, Thomas. *Leviathan*, 1651. Project Gutenberg EBook version. http://www.gutenberg. org/files/3207/3207-h/3207-h.htm#link2H_4_0115.

Holmes, Oliver Wendell, Jr. *The Common Law*. New York: Dover Publications, Inc., [1881] 1991.

Holmes, Oliver Wendell, Jr. "The Path of the Law." *Harvard Law Review* 10, no. 8 (1897): 457–478.

Holmstrom, Bengt. "Moral Hazard in Teams." *Bell Journal of Economics* 13, no. 2 (Autumn 1982): 324–340.

Hoynes, Hilary W., and Diane Whitmore Schanzenbach. "Consumption Responses to In-Kind Transfers: Evidence from the Introduction of the Food Stamp Program." *American Economic Journal: Applied Economics* 1, no. 4 (2009): 109–139.

Huang, Peter Henry. "Happiness Studies and Legal Policy." *Annual Review of Law and Social Science* 6 (2010): 405–432.

Hunt, J. G., ed. *The Essential Thomas Jefferson*. Avenal, NJ: Portland House, 1996.

Hyshka, Elaine, Tania Bubela, and T. Cameron Wild. "Prospects for Scaling-Up Supervised Injection Facilities in Canada: The Role of Evidence in Legal and Political Decision-Making." *Addiction* 108, no. 3 (Mar. 2013): 468–476.

Irons, Peter. *A People's History of the Supreme Court*. New York: Viking Penguin, 1999.

Jacobsen, Mark R., and Arthur A. van Benthem. "Vehicle Scrappage and Gasoline Policy." National Bureau of Economic Research Working Paper 19055, May 2013.

Kahneman, Daniel. *Thinking, Fast and Slow*. New York: Farrar, Straus and Giroux, 2011.

Kahneman, Daniel, Jack L. Knetsch, and Richard H. Thaler. "Experimental Tests of the Endowment Effect and the Coase Theorem." *Journal of Political Economy* 98, no. 6 (1990): 1325–1348.

Kaplan, John. *The Hardest Drug: Heroin and Public Policy*. Chicago: University of Chicago Press, 1983.

Kaplow, Louis. "On the Optimal Burden of Proof." *Journal of Political Economy* 119, no. 6 (Dec. 2011): 1104–1140.

Kaplow, Louis, and Steven Shavell. *Fairness versus Welfare*. Cambridge, MA: Harvard University Press, 2002.

Kaplow, Louis, and Steven Shavell. "Why the Legal System is Less Efficient than the Income Tax in Redistributing Income." *Journal of Legal Studies* 23, no. 2 (June 1994): 667–681.

Kassin, Saul M., Itiel E. Dror, and Jeff Kukucka. "The Forensic Confirmation Bias: Problems, Perspectives, and Proposed Solutions." *Journal of Applied Research in Memory and Cognition* 2, no. 1 (Mar. 2013): 42–52.

Kens, Paul. *Lochner v. New York: Economic Regulation on Trial.* Lawrence: University Press of Kansas, 1998.

Kessler, Judd B., and Alvin E. Roth. "Organ Allocation Policy and the Decision to Donate." *American Economic Review* 102, no. 5 (2012): 2018–2047.

Kilmer, Beau, and Keith Humphreys. "Losing Your 'License to Drink': The Radical South Dakota Approach to Heavy Drinkers Who Threaten Public Safety." *Brown Journal of World Affairs* 20, no. 1 (Fall/Winter 2013): 267–279.

Kilmer, Beau, Nancy Nicosia, Paul Heaton, and Greg Midgette. "Efficacy of Frequent Monitoring with Swift, Certain, and Modest Sanctions for Violations: Insights from South Dakota's 24/7 Sobriety Project." *American Journal of Public Health* 103, no. 1 (Jan. 2013): e37–e43.

Kleiman, Mark. "Dopey, Boozy, Smoky—and Stupid." *American Interest Online* 2, no. 3 (Jan.-Feb. 2007).

Kleiman, Mark A. R. *Against Excess: Drug Policy for Results.* New York: Basic Books, 1993.

Knight, Frank H. *Risk, Uncertainty and Profit.* Mineola, NY: Dover, [1921] 2006.

Komlos, John. "Has Creative Destruction Become More Destructive?" CESifo Working Paper Series No. 4941, Aug. 21, 2014. http://ssrn.com/abstract=2496883.

Korobkin, Russell. "A 'Traditional' and 'Behavioral' Law-and-Economics Analysis of *Williams v. Walker-Thomas Furniture Company.*" UCLA School of Law, Law & Economics Research Paper Series, Research Paper No. 03-24, 2003. http://papers.ssrn.com/sol3/papers.cfm?abstract_id=471961.

Kousky, Carolyn, and Howard Kunreuther. "Improving Flood Insurance and Flood Risk Management: Insights from St. Louis, Missouri." Resources for the Future Discussion Paper 09-07, Feb. 2009.

Krekel, Christian, and Marie L. Poprawe. "The Effect of Local Crime on Well-Being: Evidence for Germany." ETH Zurich, KOF Working Paper No. 358, June 2014.

Kremer, Michael. "Making Vaccines Pay: Creating Incentives to Stop AIDS, Tuberculosis and Malaria." *Milken Institute Review,* First Quarter, 2004, 43–53.

Kronman, Anthony T. "Contract Law and the State of Nature." *Journal of Law, Economics, & Organization* 1, no. 1 (Spring 1985): 5–32.

Krutilla, John V. "Conservation Reconsidered." *American Economic Review* 57, no. 4 (Sept. 1967): 777–786.

Kunreuther, Howard, and Mark Pauly. "Rules Rather Than Discretion: Lessons from Hurricane Katrina." National Bureau of Economic Research Working Paper Number 12503, Aug. 2006.

Lacetera, Nicola, Mario Macis, and Robert Slonim. "Economic Rewards to Motivate Blood Donations." *Science* 340 (May 24, 2013): 927–928.

Landes, William M., and Richard A. Posner. *The Economic Structure of Intellectual Property Law.* Cambridge, MA: Harvard University Press, 2003.

Langpap, Christian, and Joe Kerkvliet. "Endangered Species Conservation on Private Land: Assessing the Effectiveness of Habitat Conservation Plans." *Journal of Environmental Economics and Management* 64, no. 1 (July 2012): 1–15.

La Porta, Rafael, Florencio Lopez-de-Silanes, and Andrei Shleifer. "The Economic Consequences of Legal Origins." *Journal of Economic Literature* 46, no. 2 (2008): 285–332.

Lee, Jungmin. "The Impact of a Mandatory Cooling-off Period on Divorce." *Journal of Law and Economics* 56, no. 1 (Feb. 2013): 227–243.

Leff, Arthur Allen. "Unconscionability and the Code—The Emperor's New Clause." *University of Pennsylvania Law Review* 115, no. 4 (Feb. 1967): 485–559.

Leitzel, Jim. "Toward Drug Control: Exclusion and Buyer Licensing." *Criminal Law and Philosophy* 7 (2013): 99–119.

Leitzel, Jim. *The Political Economy of Rule Evasion and Policy Reform*. London: Routledge, 2003.

Leitzel, Jim. *Regulating Vice: Misguided Prohibitions and Realistic Controls*. New York: Cambridge University Press, 2008.

Leitzel, Jim. "Reliance and Contract Breach." *Law and Contemporary Problems* 52 (Winter 1989): 87–105.

Lennerling, Annette, Ingela Fehrman-Ekholm, and Gunnela Nordén. "Nondirected Living Kidney Donation: Experiences in a Swedish Transplant Centre." *Clinical Transplantation* 22 (2008): 304–308.

Lerner, Josh. "The Empirical Impact of Intellectual Property Rights on Innovation: Puzzles and Clues." *American Economic Review Papers and Proceedings* 99, no. 2 (2009): 343–348.

Leslie, Phillip, and Alan T. Sorensen. "The Welfare Effects of Ticket Resale." NBER Working Paper No. 15476, Nov. 2009.

Levine, Harry G., and Craig Reinarman. "From Prohibition to Regulation: Lessons from Alcohol Policy for Drug Policy." *The Milbank Quarterly* 69, no. 3 (1991): 461–494.

Levinson, Arik. "Happiness, Behavioral Economics, and Public Policy." NBER Working Paper No. 19329, Aug. 2013.

Levitt, Steven D. "The Effect of Prison Population Size on Crime Rates: Evidence from Prison Overcrowding Litigation." *Quarterly Journal of Economics* 111, no. 2 (1996): 319–351.

Levitt, Steven D. "Why Do Increased Arrest Rates Appear to Reduce Crime: Deterrence, Incapacitation, or Measurement Error?" *Economic Inquiry* 36, no. 3 (1998): 353–372.

Loewenstein, George, Daylian M. Cain, and Sunita Sah. "The Limits of Transparency: Pitfalls and Potential of Disclosing Conflicts of Interest." *American Economic Review* 101, no. 3 (2011): 423–428.

Loewenstein, George, and Peter A. Ubel. "Hedonic Adaptation and the Role of Decision and Experience Utility in Public Policy." *Journal of Public Economics* 92, nos. 8–9 (2008): 1795–1810.

Lyubomirsky, Sonja. "Hedonic Adaptation to Positive and Negative Experiences." In *The Oxford Handbook of Stress, Health, and Coping*, edited by Susan Folkman, 200–224. Oxford: Oxford University Press, 2011.

MacConmara, Malcolm P., and Kenneth A. Newell. "Medical Evaluation of the Living Donor." In *Kidney Transplantation: Principles and Practice*, 7th edn., edited by Peter J. Morris and Stuart J. Knechtle, 105–117. Edinburgh and New York: Elsevier, 2014.

Mahar, Heather. "Why Are There So Few Prenuptial Agreements?" John M. Olin Center for Law, Economics, and Business, Discussion Paper No. 436, Harvard Law School, Sept. 2003.

Mahoney, Julia D. "Altruism, Markets, and Organ Procurement." *Duke Law Journal* 72 (2009): 17–35.

Marcin, Isabel, and Andreas Nicklisch. "Testing the Endowment Effect for Default Rules." MPI Collective Goods Preprint, No. 2014/1, Jan. 2014. http://ssrn.com/abstract=2375107.

Marmoy, C. F. A. "The 'Auto-Icon' of Jeremy Bentham at University College London." *Medical History* 2 (1958): 77–86.

Marzilli Ericson, Keith M., and Andreas Fuster. "The Endowment Effect." *Annual Review of Economics* 6 (2014): 555–579.

Maskin, Eric. "The Arrow Impossibility Theorem: Where Do We Go From Here?" Arrow Lecture, Columbia University, 2009.

Matas, Arthur J., and Hassan N. Ibrahim. "The Unjustified Classification of Kidney Donors as Patients with CKD: Critique and Recommendations." *Clinical Journal of the American Society of Nephrology* 8 (Aug. 2013): 1406–1413.

McChesney, Fred S. "Snow Jobs." Library of Economics and Liberty, Oct. 15, 2001. http://
   www.econlib.org/library/Columns/Mcchesneysnow.html.
Mellström, Carl, and Magnus Johannesson. "Crowding Out in Blood Donation: Was Titmuss
   Right?" *Journal of the European Economic Association* 6, no. 4 (2008): 845–863.
Merrill, Thomas W., and Henry E. Smith. *Property*. New York: Oxford University Press, 2010.
Michel-Kerjan, Erwann O. "Catastrophe Economics: The National Flood Insurance Pro-
   gram." *Journal of Economic Perspectives* 24, no. 4 (Fall 2010): 165–186.
Mill, John Stuart. *Collected Works of John Stuart Mill*, Vol. 10: *Essays on Ethics, Religion and So-
   ciety*. Indianapolis, IN: Liberty Fund, 2006. http://oll.libertyfund.org/titles/mill-the-
   collected-works-of-john-stuart-mill-volume-x-essays-on-ethics-religion-and-society.
Mill, John Stuart. *On Liberty*. Edited by Elizabeth Rapaport. Indianapolis, IN and Cambridge:
   Hackett, [1859] 1978.
Mill, John Stuart. *Principles of Political Economy with some of their Applications to Social Philoso-
   phy*. Edited by William J. Ashley. [1848] 1909. Library of Economics and Liberty. http://
   www.econlib.org/library/Mill/mlP.html.
Mokyr, Joel. "Intellectual Property Rights, the Industrial Revolution, and the Beginnings of
   Modern Economic Growth." *American Economic Review Papers and Proceedings* 99, no. 2
   (2009): 349–355.
Morrall, John F., III. "Saving Lives: A Review of the Record." AEI-Brookings Joint Center for
   Regulatory Studies, Working Paper 03-6, July 2003.
Moser, Petra. "Innovation without Patents: Evidence from World's Fairs." *Journal of Law and
   Economics* 55, no. 1 (Feb. 2012): 43–74.
Nabokov, Vladimir. *The Original of Laura*. New York: Alfred A. Knopf, 2008.
Norton, Michael I., Daniel Mochon, and Dan Ariely. "The IKEA Effect: When Labor Leads to
   Love." *Journal of Consumer Psychology* 22, no. 3 (July 2012): 453–460.
Nozick, Robert. *Anarchy, State, and Utopia*. New York: Basic Books, 1974.
Okun, Arthur M. *Equality and Efficiency, the Big Tradeoff*. Washington, DC: Brookings Institu-
   tion Press, 1975.
Oliar, Dotan, and Christopher Sprigman. "There's No Free Laugh (Anymore): The Emergence
   of Intellectual Property Norms and the Transformation of Stand-Up Comedy." *Virginia
   Law Review* 94, no. 8 (Dec. 2008): 1787–1867.
Organ Procurement and Transplantation Network (OPTN) and Scientific Registry of Transplant Recipients (SRTR). *OPTN/SRTR 2012 Annual Data Report*. Department of Health
   and Human Services, Health Resources and Services Administration, Healthcare Systems Bureau, Division of Transplantation, June, 2014. http://srtr.transplant.hrsa.gov/
   annual_reports/2012/Default.aspx.
Packe, Michael St. John. *The Life of John Stuart Mill*. New York: Macmillan, 1954.
Parisi, Francesco. "Positive, Normative and Functional Schools in Law and Economics." *European Journal of Law and Economics* 18 (2004): 259–272.
Patzer, Rachel E., and Stuart J. Knechtle. "Results of Renal Transplantation." In *Kidney Transplantation: Principles and Practice*, 7th edn., edited by Peter J. Morris and Stuart J. Knechtle, 676–697. Edinburgh and New York: Elsevier, 2014.
Peltzman, Sam. "The Effects of Automobile Safety Regulation." *Journal of Political Economy* 83,
   no. 4 (1975): 677–725.
Peukert, Christian, Jörg Claussen, and Tobias Kretschmer. "Piracy and Movie Revenues: Evidence from Megaupload. A Tale of the Long Tail?" Beiträge zur Jahrestagung des Vereins
   für Socialpolitik 2013: Wettbewerbspolitik und Regulierung in einer globalen Wirtschaft-
   sordnung—Session: Media Economics, No. A13–V1, 2013.
Philipson, Thomas J., and Richard A. Posner. "The Economic Epidemiology of Crime." *Journal
   of Law and Economics* 39 (Oct. 1996): 405–433.
Picker, Randal C. "Of Pirates and Puffy Shirts: A Comment on 'The Piracy Paradox: Innovation and Intellectual Property in Fashion Design.'" John M. Olin Law & Economics
   Working Paper No. 328 (2d series), University of Chicago Law School, Jan. 2007.

Plott, Charles R., and Kathryn Zeiler. "Exchange Asymmetries Incorrectly Interpreted as Evidence of Endowment Effect Theory and Prospect Theory?" *American Economic Review* 97 (Sept. 2007): 1449–1466.

Polinsky, A. Mitchell, and Steven Shavell. "Legal Error, Litigation, and the Incentive to Obey the Law." *Journal of Law, Economics, and Organization* 5, no. 1 (Spring 1989): 99–108.

Posner, Richard A. *Economic Analysis of Law.* 9th edn. New York: Wolters Kluwer Law and Business, 2014.

Posner, Richard A. "Intellectual Property: The Law and Economics Approach." *Journal of Economic Perspectives* 19, no. 2 (Spring 2005): 57–73.

Radcliffe-Richards, Janet. "Commentary by Janet Radcliffe-Richards on Simon Rippon's 'Imposing Options on People in Poverty: The Harm of a Live Donor Organ Market.'" *Journal of Medical Ethics* 40, no. 3 (2014): 152–153.

Rae, John. *Life of Adam Smith.* London: Macmillan and Co., 1895.

Raustiala, Kal, and Christopher Sprigman. "The Piracy Paradox: Innovation and Intellectual Property in Fashion Design." *Virginia Law Review* 92, no. 8 (Dec. 2006): 1687–1777.

Rippon, Simon. "Imposing Options on People in Poverty: The Harm of a Live Donor Organ Market." *Journal of Medical Ethics* 40, no. 3 (2014): 145–150.):

Robinson, Terry E., and Kent C. Berridge. "Incentive-Sensitization and Addiction." *Addiction* 96 (2001): 103–114.

Robinson, Terry E., and Kent C. Berridge. "The Neural Basis of Drug Craving: An Incentive-Sensitization Theory of Addiction." *Brain Research Reviews* 18 (1993): 247–291.

Rosenblatt, Betsy. "Moral Rights Basics," Mar. 1998. http://cyber.law.harvard.edu/property/library/moralprimer.html.

Roth, Alvin E. "Repugnance as a Constraint on Markets." *Journal of Economic Perspectives* 21, no. 3 (Summer 2007): 37–58.

Rub, Guy A. "The Unconvincing Case for Resale Royalties." *Yale Law Journal Forum*, Apr. 25, 2014. http://www.yalelawjournal.org/forum/the-unconvincing-case-for-resale-royalties.

Rubin, Paul. "Why Is the Common Law Efficient?" *Journal of Legal Studies* 6, no. 1 (Jan. 1977): 51–63.

Rubin, Paul H. "Legal Systems as Frameworks for Market Exchanges." In *Handbook of New Institutional Economics*, edited by C. Ménard and M. M. Shirley, 205–228. Berlin: Springer, 2008.

Russell, Bertrand. *Education and the Good Life.* New York: Boni and Liveright, 1926.

Russell, Bertrand. *Human Society in Ethics and Politics.* London: Routledge, [1954] 1992.

Russell, Bertrand. *New Hopes for a Changing World.* New York: Simon and Schuster, 1951.

Sacks, Daniel W., Betsey Stevenson, and Justin Wolfers. "The New Stylized Facts about Income and Subjective Well-Being." Mimeo, Aug. 2, 2012.

Sakakibara, Mariko, and Lee Branstetter. "Do Stronger Patents Induce More Innovation? Evidence from the 1988 Japanese Patent Law Reforms." *Rand Journal of Economics* 32, no. 1 (Spring 2001): 77–100.

Sandel, Michael J. "Market Reasoning as Moral Reasoning: Why Economists Should Reengage with Political Philosophy." *Journal of Economic Perspectives* 27, no. 4 (Fall 2013): 121–140.

Sandel, Michael J. *What Money Can't Buy: The Moral Limits of Markets.* London and New York: Penguin Books, Allen Lane, 2012.

Sax, Joseph L. *Playing Darts with a Rembrandt: Public and Private Rights in Cultural Treasures.* Ann Arbor: University of Michigan Press, 2001.

Scafidi, Susan. "Intellectual Property and Fashion Design." *Intellectual Property and Information Wealth* 1 (2006): 115-131. http://ssrn.com/abstract=1309735.

Schulhofer-Wohl, Sam, and Miguel Garrido. "Do Newspapers Matter? Evidence from the Closure of the *Cincinnati Post.*" National Bureau of Economic Research Working Paper No. 14817, Mar. 2009.

Schumpeter, Joseph A. *Capitalism, Socialism, and Democracy*. 3d edn. New York: Harper Perennial, [1950] 2008.

Shapiro, Carl. "Navigating the Patent Thicket: Cross Licenses, Patent Pools, and Standard Setting." *Innovation Policy and the Economy* 1 (2001): 119–150.

Shavell, Steven. *Foundations of Economic Analysis of Law*. Cambridge, MA: Harvard University Press, 2004.

Sieg, Gernot. "Costs and Benefits of a Bicycle Helmet Law for Germany." Institute of Transport Economics Münster, Working Paper No. 21, Westfälische Wilhelms-Universität, Mar. 2014.

Singer, Peter. *Animal Liberation*. New York: Ecco, [1975] 2002.

Smith, Adam. *An Inquiry into the Nature and Causes of the Wealth of Nations*. Edited by Edward Cannan. Chicago: University of Chicago Press, 1976 [1776; Cannan edition, 1904].

Smith, Adam. *The Theory of Moral Sentiments*. Indianapolis, IN: Liberty Fund, [1759] 1982.

Smith, Michael D., and Rahul Telang. "Piracy or Promotion? The Impact of Broadband Internet Penetration on DVD Sales." *Information Economics and Policy* 22, no. 4 (Dec. 2010): 289–298.

Stansel, Dean, and Anthony Randazzo. "Unmasking the Mortgage Interest Deduction: Who Benefits and by How Much?" Reason Foundation, Policy Study 394, July 2011.

Stigler, George J. *Memoirs of an Unregulated Economist*. New York: Basic Books, 1988.

Stigler, George J. "The Optimum Enforcement of Laws." *Journal of Political Economy* 78, no. 3 (May–Jun. 1970): 526–536.

Strahilevitz, Lior Jacob. "'How's My Driving?' for Everyone (and Everything?)." *New York University Law Review* 81, no. 5 (2006): 1699–1765.

Strahilevitz, Lior Jacob. "The Right to Destroy." *Yale Law Journal* 114, no. 4 (Jan. 2005): 781–854.

Suber, Peter. *Open Access*. Cambridge, MA: MIT Press, 2012. Appropriately enough, this book is available in various e-formats at no charge; see http://mitpress.mit.edu/books/open-access.

Sunstein, Cass R. "Choosing Not to Choose." *Duke Law Journal* 64, no. 1 (Oct. 2014): 1–52.

Sunstein, Cass R. "Willingness to Pay Versus Welfare." *Harvard Law and Policy Review* 1, no. 2 (2007): 303–330.

Sunstein, Cass R., and Richard J. Zeckhauser. "Overreaction to Fearsome Risks." *Environmental and Resource Economics* 48, no. 3 (Mar. 2011): 435–449.

Tayebi Khosroshahi, Hamid. "Short History about Renal Transplantation Program in Iran and the World: Special Focus on World Kidney Day 2012." *Journal of Nephropathology* 1, no. 1 (2012): 5–10.

Taylor, M. Scott. "Buffalo Hunt: International Trade and the Virtual Extinction of the North American Bison." *American Economic Review* 101, no. 7 (Dec. 2011): 3162–3195.

Thaler, Richard H., and Cass R. Sunstein. *Nudge: Improving Decisions about Health, Wealth, and Happiness*. New Haven and London: Yale University Press, 2008.

Thurman, Neil, and Anna Walters. "Live Blogging—Digital Journalism's Pivotal Platform?" *Digital Journalism* 1, no. 1 (2013): 82–101.

Titmuss, Richard M. *The Gift Relationship*. London: Allen and Unwin, 1970.

Tonry, Michael. "Can Twenty-First Century Punishment Policies Be Justified in Principle?" In *Retributivism Has a Past. Has It a Future?* edited by Michael Tonry, 3–29. Oxford: Oxford University Press, 2011a.

Tonry, Michael, ed. *Retributivism Has a Past. Has It a Future?* Oxford: Oxford University Press, 2011b.

Tullock, Gordon. "The Transitional Gains Trap." *Bell Journal of Economics* 6, no. 2 (Autumn 1975): 671–678.

Usher, Dan. "The Coase Theorem is Tautological, Incoherent or Wrong." *Economics Letters* 61 (1998): 3–11.

Usher, Dan. "Why the Legal System Is Not Necessarily Less Efficient than the Income Tax in Redistributing Income." Queen's Economics Department Working Paper No, 1210, Sept. 1, 2009. http://ssrn.com/abstract=1431742.

Varian, Hal A. "Copying and Copyright." *Journal of Economic Perspectives* 19, no. 2 (Spring 2005): 121–138.

Viscusi, W. Kip. "The Lulling Effect: The Impact of Child-Resistant Packaging on Aspirin and Analgesic Ingestions." *American Economic Association Papers and Proceedings* 74, no. 2 (1984): 324–327.

Vizzard, William J. *Shots in the Dark: The Policy, Politics, and Symbolism of Gun Control.* Lanham, MD: Rowman and Littlefield Publishers, Inc., 2000.

Volokh, Alexander. "*n* Guilty Men." *University of Pennsylvania Law Review* 146 (1997): 173–216.

Wallis, C. Bradley, Kannan P. Samy, Alvin E. Roth, and Michael A. Rees. "Kidney Paired Donation." *Nephrology Dialysis Transplantation* 26 (2011): 2091–2099.

Walzer, Michael. *Spheres of Justice: A Defence of Pluralism and Equality.* Oxford: Blackwell, 1983.

Watson, Daniel S., Brenda J. Shields, and Gary A. Smith. "Snow Shovel–Related Injuries and Medical Emergencies Treated in US EDs, 1990 to 2006." *American Journal of Emergency Medicine* 29, no. 1 (2011): 11–17.

Weinstein, Neil D. "Optimistic Biases about Personal Risks." *Science,* NS, 246, no. 4935 (Dec. 8, 1989): 1232–1233.

Whalen, W. Tom, Dennis W. Carlton, Ken Heter, and Oliver Richard. "A Solution to Airport Delays." *Regulation* (Spring 2008): 30–36.

White, Mark D., ed. *Theoretical Foundations of Law and Economics.* Cambridge: Cambridge University Press, 2009.

Wiseman, Samuel R. "Pretrial Detention and the Right to Be Monitored." *Yale Law Journal* 123, no. 5 (Mar. 2014): 1344–1404.

Wolkoff, Michael J. "Property Rights to Rent Regulated Apartments: A Path Towards Decontrol." *Journal of Policy Analysis and Management* 9 (1990): 260–265.

INDEX